For my parents, Pauline and Henry

Contents

Introduction   1

Tasmania   8

Berkhamsted   16

Harrow School   25

Mind the Gap year   36

East Anglia   40

Foreign Study League   49

Bristol Old Vic Theatre School   58

BBC Radio Repertory Company   63

Homebuilding   68

Spliced   75

Tales of the Unexpected   77

Being David Archer: The audition   78

1982   80

Being David Archer: Early days   83

By the Sword Divided   86

Being David Archer: History   92

Musical auditions   94

Being David Archer: Behind the lines   96

Young parents   98

TV commercials   103

Being David Archer: Contractual obligation   113

Sitcoms   117

Being David Archer: Phil and Jill   129

The dangers of mucking around . . .   133

Being David Archer: Bristol Court Hotel   135

Swordless   137

Being David Archer: Ruth   139

Made in Heaven   142

Being David Archer: Sound effects   145

Year of the Comet   148

Sharpe's Rifles   152

Being David Archer: High drama   157

Back to school   160

Being David Archer: 'Shocking Ambridge to the Core'   166

Night Must Fall   169

Being David Archer: Deaths and recasting   171

Henry Noel Bentinck   175

Armando Iannucci   177

Being David Archer: Freelance   181

Going Deutsch   184

Being David Archer: Editors   189

Terror   193

Being David Archer: Fame   201

Shorts   204

Being David Archer: On stage   208

The Royal Bodyguard and *Twenty Twelve*   211

Casting   216

Being David Archer: Writers   218

The Year of the Roth   221

Being David Archer: Feedback   224

Voice work   228

Being David Archer: Technique   247

Quiz shows   250

Being David Archer: Perks of the job   264

Travel journalism   268

Inventions   273

Being David Archer: Rob and Helen   277

Music   280

Being David Archer: The Great Flood   283

The title   286

Being David Archer: Pip, Josh and Ben   292

An earl abroad   295

Being David Archer: And finally . . .   308

The present   310

Acknowledgements   315

Introduction

'You're on,' said the stage manager.

'What do you mean?'

'Tim Curry's got food poisoning. You're playing the Pirate King.'

'I'm the second understudy, where's Chris?'

'He's off too.'

'This is a wind-up. It's because I'm five minutes late for the half, isn't it?'

'No.'

'Really?'

'Yes.'

'Seriously?'

'They're waiting for you in wardrobe. You've got twenty minutes.'

'Oh my God.'

'Cheer up, Tim, it's not often you get to play the lead in a West End musical.'

'But I've never even rehearsed it.'

'It's in your contract, love. Now get changed.'

This is what is known as the actor's nightmare, a curse we all

1

endure; when you dream you're on stage either naked, or in an entirely unfamiliar play, or having absolutely no idea of your lines, or bonking your leading lady stark naked in a spotlight with your whole family watching from a box.

The nightmare was now actually happening.

It was 1982. An eventful year. While playing a pirate in *The Pirates of Penzance* at Drury Lane, we bought a house in north London, and I also landed the part of David Archer, son of the eponymous household in the world's longest-running radio series, *The Archers*. At the time of writing, I've now been channelling this guy for thirty-five years. It wasn't what I set out to do – I've always been happier with the sword fighting, really – but I bless the day I was lucky with that particular audition, and not just because it's given me a measure of financial security for over three decades.

I am now proud to be part of an Icon of Britain, a National Institution, and a source of excitement, enjoyment, anger and, sometimes, visceral emotional turmoil for some 5 million people every day.

So, I'd just come down on the train from Birmingham to do the matinee, having recorded an episode of *The Archers* at 9 a.m. The train was seriously overdue and, by the time I'd retrieved my bicycle at Euston, I was running very late for the first of two shows that day. The show was the West End transfer of the hit Broadway adaptation of Gilbert and Sullivan's classic, with Tim Curry, George Cole, Annie Ross, Chris Langham, Michael Praed, Bonnie Langford and Pamela Stephenson. If you ever saw that production of *The Pirates of Penzance*, I was the big bloke at the back – until that day, when I was suddenly the big bloke at the front.

I'd already done the movie. I was a pirate in that, too. At the audition for the film, this small, wired Argentinian ball of energy, choreographer Graciela Daniele, shouted, 'I want WAN HUNNERD TWENNY PO-SEN!! YANNERSTAN??!!' Luckily, I did understand, and because I was (and, indeed, still am) six foot three, and at twenty-eight was very fit and had boundless energy (cancel comparison), I gave her 130 per cent and got the part. Mainly because I didn't have to actually sing – we'd be miming to the original New York cast recordings in the film version.

I had performed in *Joseph and the Amazing Technicolor Dreamcoat* in Plymouth in 1979 but, I have to admit, I really wasn't a very good singer at the time. I got away with it, just, but always sang a wee bit flat. No one ever told me to sit on a note. Filming for months and earning pots of money (nearly all the pirates and policemen bought houses on that film) for just miming, dancing and faux fighting on a mock-up pirate ship in Shepperton Studios was about the best job a tall, energetic, not very good at singing, young-ish actor could possibly ask for.

Kevin Klein played the Pirate King. The inevitable and endless repetition of the scenes during filming meant that I at least knew the lines to the songs when it came to my turn to play the part on stage. The film's director was a man called Wilford Leach, and he wanted to do take after take from every conceivable angle, so the words were seared into my brain. When a fellow pirate, Mike Walling, asked him how many films he had directed before, he replied, 'Oh, this is my first one.' Mike came into the green room with a big thumbs up, 'We're in the money lads!' – and we were; what was scheduled as a three-week shoot took almost three months.

As Hollywood stars go, Kevin Kline is a diamond. When we once played a tedium-relieving silly game which ended with him getting slapped hard around the face, we all held our breath, waiting for a hissy fit. Instead, he smiled ruefully and said, 'I see, subtle British humour, eh?'

He came to dinner with me one evening, and when a friend of mine asked him if he was in 'this funny pirate film with Tim', he smiled his disarming Kevin-ish smile and said modestly, 'Yeah, I'm a pirate too.'

After filming had finished, Graciela told us that anyone who could actually sing had a part in the forthcoming West End show if they wanted it. I auditioned – and I was laughed at. However, the being tall and energetic bit got me in – 'Hey, we got back-op singas IN DA WINGS!!' Graciela said.

Three months later, we opened at the Theatre Royal Drury Lane to rave reviews and a sell-out nine-month season. As well as being a pirate at the back, I was asked to be second understudy for the Pirate King, which I accepted purely because it meant a slight pay rise. I never for one second thought that I would go on.

My preparation for playing the lead in a West End musical therefore was

1. I knew the words to the songs;

2. I had sung them at the piano precisely once with the musical director; and

3. I had watched the show from out front on a Wednesday matinee.

That was it.

Tim Curry's costume for the show was about as sexy as you can get. This was 1982 and glam rock and New Romanticism were in their pomp. With bouffant hair and red headband, entire tubes of mascara, blousy, frilly white shirt, tight purple breeches and waistband and the coolest, tightest, longest black leather boots you can imagine, a fabu-lously flamboyant star like Tim Curry looked like a *sex god*. The problem was that none of his kit fitted me: it was far too small.

So, I didn't look like a sex god. More like an oversized kid in a school production of *Puss in Boots*.

I have very little memory of that afternoon, but a drug called adrenaline came to my rescue all by itself. While standing on the prow of the ship as it hove round from the backdrop and the curtain went up, I seem to remember laughing at the total absurdity of the situation. I pumped out my chest, lifted my chin, jumped off the ship and my hat fell off. I strode purposefully across the stage to begin the first number and was hauled unceremoniously back by Bonnie Langford to where I should have been. This continued all through the show. Bonnie pulled me one way, Annie Ross pulled me another and Pamela Stephenson ignored me completely, as she has done to this day.

All the swordfights that I did with Tim I now had to do from the other side, so I kept missing the blade of the guy who was playing me. The jokey 'oh, the boss has missed catching the sword' shtick that the pirates all find embarrassing but usually got a big laugh just looked like the understudy had screwed up and was deeply eggy. It was only the power of the show and the professionalism of the rest of the cast that got us through.

Somehow, I survived. I asked the tech guys to record the audio as I thought it would be my one and only performance as the Pirate King, and I still have the tape. I'm not great. I just about survive but the cadenza at the end of 'I'm a Pirate King' is a train crash. I gabble my words and only through the comic genius and generosity of George Cole did any of my jokey sequence with the Major-General get any laughs. But one thing you can hear: I did have enormous energy and apparent confidence, and that, if anything, can disguise a multitude of sins.

That evening Tim was still ill but Chris Langham was back and so, as first understudy, he had to go through the whole thing himself while I went back to being a pirate. By his own admission, he had an even worse time than I did. After that a decision was made, probably by Chris himself, that I should take over as number-one understudy. The costume department started the job of making me a pair of the coolest, tightest, longest black leather boots you can imagine, but this time in a size twelve. By the time they'd done with me, I too had achieved sex-goddery.

Now, I was able to rehearse the part and I had proper sessions with the musical director. I stopped singing so flat and learned how to time the jokes. However, in Tim's continued absence, the announcement 'Ladies and gentlemen, at this evening's performance of *The Pirates of Penzance* the part of the Pirate King will be played by Timothy Bentinck' was greeted with sustained groans of disappointment, which does little for your confidence as you stand shaking in the wings.

Kevin Kline helped my confidence, though. I was faced with having to do on the West End stage what this modest but big movie star had done on Broadway, so I wanted his advice and phoned him in New York.

'Are you paying for this call?'

'Yes?'

'Put down the phone. I'll call you back.'

We talked for nearly an hour about how to do it: timing of gags, thought processes, everything from how to kick a sword up from the floor and into another character's hand, to jock-itch, thigh boots and make-up – gold dust.

Eventually, Tim became very ill and had to give up the part, so I moved down from the fourth-floor dressing room that I shared with my pirate mates into the number-one dressing room on the ground floor, with my own dresser and my name slipped in the programme. It was the same dressing room that had sheltered the egos and insecurities of many of the great names of theatre and music for hundreds of years, including, thrillingly, my direct ancestor Mrs Dorothy Jordan. When I came out of the stage door every evening, hordes of young women were there, throwing knickers at me and wanting my autograph. This was it. I was a star!

It lasted about six weeks, which included Christmas and New Year. But one day in early January I came into the theatre on a Monday afternoon, cleared my stuff out of the number-one dressing room, trudged back up to the fourth floor, put away my sexy boots and shirt and watched from the back of the stage as Oliver Tobias swaggered his way through the part that I had made my own. After the show, I walked through the stage door as he was signing autographs and fending off knickers, and no one knew who the hell I was. My first lesson in the fleeting nature of fame.

Tasmania

'I was born on a sheep station in Tasmania.' I've always loved being able to say that.

My father had taken his wife and two daughters there in 1950, and I was born in 1953. We came back two years later so I have no memory of the place, but I have dual nationality, as do both my sons. When I finally returned to the land of my birth, to do a TV commercial there in 1998, I presented my virgin Australian passport to the guy at Sydney airport.

'How long have you been overseas, mate?'

'About forty-three years.'

'Christ, hell of a gap year.'

As a young man, my father Henry had absconded from Sandhurst, stowed away on a ship to America, ridden rough on the railroad to California and become a cowboy. Then, during the war, he had been wounded twice and made a prisoner of war in Italy. Faced with the beaten-up, grey, broke England that he came back to, he gave up his job as a talks producer at the BBC when he saw an advertisement in a paper saying, 'JACKAROO WANTED ON TASMANIAN SHEEP STATION'. A jackaroo is a farmhand and trainee. My father was a Count of the Holy Roman Empire (and I am too). It was a strange choice.

Bentinck is a Dutch name. We can trace it back to a Helmich Bentinck, or Benting, who died in 1354. There are quite a few books about us but probably the most famous, or at least important, Bentinck is Hans Willem, later Earl of Portland, who came to England as the most trusted advisor of Prince William of Orange in the Glorious Revolution of 1688. There have been whisperings, handed down through history, that he was more than an advisor. This may have started because, when the young Prince was struck down with smallpox, Bentinck slept in his bed with him, as it was believed in those days that by catching a disease from someone, you took it away from them. Recent research suggests that while King William probably did 'swing both ways' – particularly with Hans Willem's great rival for William's affections, Arnold Joost van Keppel – my ancestor was a rather turgid statesman and, in the words of one historian, 'far too dull to be gay'. This didn't stop my distant cousin, Lady Anne Cavendish-Bentinck, when showing me the ancestral paintings at Welbeck, cheerily dismissing him, as we walked past his enormous portrait, with the words, '. . . and that's The Bugger'.

When the Prince was crowned King William III of England, there was a lot of tension between the English parliament and aristocracy and the new Dutch interlopers. To help assimilate his court into their new realm, he handed out titles left, right and centre. My father was never clear why Bentinck was given the title Earl of Portland, but family word-of-mouth had it that, as the Dutch fleet sailed towards their landing at Torbay, they passed close by Portland Bill in Dorset. Turning to the ship's captain, the Prince asked the name of their first sighting of England.

'That's Portland Bill, my lord.'

'Vat iss a Bill?' asked the Dutch Prince.

There followed a lengthy explanation, which included the fact that Bill was also a diminutive of William, the name the Prince shared with my ancestor.

'Den I shall make you Earl off Portland, Bill!'

Cue helpless Dutch hilarity, probably the joke of the year, endlessly repeated to hose-wetting effect at parties throughout the Empire. This is the only known example of a joke in the entire 700-year history of my family, giving weight to the 'too dull to be gay' defence.

I have recently found out from the University of Nottingham that this is nonsense: the title was re-established through a connection with Hans Willem's first wife, Anne Villiers. Also, the Prince's first sight of land was Kent.

Hans Willem's son, William, was made Duke of Portland and his descendants married well, to the Harley, Scott and Cavendish families, and ended up with large estates in Scotland and Nottinghamshire, the seat of the family being Welbeck Abbey near Worksop. When the last duke died in 1990, there were no descendants of Hans Willem's son left, so the dukedom died out. However, the first Earl had married twice and we are the descendants of that second union, so at the age of seventy, Pa became the 11th Earl of Portland, a title I inherited. This came with a seat in the House of Lords, though without land or income. I'm often asked why not, and the answer seems quite clear – the deceased duke was my father's sixth cousin twice removed. Would you expect to inherit anything from your sixth cousin twice removed? Do you even know who any of your sixth cousins twice removed are? Or what 'twice removed' actually means? It does, however, explain why I'm a jobbing actor and not managing an estate from a Subaru.

So, we are a family of counts. The Holy Roman Empire bit is complicated but doesn't mean Catholic. My Protestant great-grandfather was so formidably religious he gave up his Dutch castle and his entire inheritance for his belief. His son, my grandfather, was too dim to get the connection and continued being a slave to Jesus. My grandmother came from the Catholic Noel family, who disinherited her when she married a Protestant. When your father's the Earl of Gainsborough, being disinherited by him makes a difference. My father was therefore brought up by these impoverished warring Christian parents who had lost everything in the name of the Lord, and, understandably, the moment he became sentient he also became a staunch atheist. He married the daughter of a Yorkshire industrialist whose business had gone down the Swanee, which makes me a nicely mongreled half toff, half Sheffield steel.

My father's parents both died before he was out of his teens, and what bits of family stuff that were left, such as a house, some Gainsboroughs, a Titian and a Romney, were all sold by my sweet but totally naive great-uncle Arthur for practically nothing. He had become my father's guardian and he basically sold the entire inheritance in order to pay the death duties – Arthur's famous sayings have lived on, but his dismissal of these treasures with the words, 'not worth much, a few paintin's and a bit of rough shootin' for the boy' has lived on in infamy. It should be said that Arthur was also pretty much responsible for the Iraq wars, having been an important part of the British mandate that drew a straight line between Iraq, Kurdistan and Turkey. As we know, this led to more than just a 'bit of rough shootin''.

Arthur took his role as guardian very seriously. He once collected Pa from a party in Belgravia, from where they were due to drive to Scotland in his beautiful Lagonda. As they were walking towards the car, a pretty young French girl asked my father for directions. In the thirties, there were a lot of prostitutes in London, and a great many of them were French. Fearing 'the worst', Arthur grabbed Pa in the middle of his explanation to this perfectly innocent tourist, threw him into the car, reversed into a taxi and sped off into the night, engine roaring.

They drove in silence until they got to the A1, the romantically named Great North Road, when Arthur said, 'Now look here, Henry.' This usually presaged trouble. 'Were there girls at this party?'

'Yes, Uncle Arthur, of course there were girls.'

'Harrumph.'

They continued to travel in strained silence until they reached Scotch Corner, about eight hours later, when Arthur, who could contain himself no longer, suddenly shouted very loudly, 'Did they show their breasts?!!'

Arthur was a tragic relic of an aristocratic Edwardian childhood who, despite being a highly decorated major-general in the Coldstream Guards, badly wounded in the Boer and Great Wars, was quite simply out of his depth in the meritocratic twentieth century. One evening, Arthur had got tickets for a West End show. When they couldn't get a taxi, Pa suggested they take a bus. Arthur had never been on a bus in his life. When they got on, Arthur said to the conductor, 'Do you go to Piccadilly Circus?' The fact that the number 42 had 'Piccadilly Circus' written on the front of it hadn't registered with him. 'Yes, we do,' answered the conductor patiently. 'Will you take us?' asked Arthur, kindly. The fare was tuppence each, so Arthur gave the conductor sixpence and told him to keep the change.

I was brought up with these tales of odd relations. Arthur's sister Ursula drove around Europe in a VW Beetle, teaching the word of the Lord. She never discovered fourth gear so was a serious danger on speed-limit-free autobahns, going flat out in third in the fast lane – about forty. She picked up every hitchhiker she passed and one day a young man threatened her with a knife. She calmly pulled over to the hard shoulder, leant across him to the glovebox, got out a bible and gave it to the perplexed would-be mugger with the words, 'Now I don't believe you have read this. I want you to get out now, take this Bible with you, and when you have studied it thoroughly, come back to me and we will talk further. My address is on the flyleaf.' My great-aunts and -uncles were all devoted to God in such an all-embracing way that their own lives, education, intellect and possessions were entirely secondary to their faith, which is why my father was so frustrated that he had no one in the family who he liked talking to, and the ones he did have anything to do with had managed to throw away his entire inheritance out of sheer ignorance.

So, when my parents left for Australia in 1950, they took just one crate of paintings and furniture to a modest settlement in the midlands of Tasmania. *One* crate. This was all this *nouveau pauvre* aristocrat had been left after a succession of forebears had managed to lose great castles full of the stuff.

So, I was born in a small hospital in Campbell Town, Tasmania, on 1 June 1953. As my family returned to England just two years later, the Australian adventure was like a part of my life that I'd completely missed out on. There were endless family stories of Hupmobiles and corrugated roads, of riding fast horses and climbing mountains, and two photograph albums of black-and-white pictures taken on my mum's Box Brownie camera, with me as a baby in this wonderful place that, to me, was so far away it might have been on

Mars. My elder sisters, Sorrel and Anna, were full of memories, but I had none.

When I did finally get back there, some forty years later, I walked up the path to the hospital and approached the receptionist. She looked up at me and immediately said, 'Oh, are you Tim Bentinck?'

I was shocked. Had my birth made that much impression? It turned out that she was the wife of the old friend of the family with whom I'd arranged to stay that night. When I asked her which room I'd been born in, she told me that the old maternity ward had been knocked down years before. She pointed out of the window at the car park. 'You'd have probably been born just underneath that little red Mazda over there.'

Wandering around Barton, the sheep station where we lived, about ten miles north of Campbell Town, I matched the locations of all the black-and-white photos of me as a baby to their present-day reality. The place was just the same, but in colour. When I dived into Broadwater, the wide, deep part of the river that ran through the estate, I saw in my mind the photo of me floating there aged one with my pa, and it completed a circle, restoring part of my childhood.

The owners kindly left me to my own thoughts, which were sad and jumbled and confused. I tried to picture my mum – naughty, funny, sexy, smoky Pauline Mellowes from Yorkshire, the aesthete, the jazz lover, singer, writer, the play-loving 'pretty one', as described by her older sister Pinkie. What on earth would she have made of sheep-shearing Aussie farmers, stuck in the heat in the middle of nowhere with no one to talk to, two young children and a baby on the way? How had my father persuaded her? He was always thinking ahead and in the post-war years with the fear of MAD – Mutually Assured Destruction – he had read somewhere that the only place in the world that would be almost free from the resultant radiation was Tasmania. That's why he went. In doing so, he made what became known as Pa's Great Mistake.

As far as I can make out, when Pa (broke aristocrat) married Mum (daughter of once wealthy Yorkshire industrialist), said industrialist gave his daughter a sum of money to be used to buy a house. This money was in a form of trust called a Marriage Settlement, administered by a law firm called Bird and Bird (names which I heard my parents utter in the same way a Jewish family might refer to Himmler). Ever a one for the greater picture and often impatient with the petty details like contracts, Pa's Great Mistake was not to read the small print.

He was going off to Tassie to be a farm labourer, but that was just while he pursued his real goal: he was out there to buy a farm with thousands of acres, ride the range and start a dynasty. The small print, however, decreed that any property purchased with said Settlement was to be 'within the borders of the United Kingdom'. The pragmatic Grandpa Mellowes didn't trust this intellectual, flighty, handsome southern fop and wasn't about to see his daughter whisked off to the colonies. That's why Pa stayed a jackaroo for four years. Twit.

So, in 1955, he made an enormous crate out of Tasmanian oak, painted 'HB London' on the side of it, filled it with all the family furniture and paintings, and came home. I know this because there's a photo of him up a ladder painting the words on the crate. After he died, of cancer in 1997, I inherited his enormous book collection, the bookshelves of which were made from this packing case. As I was dismantling them and stacking them together, I found the shelves with the writing on them, which was impossibly moving.

Berkhamsted

Back in England, my parents rented a house in Finchley while they went house-hunting. In fact, 'house-hunting' was one of the first phrases I remember, because that's all the grown-ups seemed to do all day. I used to wonder what sort of House they would eventually catch, and whether or not it might be a dangerous sort of House once they'd found it. It turned out to be quite benign, a four-bedroom detached house called 'Thorn Bank' in a quarter-acre of garden, just outside a village called Potten End, near Berkhamsted.

The garden was my playground, my fantasy world, with a sandpit and Wendy house, where I built camps and treehouses and later a stage with a curtain for putting on plays that I had written. The kitchen, where we ate, was the scene of great philosophical debates with my parents' friends, and sisters' boyfriends, with diagrams written in pencil on the blue Formica top of the dining table. It was also the place where, in January 1967, waiting to be taken back for my second term at boarding school, my father came downstairs and told me that my mother was dead. She had taken an overdose. I still don't know why they never gave her a funeral.

* * *

Until that day, my childhood had been pretty happy. After a rocky first day at a kindergarten called Rothesay in Berkhamsted, when I refused to let go of my father's hand and had to be dragged, screaming, into morning prayers, I settled down to a life of conkers, marbles, swimming, fighting and football. I do have some vague memories of sitting in classrooms while formidable women called Miss and dotty old gents with military titles droned on about things that scared me stiff because I didn't understand them, like Maths, which is odd given my later utter delight in computer programming. There are certain smells that take me straight back to my schooldays. Rothesay is wet leaves on new tarmac (they had just relaid the playground when I arrived), Berkhamsted Prep School is wet white woollen polo-neck jerseys after games, and Harrow is an incriminating mixture of cigarettes and burning electrical motors from the overworked Vent-Axia extractor fan in the first-floor bogs.

The countryside around our house was beautiful, and for an adventurous child it was a bucolic idyll, of which I was the king and my bicycle was a thoroughbred charger. I biked everywhere. My best friend Johnse (his name was Johnson Merrix, a moniker with which his mother used to assault him in full when angry – he's been a relieved John for a while now) and I used to build camps. Our playground was a mixture of the paths, bracken and woods of common land, and the bicycling heaven of the fairways and bunkers of the local golf course. The area had been used to train the troops before they set off for the front in the Great War, so it was dotted with zigzag trenches, foxholes, slit trenches and bomb craters. Our camps were made by covering these holes with branches and leaves – a technique learned from Pooh when making Heffalump traps. I can't really remember what we did when inside them; we were too young to smoke; maybe it was a desire to return to the womb or an early manifestation of nest-building, a trait which has been an important part of my life – building a home, making things, repairing, being practical. Basically, it was nine-year-old DIY.

I loved my bike for the total freedom it gave me. Some of the shell craters made amazing bike courses, like modern-day skateboard parks, and we would spend hours finessing our techniques and timing our runs. I used to bicycle to school, which in the morning meant crossing the common, then a death-defyingly fast downhill run of about a mile, past the Norman Berkhamsted Castle and into the town. Going back was a grinding slog, but my God I was fit. My first bike was a second-hand boneshaker, but putting black-and-white check tape down the side made it go like a rocket. When I was finally given a new one – a Raleigh three-speed – the twist-grip gears were about the most futuristic, coolest things I had ever seen. It felt like being on a motorbike. I learned to do wheelies and I saved up my pocket money to get special off-road tyres, which slowed the bike down a lot but looked great when covered with mud. Instant smell-memory: 3-in-One oil. I never knew what three things it did, but the fact that you were getting three things for the price of one made it important, grown-up and highly technical. A must for boys who wanted to be spaceship-pilots like Dan Dare, racing drivers like Stirling Moss, pilots like Biggles or land-speed record holders like Malcolm Campbell. A world of fantasy and invention, the joy of Wednesdays when the *Eagle* comic would arrive, and the sadness of Thursdays knowing you had another whole week to wait for the next one.

We would watch *Doctor Who*, *Robin Hood* and Westerns – classic black-and-white cowboy shows on a small screen. I'd lie on the floor about a foot from the tiny TV and live every minute of *Bronco Lane*,

Rawhide, *The Lone Ranger* and *Bonanza* and, as you only saw it the once – no replay, no catch-up – you had to literally replay it yourself. So I'd strap on ma six-gun, pull on ma chaps, slip on ma weskit and flip on ma Stetson. With my trusty steed 'Raleigh Roadster', I was ready. First, I had to check for Injuns. Keeping low, I gained the cover of the hedge. From there, I made my way slowly and quietly to the top of the garden and the overhanging bough that I could climb up to reach the extensive, camouflaged treehouse I had built. I could reconnoitre the whole garden, judging whether it would be safe to continue the mission on to the Wendy house. To keep ready for any trouble, I would practise my quick draw. Johnse and I would have shoot-outs, and of course whoever went, 'Peeeew, peeeew' first, won. I became lethally quick: I was like the gunfighter Johnny Ringo. This skill was to bear fruit some forty years later when I was in a Western myself. The problem was I couldn't stop going 'Peeeew, peeeew!' even in tight close-up. Some things are ingrained.

We had a beagle called Jasper and a black cat called Oospoo. Jasper was great: he could roam free and would be called back for food in the evening with a bugle. That's why I can play the bugle – again, nothing wasted. One day, he came back in the van of a farmer who said the next time he chased his bloody sheep he'd 'shoot the bastard hound!' As a result, I have a vague recollection of taking Jasper for a walk through a field, showing him a sheep, and saying, 'NO! UNDERSTAND? NO!'

My first paid job was working on a farm in Nettleden. This gave me the farming experience I still use in my imagination for *The Archers*, and in my mind the farm remains the location of the yard at Brookfield. Later, when my father and stepmother created an organic smallholding in Devon, I did more farm work, but the traditional family farm at Nettleden, with its cows, sheep and pigs, is also a great source of inspiration. There was a big bloke with massive sideburns and a strong old Hertfordshire accent called Jess, and a weaselly, naughty kid called Nobby who used to take me out poaching. All my scenes with Jethro and later Bert Fry have resonances with those two, and that's where I learned to drive a tractor, muck out a pig sty, build a barbed-wire fence (I have the scars to prove it), toss a bale to the top of a haystack and roll a crafty fag.

I've always been able to imagine a mile in my head because, just down the road from our house, was 'The Mad Mile' – a stretch of almost straight country road on which my father, and later I, used to test the speed of our Beetle. The answer was always the same, about 68 mph, top whack. His other trick was to see how late he could leave it before braking for the T-junction. He'd worked out that if he hit the anchors at the second he passed the T-junction sign, he'd stop just in time. One night he was returning from work, over the limit (the norm in those days), missed the sign due to thick fog and went straight through the fence at the end and into a field. The barbed wire on the top of the fence ripped the sunshine roof clean off and the rest of the car was battered and bruised. In the morning, when I got up to find the pitiable remains of my favourite thing in the world, I stormed into my parents' bedroom, purple with rage and streaming tears, and shouted, 'What have you done to Folksie?!' A few days later, no doubt to make up for his idiocy, Pa bought me a toy Beetle. Not a Corgi, Dinky or Matchbox, but a large, blue, beautiful model with a pull-back engine and opening doors. Within a week I had taken a hammer to it and bashed it to make it look like our own. I have it still.

It was typical of my father that, having gone through a war where the Germans had nearly killed him, taken him prisoner and amused themselves by subjecting him to a mock execution, the first car he had bought when we got back from Tassie was Hitler's iconic People's Car, the VW Beetle. Compared to everything else on the road in the late fifties, it looked like a spaceship. Pa was fascinated by modern things and the future, so to him it made perfect sense. Crowds would gather when we stopped at traffic lights, asking what on earth it was. It was metallic bronze and I was brought up to the sound of its air-cooled flat-four engine, as my place was the 'back-back' – the luggage space behind the back seat which was like a cot, and I would sleep there on long journeys. And boy did we have some long journeys.

Every Christmas we would drive up to visit our cousins in Forfar, Scotland. It's only an eight-hour drive these days, but in the 1960s it meant a marathon journey on the Great North Road with a family of five and all their clothes, plus Christmas presents, jammed into a tiny Beetle with an underpowered 1200cc engine and a six-volt battery. The headlights were only slightly brighter than candles but we would drive through the whole night, often in freezing hail, fog or snow. One time, it was so cold that the windscreen wipers froze up and my father, damned if he was going to stop because he'd managed to overtake a lorry four miles back after an hour of trying, got my mum to stick her head up through the sunshine roof to free the wipers.

The reason we had all managed to fit in the car was because my mother had won the packing prize at school. Every spare space in the car was used, even around the engine. Wine bottles and Christmas crackers were fitted round the fuel tank, which made Christmas lunch at Fotheringham a spectacular affair when the petrol-soaked crackers were pulled.

Scotland was magical. Flinging curling stones down bumpy frozen lochs, driving wildly around the estate in a Jag that smelled of oil and leather, playing in the massive loft full of generations of memories, and togging up for fancy-dress dinners in the clothes we found there.

The other great thing about our car was that I was allowed to drive it from a very young age. Can you imagine the pride, aged about ten, on hearing your father say, 'Timmy, can you get the car out please?' I would rush out, open the garage doors, start the car, back it out ten yards, turn the wheel, put it in first, drive forward another ten yards and stop it outside the front door. I passed my test about a week after my seventeenth birthday and got my HGV Class 2 licence when I was twenty-three. One of my great regrets is not being a Formula One driver. It all started with that Beetle.

After Rothesay, I went to Berkhamsted Prep and then Junior School. I had a pretty good time, at least until the last year, but my standout memories are of being punished. One teacher was very partial to grabbing chunks of our hair and twisting it until it nearly came out. His other hobby was rapping us hard on the back of the hand with a ruler. The headmaster's beatings had an especially perverse cruelty about them. You would wait on a bench in the table-tennis room, which smelled of lino and polish, and be summoned into the head-master's study, which smelled of pipe smoke and leather. You would then take down your trousers and underpants and bend over the back of a leather armchair and be hit six times, hard, with a cane. I remember him actually saying, 'This hurts me more than it does you,' and I had to shake his hand at the end and say 'Thank you, sir.'

The decision to send me to Harrow had a disastrous effect on my last year at Berkhamsted. The norm for the boys was to go from the Junior School straight into the Senior School, but my parents had other things in mind. I never asked my father about it and now it's too late. It's not as though he could afford the fees – his salary as an adman at J. Walter Thompson was ridiculously small as he never asked for a raise and remained stupidly loyal to them. I believe he got help from richer relations, one of whom admonished me once for not thanking her – I would have done if I'd known.

Once my friends found out I was going to a posh school, and was having to take private Latin lessons to get me through Common Entrance, they ceased to be my friends. I was sent to Coventry, teased, baited and mentally bullied. The most hurtful thing of all was that my closest friend, a boy called Jeremy, became the ringleader of my tormentors. I used to hide during break so they couldn't gang up on me, and no one came to my birthday party that last year.

Jeremy and I had acted in lots of school plays together. I distinctly remember the first one, *The Dear Departed* by Stanley Houghton, in which we were both playing women. He got a huge laugh when he shot out of the wings and leapt into my arms in fear of being caught by the baddy. It took trust and friendship. After the first night, I went outside to look for my parents, forgetting to take off my make-up, and found myself being noticed by the departing audience. I came back inside and remarked on the attention I was getting. 'Oh, I'm not interested in that sort of thing,' Jeremy replied superciliously, putting me in my place and making me wonder if that was the 'sort of thing' that I wanted. Fifty years later and still an actor, I suppose the answer must be yes, a bit.

The change from best friend to chief tormentor was harsh and cruel, and I never forgave him. His treachery stuck with me for a long time, but when I discovered, well into my forties, that he had been killed in a car accident, I didn't know how to feel. I was shocked and saddened at his death, but, selfishly, I also felt cheated of confronting him with his betrayal of our friendship. I'm sure that as an adult he would have apologised, and I could have laid that period of my life to rest, but he wasn't able to, so it still hurts. It explains why I was so oversensitive to bullying when my two boys were at school, and why I have such a dislike for the cowardice of trolls and cyber-bullies today.

Another lesson learned at that school was that parents should be very careful about complaining, as it's usually the child who suffers. I once got full marks on a test in maths, which was highly unusual but I'd done some work for a change. I was accused of cheating and given 0/10 and a punishment. Upset, I told my mother, who complained bitterly to the teacher. The result was that at the next test, where I got my usual middling marks, the teacher said, 'Bentinck, 5/10. However, we'd better give you full marks. We don't want your *mother* complaining again, do we?' Bastard.

Harrow School

When my father dropped me off on day one at Harrow in 1966, he remarked, 'Hasn't changed much since my time' – his time being 1932–7, which meant it hadn't changed much since the nineteenth century. The main difference, which he never stopped going on about, was that we had central heating, whereas they froze in Harry Potter-like dormitories with open fires and an allowance of about one lump of coal per week.

The school is divided up into houses of about sixty boys each. I was in Moretons, which is right smack in the middle, making getting to classrooms a lot easier than for the boys at the end of Harrow Hill. When I arrived I was put in a room with two other wide-eyed innocents. The houses are like rabbit warrens with bits added on over the centuries, so that finding my way around took months to learn. This made responding to 'boy calls' even harder. The fagging system at Harrow was complex but more or less phased out by the time I left. This was annoying because I willingly submitted to being treated like a virtual slave for my first year only because I knew that when I got to be a sixth former, I too would have someone to clean my shoes, make my tea, go shopping, run errands, clean my room and generally do as they're told. I had to do all that shit, and never got to dole it out later.

Those were 'private' fags. A boy call was made by a sixth-former whose private fag was out or unavailable and it went like this. Said sixth-former stands outside his room and shouts, 'BOY, BOY, BOY, BOY, BOY!' upon which anyone in their first year has to drop what they are doing or, if they're on the bog, stop mid-effort, and run at full speed through the warren of corridors to where the shouting is coming from. Last boy there gets the job. This explains why I and my contemporaries were highly skilled at leaping down an entire flight of stairs in one go, and tended to win at rugby.

I can't say that I hated Harrow. I made some very good friends, some of whom remain dear to me to this day. My mum took her own life just after my first term at boarding school – maybe she wasn't too keen on the last of her children leaving home, and was alone and sad. It was tough, but those friends helped me through, especially Noël Diacono, who was my new room-mate that term. He was essentially brutal and didn't allow me time to wallow in sadness, but he knew what he was doing. Now in our sixties, he's the brother I never had.

I once read a psychiatrist saying that five years at a boys' boarding school does untold psychological damage, ruins sex lives, screws up a man's ability to have relationships and triggers a budding psycho-path into full-on barking lunacy. Well, no one who decides to be an actor can be described as completely normal, but I seem to have survived, if not unscathed, then just about able to cope. Part of the reason for that has been the love of my older sisters, Sorrel and Anna, whom I adore, an easy and happy life with my mother in the short time I had with her, a close relationship with my father, then, later, the incredible luck of meeting my beloved Judy when I was twenty-one, and the joy of bringing up our amazing boys, Will'm and Jasper.

I perfectly understand why some people think of boys who went to places like Harrow and Eton as out-of-touch, privileged toffs, without a care in the world. Funnily enough, that's exactly what we thought of Etonians. Most of my friends' parents weren't rich but had scrimped and saved from fairly modest middle-class incomes to send their sons there, and had nothing left over for any luxuries. That's not to say that some kids weren't minted, but as a rule the brash rich tended to be disliked and it was considered bad form to boast of wealth. Of course, everything is relative and we had no understanding of real poverty or suffering; the only ethnic minorities we ever met were African or Arab princes and kings; and a lot of boys were picked up at the end of term in Bentleys and Jags, although my pa brilliantly used to turn up in winter in his rusty convertible Beetle with the hood down, long white hair and beard flowing, wearing a black eyepatch and his grandfather's Canadian racoon-skin coat, with massive furry collar turned up.

Sports were an important part of life at Harrow. I was quite good at most sports, but not outstanding. The one thing at which I excelled was swimming. I learned how to swim fast from Pa, who had the most graceful freestyle stroke, and it is written of my Great-Uncle Henry, who died at the Somme, that to witness 'Bentinck off the high board was worth travelling miles to see' according to the school magazine, the *Harrovian*. The Harrow pool was called Ducker, as it used to be a duck pond. Before it was abandoned in the seventies, it was the longest outdoor private pool in Europe, some 250 yards long, incorporating a 50-yard racing section, and was unheated. It was here that my father found himself in the thirties swimming naked against the Hitler Youth (swimming trunks were only made compulsory in the late 1950s when they built the nearby hospital that overlooks the pool). During the war, my father was comforted by the knowledge that 'extremely cold water has the same shrivelling effect on a Nazi as it does on a Harrovian'. It was inspiring to find in the changing rooms one's own father's name carved on the wooden boards for cups and prizes won, and I set out to emulate him.

I was used to cold water as our local pool, the Deer Leap in Little Gaddesden, was an unheated outdoor lido – blissful on summer days but so cold it made your head ache if you swam too fast. The Berkhamsted School pool, by contrast, was indoor, heated and only 25 yards long. I'd been swimming captain there and also had the school underwater distance record, so I arrived at Harrow thinking I was the bee's knees. I had a rude awakening. One fifty-yard length of the pool in near freezing water was a massive shock to the system, but probably explained why the school won everything – we just wanted to get out of the bloody water as soon as we could.

I was the fastest boy ever to swim in that pool, as I still held the individual medley and freestyle records when they shut it down and built an indoor replacement. I also swam the last ever length there when, many years later, my dear friend Noël and I, on a nostalgic, alcohol-fuelled ramble about the old place, scrambled through undergrowth to find the pool ruinous, abandoned, but so full of memories. There was about three feet of rainwater, so I stripped off to the buff and swam the last length. My great-uncle had spent his final week's leave from the Front at the pool, so there was a palpable sense of sadness and closure in that act.

Having a cool dad but having lost my mum; being a swimmer and a smoker (the two went inextricably together); being not great at footie but a demonic tackler; playing the guitar; having a tuck box full of Mr Kipling's Almond Slices (probably the most delicious thing ever made) left over from one of Pa's advertising shoots; doing Modern Languages – these things made me accepted in such relieving contrast to the tormented, excluded year I'd come from.

Of course, I look back now with rose-tinted glasses, but there were satisfying moments, including getting into a bath full of hot muddy water after freezing games of rugby or Harrow Football, then having tea and toast before setting off in the dark for more lessons, bruised and bleeding but wrapped up in the traditional long Harrow scarf. In a perverse way, the feeling of having survived without having any limbs ripped off was a good one.

And Ducker was magical, beautiful, serene. When we weren't racing or diving, there were 'log mills', a mill is a fight, and a log is a log. There were logs floating in the water and teams of about twenty boys would fight each other to get a log to their side of the pool. The log had splinters, the pool was rough concrete, and like so many things which 'wouldn't be allowed today', it was great.

As the sun set, we'd walk back to the Hill, avoiding the cow pats on the football fields that were grazed by Friesians, munching our Ducker Biscuits – huge rich-tea wheels that cost a penny each – and a Coke that was sixpence, bought from the small hatch in the door of the pool-keeper's cottage, run by Mr Campkin, who had been there in my father's day and remembered his swimming. Mr Campkin had treasures of chocolate inside, which you could just see through the hatch but could only afford on special occasions. Glowing and exhausted, we walked across fields and up to our rooms in the huge houses on top of the Hill.

All of that was pretty blissful.

On the other hand, I was pretty much constantly homesick. I just counted down the days until I could go home. There was a thing called 'Exeat Weekends', when our parents would come and collect us on Friday night, and we had to be back on Sunday evening. Even the word 'evening' felt like a very grown-up luxury, to be allowed back so late. I would feel the joy of release on the Friday night when I'd hear from way up the road the sound of the familiar VW engine of my childhood come gurgling round the corner, and I'd rush down with my bag and leap in the car before Pa had hardly stopped, and we'd be away from what was essentially a prison term, locked up in a building, with no choice but to stay, beaten if we misbehaved, made to attend classes, chapel and cadet force, required to wear starched collar and tails, compulsory exercise, no drinking, no girls, no smoking (!) – no wonder we wanted to go home.

In the first summer holiday after Mum died, my father borrowed a Commer camper van and we set off together to tour round Eastern Europe. I never asked him why, but I imagine it was a desire for a father/son bonding exercise and guilt about my parents' deteriorating relationship, which had contributed to my mum's depression and suicide. That summer I wrote a poem that began:

> I went round Eastern Europe in a Commer with
> my Dad.
> It was nineteen sixty-seven, my mum had gone
> to heaven,
> We saw the sights in black and white and both
> of us were feeling
> Understandably
> Quite sad.

It was an odd trip to take in the years of the cold war: East Germany, Poland, Czechoslovakia, Austria, Switzerland and back through France. We had an amazing 1960s Philips Mignon portable record player that purported to play 45s on the move. It was very futuristic as you slid the record in like a modern car CD player, and it had dampers to stop it jumping. My dad used to like to play Scott McKenzie's 'San Francisco (Be Sure To Wear Flowers In Your Hair)' because it filled him with hope for a better post-war future, run by peace-loving hippies. I got into trouble for leaving the discs on the dashboard in the sun, and they all warped except Nancy Sinatra's 'You Only Live Twice'. I wrote in the poem:

> Of all the songs that melted in the dormobile
>> that day
> The one song that survived it was the one that
>> made him cry.
> The one I'd brought, when he'd asked not,
>> the Bond theme about living twice.
> Because my
> Mother hadn't.

Memories of that trip include his outrage at having a massive military bayonet confiscated at the East German border, doing black-market cash deals with a Polish woman in a petrol station toilet, me being pulled off the roof of the camper as I took photographs of Soviet troops parachuting into the Danube, and pouring water from the sink into the radiator (the engine was between the front seats) as we puffed and steamed our way over the Alps.

Happier times with my father were spent at home and abroad on the film sets for the TV commercials he produced for J. Walter Thompson. These included ads for Mother's Pride, with Dusty Springfield, Joe Brown and Andy Stewart, and Mr Kipling (it was Pa who wrote the lines 'Mr Kipling makes exceedingly good cakes' and cast the inimitable voice of James Hayter).

These days TV commercials don't generate the iconic status that they used to, but back then some ads became part of the national consciousness. If you say to anyone of my generation, 'Do you remember the Nimble balloon adverts?' they will nearly all say yes. The strapline was 'Real bread, but lighter'. 'Bingo,' thought Pa, 'strap it to a balloon.'

Expanding on this idea, he imagined a girl eating a Nimble sandwich in a balloon basket with a beautiful Spanish castle in the background. Why a Spanish castle? Probably because Pa fancied a trip to Spain. In those pre-green screen days and with massive budgets, films were made in exotic locations simply for the jolly! Which is how he found himself in Segovia with a hydrogen balloon, a film crew and me. It was an amazing adventure for a fourteen-year-old, and it's probably why I feel so at home on a film set to this day.

On the first day, they inflated the balloon with hydrogen bottles but discovered the first major problem: the 'Nimble Bread' banner was so small you couldn't read the lettering. Cue Bentinck improvisation skills. He got the art director to go around the town buying as many large white cotton sheets as he could find. He then co-opted the hotel ballroom and laid them out on the floor where the art director pencilled out the new lettering. Next, he found a willing local with a sewing machine to stitch them all together, then overnight got everyone, including me, to work with buckets of paint filling in the lettering. By the morning it was dry and ready.

In the ad, you can see a flock of rooks flying past as the balloon takes off with Segovia Castle in the background. That was me in a wood, armed with a walkie-talkie. On 'action', I had to set off firecrackers so that the rooks flew past, in the right direction, at the exact right time. I was terrified I'd get it wrong but it worked. Just imagine today letting the producer's fourteen-year-old be in charge of something like that. Today, the entire thing would be done on a computer anyway, which is why it's not so much fun doing adverts any more!

Once the balloon was airborne, the second problem became apparent. Where exactly was it going to end up? It was the balloon crew department's job to retrieve it. An incredibly cool babe-magnet and ex-soldier called John Spear followed it across all terrain with the aid of a four-wheel-drive Land Rover and binoculars, but he was amazed to find that, having bounced and skidded across impenetrable Spanish desert for hours, he'd been beaten to the balloon's final resting spot by a film producer with a black eyepatch and his young son. Our only resources had been a beaten-up convertible Beetle and the question, 'Ha visto un globo?' The phrase has gone down in family history.

The Nimble girl was an incredibly brave model from London called Emily Cumming. She wasn't a stunt girl or a balloon expert, and for the long shots of the balloon in flight, she was replaced by Christine Turnbull, the daughter of the balloon manufacturer, Gerry. However, the following year they used a hot-air balloon in Switzerland, and that was when Emily earned everyone's admiration for her extraordinary bravery. This time, instead of a castle as a backdrop, Pa wanted the Eiger. So, they built a steel-frame mock-up of the bottom of the balloon, which was then suspended from a helicopter. Emily was slung beneath the steel frame, and the whole contraption was then lifted to a photogenic spot, about fourteen thousand feet high, in front of the mountain. These days she'd be wearing a parachute harness and every safety device known to man would be employed; and no way on earth a totally inexperienced but immensely brave model would be hand-cued, from another helicopter filming her a few yards away, to reach into a small hidden backpack, take out a slimming sandwich and eat it as though she were taking tea on the lawn. In fact her harness was just a few straps sewn together, designed by my father. Terrifying.

The location for the very first Nimble ad was less glamorous, and involved a very young Joanna Lumley diving into a freezing and muddy river in Gloucestershire. I was there too, and Joanna held my hand. I've been in love with her ever since.

So at least I was having some fun in the holidays, which took my mind off missing Mum.

I was finally released from Harrow in 1971. I was amazed to find that fellow pupils whom I thought I knew were setting off to become accountants or to work in banking. I thought they were bonkers, but of course most of them are now multi-millionaires who retired at forty. The friends from Harrow that I've kept in touch with are more like me: teachers, charity workers, psychologists, alcoholic writers, hippie drop-outs, that kind of thing. Mind you, there's a smattering of eccentric lawyers, lords and landowners who are good chums too!

The subject of my schooling came up when I worked with a communist-voting actress called Marjorie Yates in a production of *Hedda Gabler* at the King's Head Theatre in London. Hedda was played by Elizabeth Quinn, the profoundly deaf actress famous for *Children of a Lesser God*. I played her loving husband, Tesman, which was terrifying as she couldn't hear a word any of the cast were saying, so if anything went wrong, as can happen, a line missed or misspoken, where a hearing actor adjusts accordingly – she couldn't adjust accordingly. Still that's acting: a lot of the time it's just balls-out terror. One night in the dressing room, Marjorie asked me where I'd been to school. When I said Harrow, she said, 'Oh, so that's why you're so fucking confident.' That got me thinking. Was I able, insanely and without the talent to justify it, to walk out on stage just because of a confidence I'd gained at school? The younger me would have said, no, I did it all myself, but perhaps I might not otherwise have had the chutzpah to have made the bloody stupid decision to be a freelance, hand-to-mouth, jobbing actor, trading on a fleeting artistry that will fade with age while still hoping to be finally discovered by Spielberg.

Mind you, it's been fun.

Mind the Gap year

I got lousy grades in my A levels so if I was to have any chance of going to university, I'd have to resit them. I found this out in a phone box on a beach in Sardinia during a serious bout of food poisoning. I was hungry, broke, living in a tent, feeling like I was dying, and I had to decide whether to come home and do the exams again instead of continuing my journey to India.

I was eighteen, and after hitchhiking and working around Europe for a few months I'd bought my first car, a VW 1500N step-back, the saloon version of the Variant, and I had set off down the Indian hippie trail, stopping every now and then to earn enough money for food and petrol to get me to my next stop. I'd spent a fortnight in Florence where I'd worked handing out leaflets for a discotheque. The deal was that if I could get British and American girls to go for free, the local men would pay in droves to get in. I'd write my name on the leaflet and get paid for everyone that took me up on it. So essentially I was being paid to chat up all the girls in Florence! I found a cheap café that did spaghetti bolognese and a glass of wine for a few lire, which has given me a life-long love of the combination.

I stayed in a campsite just outside town, and when I tried to leave without paying, the poor bloke on the gate accepted as surety for my return my much-loved but essentially valueless *Man from U.N.C.L.E.* identification card. I still feel guilty about that.

I took the ferry to Sardinia where my sister Sorrel had got me a job as a child-minder and cleaner for an Italian family. She came to visit me but had no idea where I was, so in typically forthright fashion she simply walked through the town yelling my name. When the job ended and Sorrel had left, I finished up in my tent on a beach, where I now had to make a big decision about my future. After a lot of soul-searching I decided to come home. I drove back up Italy, over the Alps, and was halfway through Germany when the front-right wheel bearing seized solid on the autobahn. By amazing chance, I had stopped within sight of a major VW dealership. I stood in wonder as the chief mechanic sat by my jacked-up car like a surgeon with his patient, as fawning underlings slapped spanners into his hand like nurses with scalpels. Finally, he resorted to a blow torch and burned the entire wheel assembly clean off and replaced the whole thing. The entire procedure took about an hour and I remember wondering how on earth they had lost the war.

I was aiming to get back in time for my old friend Jamie Borthwick's birthday party the following night, so I kept driving, napping in the car when my eyelids started to droop. In Holland at 4 a.m. I ran out of fuel by a dyke and had to hitchhike to the nearest petrol station, sleeping by a pump until it opened. I reached Calais mid-morning, only to be told that all the ferries were full until the next day. I'd been through enough; I wasn't going to miss the party. I drove to Dunkirk, figuring it to be a historically good place to get to England from. Amazingly I found a merchant ship that was loading goods onto its deck and blagged a lift. I drove the car onto a large net, and they hoisted us both aboard. I lunched with the captain in some style and was dumped on the Dover docks a few hours later.

In those days, Dover to Brancaster in north Norfolk was a good six hours, but setting off at two I reckoned I'd be just in time. I nearly didn't make it. On the north Norfolk coast road about a mile from my destination there's a rather hairy chicane, and, pumped up with a massive sense of achievement at having made it from Sardinia in one go, I approached it at about sixty and went straight into the ditch. Still my luck held; a passing tractor hauled me out and I drove the last mile to the party, only to find it was a black-tie event. Resplendent in oily T-shirt, jeans, greasy hair and thick stubble, I was fit, tanned and safe so I couldn't have cared less.

I had managed a 'B' in English and my French just needed some more work, but I'd failed my German, so my father arranged for me to stay with cousins in Hamburg for two months. Wilhelm and Ise von Ilsemann, together with their children Andrea and Godard, had been briefed by Pa not to speak English with me at all. I didn't know this and thought, right until my last day, that he had stupidly managed to find the ONLY well-educated family in Germany that didn't have a word of English. Wilhelm was a director of Shell and he got me a job in market research.

It wasn't all work though. I was taken out for weekend adventures by a wonderfully eccentric cousin called Baron Joska Pintschovius and his barking-mad friend, the artist, satirist and radio comedian Heino Jaeger. They were older than me and had grown up to believe that the death and destruction that fell from the skies as they played in the ruins of Hamburg was normality. When the Allied bombardment was over they both experienced a kind of post-traumatic stress disorder in reverse, in that they found they missed it. Heino's art is predominantly to do with the iconography of bombs, destruction, war and Nazis, and when we went off in Joska's smoke-filled Mercedes for the day, we were on the hunt for bunkers, steel helmets and swastikas. When they came to visit me at university the following year, it was as if the concrete campus just outside Norwich had been built specifically for them.

'Da! Da ist noch ein bunker!'

East Anglia

The University of East Anglia (UEA) looks something like a spaceship that has landed on a golf course. Designed by Denys Lasdun, it shares its architectural style with the National Theatre on the South Bank, which he built some ten years later. Rough concrete, steel and carpet – the perfect 'bunker' for my war-damaged German friends.

I arrived in 1972 and read History of Art, not because I initially had any special interest in art, but because I knew I wasn't going to be a scientist and I was done with studying languages.

I often wonder if the whole 'confident' thing wasn't just my enormous relief at being free. After all, not many Harrovians went to UEA – I'd been attracted to the university because there'd been a student sit-in the previous year and that sounded so radical and anti-establishment. If I had been more industrious, I might just have scraped into Oxbridge, but at the time it seemed to me to be an extension of Harrow, with possibly a few girls thrown in. Tales of having to avoid college porters and sneaking out at night didn't appeal to me. At UEA, I had a car and could come and go as I pleased. Academic demands aside, my days were my own and I filled them as I wished; I played Frisbee, went water-skiing in the local gravel pits, played guitar, went to concerts, rehearsed and performed plays. Even the lectures and seminars were given and led by people who loved their subjects and discussed them with you on equal terms; it was very different from the teacher/pupil relationship that I had endured at school – I was learning how to learn. Perhaps I wasn't so much confident as full of the joy of life – I was happy for a change.

Unfortunately, the self-assuredness didn't extend to dating. Maybe that shrink's assessment of public schoolboys is right about one thing: I was always hopeless at getting girls into bed. I once popped the question to a girl I fancied wildly at about two in the morning after we'd spent the whole evening talking and listening to music. 'Christ,' she said, 'I thought you'd never ask.' I look at pictures of me in those days and I suppose I was a fairly handsome chap, but I didn't think so at the time, and never dreamed that anyone fancied me back. That's not to say I was awkward with girls, quite the opposite: I just didn't want to offend them!

In my first year, I shared a room in the iconic ziggurat residence of Norfolk Terrace with Dave Robinson. I don't know if the authorities did this on purpose but Dave Robinson and I had completely different backgrounds and interests. He was from a state school, he had long black hair and a moustache, and was reading physics and chemistry. The only things we had in common were getting wrecked and watching Monty Python. Which was enough really. He'd never met anyone like me before and vice versa, but he was a lovely bright lad and we learned a lot from each other. I was astonished and relieved to find myself surrounded by northerners, communists, women, cockneys, Glaswegians, Asians and black people who weren't royal; I discovered a whole new world and I loved it.

It's quite odd doing a degree in something you know absolutely nothing about, and I had a huge amount of catching up to do on the history of art, but the great joy was that I was doing it because I wanted to, not because I was being forced; it was my idea and mine alone. I discovered that I loved architecture. Maybe this is because I like to make things; I want to see the physical skill in something and wonder 'How did you do that?' I like the idea of 'finding the figure' within a stone carving, as though it was always there and just needs the artist to reveal it. I love the strange importance of proportion, and the mystery of why the Golden Ratio just feels 'right'. I have a sneaking regard for Rachel Whiteread's *House* – filling a terraced house with concrete and then knocking the walls and roof away to display a concrete version of the space inside. And I love buildings because they are like the sea and the sky, they are seen by everyone who passes by; they are the same now as when they were first built and somehow embody the zeitgeist of the period. Buildings are like time travel, especially ruins which, in their decay, seem to express the past so much better than the roped-off furniture and paintings of a National Trust stately home. I've also always wanted to build my own house, from scratch. Now that would be my kind of art!

I found that I wasn't that turned on by paintings. To this day, I'm not a fan of non-figurative and more abstract art. It was pretty clear to me very early on that whatever I was going to end up doing for the rest of my life, it wasn't going to involve dealing with other peoples' art, I wanted to be the one who created stuff. There aren't many jobs for which a degree in History of Art qualifies you anyway – academia was not my world and otherwise working for Christie's, Sotheby's or an art gallery was not a seductive prospect either. Nonetheless, I enjoyed the detective part of finding a painting's provenance and the research required to find how an artist was influenced in his life, and I enjoyed the discussions and gaining a deeper understanding of art. Just being able to bandy about the word 'painterly' made me feel like I was a real undergraduate, able to verbally spar with academics on Radio 4 discussion programmes who can't get through a sentence without saying 'in a sense'. Such are the linguistic shibboleths of learning, worn like badges or secret handshakes of identification, and I enjoyed being accepted into this new club.

However, the theatre at UEA was where I was happiest. On the first day, at the Freshers' Fair, I joined the Drama Society, and that was where all my focus lay for the next three years. We did a play every term and it was really what I lived for. At Harrow, I used to devise and produce end-of-term sketch shows with music, but I only ever did one school play. I'd always been good at accents, voices and mimicry and just wanted to make people laugh. Shakespeare had seemed impenetrable and was performed only by a small coterie of classicists and scholars, and if you weren't part of their circle, you didn't get invited. The UEA Drama Society was more like a rep company, a mongrel assemblage of oddballs who were having loads of fun. This was where I cut my teeth and discovered my strengths and weaknesses.

I discovered drying. I now know that you can walk on stage for the umpteenth performance of a play, get to a line that you have delivered perfectly every night for months and suddenly find yourself enveloped in a dark blanket of memory loss. You experience not just the loss of the line, but everything – who you are, where you are, what the play is, what you had for lunch – nothing remains. The first time it happened to me was on the first night of Joe Orton's *The Ruffian on the Stair* – I just stopped. It instantly shattered my blithe confidence, and to this day drying is one of my worst fears. It can have you shaking in the wings, and, unfortunately, it gets worse with age: Laurence Olivier, as a younger man, once said to Anthony Hopkins, 'Remember, nerves are vanity – you're wondering what people think of you; to hell with them, just jump off the edge.' But in old age he could barely go on, and directed the other actors on stage not to look at him, so terrified was he of drying. Much later, I discovered how to stop this. If your head is in the right place, the lines are only a guide to what the character is thinking, and since you are *being* that character, not just pretending to be him, then it's much harder to forget a line as this would mean also forgetting who you actually *are* and what you believe. That's the theory anyway.

I discovered corpsing. In James Saunders's *A Scent of Flowers* there's a scene where a coffin is lowered into a grave. Just prior to this, the 'corpse' walks, trance-like, past the mourners and into her final resting place – all very symbolic. In our production, as we solemnly lowered the heavy oak coffin, borrowed from a local undertaker, my fellow pallbearer's foot slipped and he dropped his end of the coffin straight on top of the unfortunate corpse. The audience then heard the deceased, played by Belinda Oliver, scream, 'FUCK!' I looked for help to the guilty party, a Scottish bloke with an impish face, which was now streaming with tears. I turned upstage to find that the mourners were no longer gazing sorrowfully, but instead had turned their backs on the audience in a forlorn attempt at concealing their convulsions. When they began to emit a strange, strangulated mewling, the vicar broke down and began to weep openly with laughter. Just when we thought it couldn't get any worse, the injured corpse suddenly arose from her grave and, with the words 'Sorry, but I'm actually bleeding', staggered off the stage. I really don't think I've ever heard an audience laugh so long or so loud.

I also discovered 'The Pint After the Show', which is without doubt the most sublime drink in the world. There's an old actor's tale of a seasoned thespian who offers a young actor a drink before they go on. When the youngster politely refuses, the old boy asks in horror, 'You mean you're going on *alone?*' Drinking before the show is not to be recommended; I've tried it and it doesn't help, but drinking afterwards is pretty much the entire point. Relief, achievement, pride, release, basically not being shit scared any more – all these things go so well with a pint or three. I'm sure there must be actors who don't touch a drop, but personally I've only ever met the ones who have been told to stop by their doctors.

Where did this love of performing come from? Thankfully I have one recording of my mother's voice. On it, I'm aged about twelve and I'm showing her how our new Grundig reel-to-reel tape recorder worked. The banter between us is lovely, we do Pete & Dud voices, and she reels off great swathes of Shakespeare, rueing the fact that at that very minute she is missing seeing Richard Burton playing Dr Faustus in Oxford. My mum adored the theatre and could easily have been an actress, and when my sister Anna went into the business, I was hooked. Strange how it took me three years of not enjoying History of Art to come to the conclusion.

In my second year, I shared a houseboat with another Robinson, Michael. My friendship with Mike began during my very first night at the student bar when I dropped the 10p I was going to feed into the jukebox. Mike picked up the coin and told me I could have it back as long as I played something decent which, of course, was David Bowie. I was a Bowie freak – the first Ziggy Stardust concert that I went to was at the Friars Club in Aylesbury in 1972 and had a profound effect on me: I got both my ears pierced and dyed my hair – my father actually fell over when he first saw me, which, considering what a rebel he'd been, was quite a result. (One of the ear piercings went septic and I ended up wearing a single big gold earring in my right ear for years afterwards. What everyone failed to tell me was it signified that you were gay, which I wasn't, but it explained the friendly looks I used to get on Old Compton Street.) Luckily Mike approved of my choice of song and we've remained friends ever since. The houseboat, which was once owned by George Formby, was moored on the river Bure near Horning. It looked like a railway carriage, with a large room at one end and three bedrooms off a corridor that ran the length of the boat. It had gas heaters and the electricity came from a small Honda generator. The owner was a drummer who worked on cruise ships, and after a thorough briefing in September, he left us to it and went off to the Caribbean for nine months, with no way of getting in touch with him. Within a week, the generator packed up, leaving us to survive on a dangerous system of car batteries and a 12 to 240 volt converter. Dangerous because the boat leaked permanently and was only kept afloat by an electrical bilge pump, so if the batteries ran down, we would sink.

Our days therefore went like this. Wake up in freezing damp room and turn on gas fire. When room warm enough to get out of bed, put on two layers of clothes and make tea on gas hob. Put two batteries in dinghy and row 200 yards upstream to where VW Beetle was parked. Drive to Roy's Garage in Wroxham (everything in Wroxham was owned by Roy) and put the batteries on trickle charge. Drive into uni and go to shower block. Stand under hot shower until thawed out, clean teeth and head off to lectures/seminars/rehearsals/somewhere warm. Head back to Wroxham before garage shuts at five. Collect charged batteries and put in dinghy. Row back to boat and add batteries to four others wired in series connected to said transformer. Get half an hour of telly or four hours of music from 240-volt output, leaving just enough for dim lights and bilge pump to work.

Sometimes I'd persuade a girl who had been attracted by my wellies, thick jumper and tales of my glamorous houseboat life to accept an invitation to share a takeaway on said boat. She'd end up staying the night only because she couldn't really row back and hitchhike in the dark. It's a pity there was a spare room.

I spent hours fixing that boat: re-felting half of the roof, painting it and keeping it afloat. One day, though, I wired the batteries up wrong and the converter exploded. No more telly or music, and when the owner finally returned, bronzed from his cruising, all I got from him was a bollocking for 'screwing up the electrics'.

We soon moved back onto the university campus, but that had its own perils. One term, a whole lot of us went down with hepatitis A from infected food in the refectory. It used to be called 'infectious hepatitis', and while nothing like as serious as hep C, it means that you have to be isolated from everyone, so I wasn't allowed to remain in residence and went to stay with my friend Maggie Wheeler in a cottage at Caistor St Edmund. I had my own plates and cutlery and had to live in solitary confinement. I was treated by a naturopath called Shyam Singha, who put me on a diet of boiled onions, Vichy water and live goat's yoghurt for a week, followed by raw food only for another week. As for alcohol, I was limited to one unit of vodka a day for six months. I recovered quickly – unlike some of my *Archers* colleagues who contracted the same virus when they went to collect their Sony Award for Broadcasting in the late eighties. They pooh-poohed my suggested cure and some have sadly remained weak-livered ever since. Singha was a controversial character, and some said he was a fraud, but the simplicity of the diet, I think, helped to purge out the toxins.

University life was filled with great days and great friends. I devised and performed sketch shows along with Maggie, my close friend and fellow Bowie nut Philip Bird, Arthur Smith, later of BBC comedy fame, the force of nature that is Adam Wide, and other friends. I hung out as a threesome with two girls called Alexandra and Clare, until Clare and I went non-platonic and I moved into her flat above a fish shop.

Work occasionally interrupted my university life. I did my thesis on 'Berlin Cinema Architecture', which meant the university paid for me to spend two weeks in West and East Berlin, researching cinemas, many of which had either been destroyed or heavily damaged during the wartime bombing. Some had been converted to other uses: I wanted to get a photo of an auditorium that was now a porn cinema, but they wouldn't let me, so I paid for a ticket to watch the matinee. I'd never seen porn before – it wasn't exactly hardcore, just bad acting and jiggly breasts – and after a while I walked down to the front, turned around and took a flash photo of the interesting thirties décor. Unfortunately, the small, dirty mac-wearing audience were not best pleased at being caught on film and I was chased out through the fire exit. Great photo though!

I got a 2:2, but I have never used my degree since. I regret that I don't even have a graduation picture, as the university had decided that, instead of wearing flowing black gowns and mortar boards, we should be modern and cool and be attired in ghastly blue and green polyester cloaks and tricorns. I didn't bother to show up.

Foreign Study League

While at UEA, I saw an advert on the 'Jobs Offered' notice board for a company called Foreign Study League (FSL), an offshoot of *Readers' Digest*, that organised European trips for American school kids as part of their study curriculum. They needed people to work in the office and in the field as tour reps. I thought it looked like fun and made a mental note to go along the next day at 5 p.m. when the interviews would take place. I'm not sure how that mental note got deleted, but, at 6.30, I remembered and kicked myself for having forgotten. Then a tiny little thought completely changed my whole life: 'Hmm, maybe I'll just pop down there anyway because, you never know, they might still be interviewing.' So I did, and they were, and I got the job working in tourism for the next three summers. I was based in London and New York, and got to drive minibuses around the States and Canada. As a result, I also met my future wife, bought the house that we still live in, and had two children. And this was all down to one little thought.

When I was at Harrow, we had fold-down beds, which had a tendency to collapse when sat on hard. One day, Noël sat down hard on mine and it landed on my big toe. The doctor told me he would have to remove the nail. He broke the needle of the syringe injecting it with local anaesthetic, so it was fully sensitive when he yanked the nail clean out. I believe it's a fairly well-known form of torture – I still remember the pain. So from that time on I've always had a damaged big toenail that doesn't grow properly and is not a pretty sight. I'm also a great one for not wearing shoes, so when Judy Emerson walked into the FSL office on her first day, she didn't immediately think that she'd one day marry the bloke with the wonky toenail sticking out from under his desk, gold earring and stripy hair.

I, however, instantly fell for the girl with the frizzy perm, kooky smile and come-to-bed eyes. She remained oblivious until I rescued her by bringing the sixty packed lunches she'd forgotten down to her group of students at the port in Dover. We saw them off onto the hovercraft, and laughed at how grateful the poor kids were to have finally got their pretty woeful pre-packed meals, and she started to see beyond my calamitous exterior. Two weeks later we shared my tiny bed in University of London's Goldsmid House on Oxford Street, accompanied by the roar of traffic and the cries of an ice-cream seller from the street below. We were twenty-one. We've been together, through a lot, ever since.

FSL was a great job. It taught me professional organisation – making and checking bookings, finding people and passports, and going to the US Embassy when we couldn't find one or the other. After a while, I was promoted to 'Airport Rep' and I had a security pass at Gatwick Airport. This meant that when a student arrived from the States on a jumbo jet, the first English voice he or she heard was me, standing on a luggage trolley, welcoming them to these shores. On one occasion, a kid who looked like something out of the Waltons, dressed in dungarees with long blond hair and an imaginary straw stuck between his teeth, came up to me after such a speech and said, with a thick Tennessee accent, 'Goddam, y'all speak good English. They teach it to you in the schools over here?'

The following summer, 1976, I worked for the same company, but this time organising European tourists in New York. My boss was the utterly delightful and eccentric Fran Lazar, who very soon came to be a kind of mother figure to me, indeed to everyone who worked there. Small, feisty and funny, she could get anything from anyone, and she taught me a lot about chutzpah. On the flight from London, I remember saying to the person sitting next to me that my idea of New York was that if you left your hotel after dark, you'd be shot, and I did actually see someone get shot within hours of my arrival. Nonetheless, I was incredibly naive. Once, after watching the Independence Day fireworks from Battery Park, I managed to walk my party of tourists deep into the Lower East Side, at that time a dangerous ghetto. A friendly local stopped us and said, 'Man, where you heading?' 'That way,' I replied, pointing ahead. 'No man, y'all turnin' around an' headin' back the way you came. Lord, it's a miracle you got this far.'

Fran's husband Stan Feig used to organise the Schaefer Music Festival in Central Park, and I got to see Cheech and Chong, Kingfish, Donovan and B. B. King, all for free. At the B. B. King concert, I was taking my seat and a big black dude sitting behind me, dripping with gold, in a white suit and fedora hat, said to one of his minions, quite audibly, 'I hate whites at my concerts.' Without hesitating I turned and said, 'No, it's all right man, I'm not white, I'm English.' There was a pause, a long pause, during which my knees slowly turned to jelly, but then he just burst out laughing. By the end of the concert, having partaken of some of his extremely fine weed, we were, as Ving Rhames says in Pulp Fiction, 'cool'. Confidence and naivety can either get you far, or dead.

Death also threatened on a weekend office adventure on a houseboat on Lake Ticonderoga. This was where I learned how to navigate an unseaworthy, square, underpowered small bungalow through a force-seven gale and huge waves. I had to fight my English co-worker for the steering wheel as his belief that you should present the boat sideways on to the waves was putting us in very serious danger of capsizing, and everything not tied down on deck got swept away. Good team bonding exercise, though, and I got very good at boat parking.

The following summer I got one of the best jobs I've ever had, driving for Trek America. I flew from London to Los Angeles and joined a mixed party of English, American, Australian and Japanese tourists for a three-week trip to New York through the southern states, learning the job from the English driver. We were in a thirteen-seater Dodge minibus loaded with camping gear on the roof, and we went from one campsite to another, driving around 300 miles per day. When I picked up my own group from a hotel in downtown NYC, the mainly Antipodean party were less than impressed at having a Pom drive them, and the fact that we were now driving the northern route meant I'd never been to any of the places we were visiting on the way. The convention that they took it in turns to put my tent up at the end of the day wasn't accepted as cheerily as it had been on my training run, and the fact that I'd forgotten to bring my driving licence from the UK meant that I had to be extremely careful not to get stopped by anyone in uniform.

I managed to convince the party that a 150-mile detour to Wounded Knee was a good idea, solely on the basis that I'd heard of the book *Bury My Heart at Wounded Knee* and thought it sounded impossibly romantic. Great name, crap place. In 1977, there was absolutely nothing there. One shack. Closed. On the other hand, driving through the night to witness sunrise at the Painted Desert was worth every minute. It is the most extraordinary place, with a sort of pre-historic beauty. I was the only one awake. I parked the van. 'Hey guys, wake up and check this out!' A few disgruntled raised heads. Roo slurred, 'Oh yeah?' Then silence. Then more sleep.

As we crossed over the Golden Gate Bridge, what should come on the radio? Scott McKenzie singing 'San Francisco', reminding me of my pa and the melted 45 in the portable record player. Saying goodbye to the group before picking up my next lot for the return journey, I finally admitted that I'd never done the trip before. 'Strewth,' said Roo, 'I'd never have known. You ought to be an actor.'

Meanwhile, for the second time in his life, my father had decided to again up sticks and drastically change his life. The first time – taking the family to Tasmania – had been for fear of a nuclear war. This time, he foresaw a world famine, which only the self-sufficient would survive. So he sold the house in Potten End, my stepmother Jenny sold her flat in London, and they bought a ten-acre smallholding in Devon and headed off west to live 'The Good Life'. This time, I was involved with the house-hunting, and an extra-ordinary set of requirements needed to be fulfilled. Firstly, it had to have a fast-flowing stream so that he could use the water to generate electricity. It needed enough land to be able to produce food and to farm sheep, turkeys, pigs, a house cow, chickens and ducks. Finally, and most disturbingly, it needed a 'killing ground' to defend the place from the marauding gangs that would be coming for us once the Great Famine had begun. I'll never forget the look on the estate agent's face when he overheard my father approving the view from an upstairs bedroom as 'a perfect spot for the Bren gun'.

It was to be an organic farm, this in the days before organic became fashionable and farming without pesticides was a forgotten art. We went to the Centre for Alternative Technology in Wales to find out about wind turbines, solar panels and the rest, and Pa read countless books on sustainable lifestyles and joined the Soil Association. Finding a hilltop fortress with running water proved impossible so they settled on a beautiful Devon cob and thatch long-house called Wigham that nestled on the side of a hill just outside the village of Morchard Bishop. It had been run as a dog kennels and in the year after university and in our holidays from drama school Judy and I stayed there to help them turn it into an organic smallholding. We tilled the fields with a two-furrow plough and harrow pulled by a lovely old grey petrol Ferguson tractor. We hand-milked 'Easy', the beautiful Jersey cow, and made butter and clotted cream. Pa harvested the wheat with a scythe and piled up stooks, which we threshed by hand. We built pigsties and bought in Tamworths that had piglets the same colour as the Labrador, 'Chumleigh', who as a result got confused and thought that he was a pig too. We raised, sheared, weighed, dagged and ate lambs; kept hens for their eggs; and I learned how to wring a chicken's neck (it's much harder than it looks). Judy too learned skills she still uses today.

In order to make some money, Pa and Jenny ran the place as a guesthouse. It became enormously popular because all the food was home-produced and my stepmother was a wonderful cook. However, they never turned it into a successful business because they didn't charge enough, and my father slowly turned into a Fawlty-esque host, hating having to play the part of fawning waiter after spending the day where he was happiest – out in the fields, working.

Happy memories, driving the short-wheelbase Land Rover to the abattoir with a pig in the trailer, and coming back with supper; trudging through drifts with our cat in a basket strapped to my back when the house had been completely cut off by snow, getting to the small station just in time for the only train that day, clambering aboard feeling like Scott of the Antarctic, observed with disdain by commuters in their shirt-sleeves; nailing down lethal corrugated iron sheets in a gale that was threatening to blow the whole roof off; plucking ducks until our thumbs were raw; coming down to breakfast wearing a crash helmet to stop getting brain damage from constantly hitting my head on the low beams and doorways; building a bedroom above the workshop with a trapdoor entrance; table tennis in the barn; then down to the pub in the evening with local tales, roaring fires and strong Devon ale. Proper job.

So much of that experience is still in my imagination today in *The Archers* recording studio, where the straw is tape, the cow is a sound effect, and the physical work is done for me by someone else. It helps if you can see the reality. It's like mime on stage – if you can see the brick wall in front of you, then so can the audience, but if you just pretend you can see it, they can't.

In the summer of 1976, Judy and I went on holiday to Morocco. We took the coach to northern Spain, then hitchhiked down to Algeciras, took the ferry to Ceuta, then a local bus into Tétouan. Stepping out of the bus was like travelling back in time and gave an arresting meaning to the term 'culture shock'. It was the first time either of us had been outside a Christian country and the noise, clothes, smells and people were like nothing we had ever known. We were immediately royally ripped off and got serious food poisoning, which made the continuing bus journey to the Rif mountains a formidable exercise in the control of bodily functions. It was hardly surprising that western tourists were seen as easy game, but as we headed south we experienced nothing but friendliness and generosity, the poorest people sharing their bread and soup with us to break Ramadan, and in the mountains, cool air, water fountains and delicious food in hotels that felt like private homes being shared with honoured guests.

Back in Tétouan, our stomachs hardened to the local fare, we met an Australian guy (I'll call him Jeff) who had a plan to buy a Mercedes in Germany, drive it down to Persia and sell it for twice the price. Not having a licence, he needed a driver, and Muggins here, always on for an adventure, volunteered. I gave him my father's address and forgot all about him until a few weeks later when he turned up on the doorstep of the farm in Devon. Pa took an instant dislike to him and put him to work in the fields, which was not Jeff's thing at all. When I announced that I was going to drive this workshy ruby smuggler (as I found out later) from Frankfurt to Tehran, father and son had a flaming row. He accused me of being impetuous and reckless; I replied that I was simply following in his footsteps and a man who had absconded from Sandhurst, stowed away on a ship to America, ridden rough on the railroad to California and become a cowboy, then fought in a war, was not in a position to lecture me on putting myself in the way of danger. It wasn't until I became a father myself that I realised where he was coming from.

The trip didn't start well. We bought the Merc, rather the worse for wear, at night, from a very dodgy dealer for a suspiciously low price. In the cold light of day, we noticed the bad paint job covering up the rust. At the same time, the Iranian revolution was happening and even if we'd got to Tehran in once piece and sold the rust-bucket, we'd never have got the money out of the country, so Jeff announced we were going back to Morocco, which was *not* what I'd signed up for. I don't know where I get it from, but to this day I have a natural affinity for the underdog and a lack of ruthlessness. I would never have made a businessman and the family motto of fearing dishonour has given me an aversion for dishonesty and also for behaving like a dick. So I said yes, and off to North Africa we went.

Through Germany, France and Spain and once again on the ferry to Ceuta: two young men in a Mercedes with no baggage. At customs, they went through us with a fine-tooth comb. Jeff told me to give them a false address. This was getting worrying. In Tétouan we were flagged down by one man after another. 'You sell car?' Then tea, hashish, haggling and an offer of money just below what we had bought it for – because of the rust. This went on for two days until Jeff announced, 'Sod it, we're going to Iran.' I wasn't, I'd had enough and he was becoming a bit of a pain anyway. I said I'd drive him to the airport at Malaga where he would buy me the flight home and find some other willing dupe to take him on from there.

Coming back, the Spanish customs saw these two stoned idiots in their rusty Merc who had been in Morocco for forty-eight hours and quite literally took the car to pieces. We spent the best part of a day in a garage as they went through every square inch of panelling, upholstery, tyres, linings – they wrecked the car but finally, and very reluctantly, were forced to let us go. Sitting relieved on the terrace of a beachside café in Algeciras, Jeff casually reached into his nether regions and pulled out a small lump of hash. 'Christ, I need this,' he remarked casually as he skinned up. I nearly killed him.

Bristol Old Vic Theatre School

In the seventies there were things called 'grants'. Unheard of today, it meant that anyone could have free university tuition. The Tories stopped all that in 1989 so my two sons are now saddled with debt. Thanks, Maggie. There were still two hurdles for me to cross to get to a good drama school. One was the audition for the Bristol Old Vic Theatre School, the next was one for the London County Council, which meant that not only did I have to convince my future tutors that I was any good, but also a bewildered bank of civil servants, whose qualifications for judging budding thesps were iffy to say the least.

Having been accepted by Bristol I thought this would be a breeze. I boldly went into my Shakespeare piece, amazed them with my broad cockney modern piece, and fooled them into thinking I could sing with vast amounts of energy and sleight of throat. They were not impressed. Their leader then said, 'Hmm. And have you any other strings to your bow?' When I told them I had an HGV Class 2 lorry-driving licence, they all started nodding with approval and I got the grant.

This was another occasion on which to thank my father. I'd been signing on for a bit and was getting very bored from occasional jobs stacking shelves, door-to-door selling and farm labouring, so he lent me the money to do a truck-driving course. By registering with somewhere like Manpower you could get work daily, and drive different trucks to different places and never get into trouble if you had any kind of 'incident'. I've had three of these: turning a truck round in a petrol station in Wales and wiping out all the fluorescent lamps in the canopy; jettisoning an entire load of yeast on the M4; and destroying a parked car by misjudging the truck's width in Clifton. Despite these slight errors, I improved and paid my father back from my first month's earnings.

It was odd being a posh-boy trucker. One time I was sent as the agency driver to a scaffolding firm. I was taken into the yard and shown how to lay the back part of a flatbed truck laden with scaffolding onto the ground. A complex procedure featuring hydraulics and cables. My lesson lasted about ten minutes and I was then sent off on my first delivery. The address was a leafy suburb outside Clevedon and I had to lay the bed on a narrow road outside the house. In order to leave enough room for cars to get by, part of the bed landed on the verge, and some flowers got crushed. Jubilant that I'd actually managed to get the load off the truck, I was then assailed by the furious owner for having destroyed her flowerbed. It was revealing to find how a rude, arrogant, upper-middle-class harridan could be silenced by being out-poshed. She simply couldn't believe what she was hearing.

In my first year at Bristol, I shared a flat with Judy, a Welshman called Russell Roberts, a tall god-fearing Australian called Kim Wright, and a lanky, athletic, good-looking lad called Daniel Day-Lewis. Whatever happened to him?

The funny thing about drama school is that people who were just your mates – with their insecurities and weaknesses laid bare for you to see – can turn into international movie stars just a few years later. Dan's career has been exceptional, but quite a few of us have done all right – Greta Scacchi, Miranda Richardson, Amanda Redman, Nicholas Farrell, Jenny Seagrove and others. The *not* funny thing is the large majority who didn't. Some have continued to work without becoming well known but the majority have given acting up and done something sensible instead.

The training was wonderful. I remember thinking at the time that everyone should do this course, actor or not. Singing, dancing, voice production, acting, reading and understanding plays, losing the fear and the self-consciousness, all of these things leading to the tantalisingly exciting idea that, if we worked hard, but above all if we got really lucky, one day fools, idiots, suckers and mad people would actually pay us, sometimes a LOT of money, just to play Cowboys and Indians for the rest of our lives.

The scary thing is how much of it is down to luck. I'm not saying that the people who have become successful aren't hard-working and talented, it's just that at Bristol, for those two years, no one could have predicted which ones would make it. In the final shows, no one really stood out as different from the rest, even Daniel. His first professional role was as a walk-on in some little-known Restoration play at the Bristol Old Vic, where his only line was, 'The carriage awaits, m'lady.' Being Dan, he probably went over and over the role, working out who this messenger was, his back-story, his motivation for saying the line, what kind of carriage it was, the colour, how many horses, whether it was nearly ready, just coming round the corner, or if it had been waiting there for hours and the horses getting hungry, and the postilions impatient and bitching.

So armed, on press night he strode on stage and, with all the bravura confidence of a future three-times Oscar winner, intoned, 'The lady awaits, m'carriage.'

In Bristol, hands roughened by hard farm work, I was loving learning how to be an actor. The theatre school has consistently produced good ones, and there's a reason for that: his name was Rudi Shelly. This tiny, ancient, bustling, waspish martinet, an Austrian Jew who had escaped the Nazis, with the body of a dancer, dressed in a Norfolk jacket, used to drive us to tears of boredom, but every one of us has found that he was right about pretty much everything. Underneath the carapace of tetchiness, he had a heart of gold. He had little adages that summed up whole classes or even terms, including the most fundamental one: 'Acting is the art of reacting.' Meaning you only do anything as a result of a reaction – to what someone says, to what they do, to what you think, to circumstances – and that requires you to *listen*.

Then there was the wonderful 'Watch out, actor about!' and 'Ducky, your technique is showing!' What every actor strives for is to make it appear that we're not acting at all. Very few achieve it. Dan Day-Lewis is one of them. Bastard!

In my final show at Bristol I played 'Master Hammon' in *The Shoemaker's Holiday* by Thomas Dekker. He opens the second half with a soliloquy and the school's principal, Nat Brenner, told me that this was the funniest scene in the play. I simply couldn't see it, but Nat took me through it line by line, using all the techniques that we'd been taught: where to pause, why, and finding out from the text alone what the playwright intended in terms of subtext, innuendo and double entendre. I still had little confidence that Nat was right, but sure enough, on opening night, I had the audience eating out of my hand, a laugh at every line, like doing stand-up comedy. It was so exciting. I was sharing a dressing room with dear friend David Heap, who had been listening on the tannoy. When I came back into the room he smiled and said, 'And just think, they're going to pay us to do this!'

After that, armed with numerous O levels, three A levels, a degree in the History of Art, two years at drama school and a radio competition prize, at the age of twenty-six I ventured forth for an actor's life. What the hell was I thinking?

BBC Radio Repertory Company

Being in the right place at the right time is horribly important. I've starred in sitcoms that sank without trace, dramas that no one watched and costume dramas that didn't quite catch the public's attention. The huge successes I've worked on, like *The Thick of It* and *Twenty Twelve*, have been in minor roles, so I've never built a starring reputation. I wanted to be a movie star, of course, but haven't quite stood out enough in the movies I've done so far. Maybe my 'Witness' in *Fantastic Beasts and Where to Find Them* will unlock the Hollywood door! I did get lucky twice, though, and that has been enough to keep me in work all this time.

The first bit of luck was winning the BBC Carleton Hobbs Bursary Award while I was at Bristol. This is a competition open to final-year drama-school students and one male and one female winner are offered a six-month contract with the BBC Radio Repertory Company, which in those days gave you an automatic Equity card – gold dust then, though not such a necessity today. My sister Anna was the first of our family to take up the profession, and her advice to me about how to go about the audition was invaluable

Being David Archer

– she told me they were after versatility, so I tried to make my two pieces sound as though they came from two entirely different actors. I did a speech from Barrie Keefe's *Gotcha* about an angry young man sitting astride a motorbike with a lit cigarette held above the cap-less petrol tank. 'Wot about people 'oo don't do A levels? Wot about ME? EH?!' I then went straight into a very gentle, reflective RP Shakespeare soliloquy. I remember them sounding very different, so I thank/blame my darling sister for that advice, depending on however much/little work I'm getting at the time.

The bursary led to doing voiceovers and the whole world of voice acting, and thence to the second bit of luck, being asked to audition for *The Archers*. I have one man to thank for that luck and his name is Anthony Hyde.

He was the actual winner of the radio bursary competition and I came second, but he turned it down, presumably because he didn't want to sign up for six months with the BBC Radio Repertory Company, so they offered it to me. I've met him once since, when we were in an episode of *Sharpe* with Sean Bean, filming in Crimea. I thanked him then – I'm not sure how he took it. He's since given up acting. He could have been David Archer.

The first radio play I did was *Westward Ho!* by Charles Kingsley in 1979. It was recorded in the wonderful Christchurch Studios in Bristol. I was playing a short fat boy with a squeaky voice – about as different from me as you could get. That's just one of the many different things about radio acting: you don't have to look the part. Over the years, so many people have told me I don't look like David Archer and of course it's true: if there are five million listeners, then there are five million David Archers living in their imaginations – and none of them look like me.

It is said that on radio you have to be able to 'raise one eyebrow

64

with your voice' – as there are no visual clues, you need to suggest movement, facial expression and feelings with voice and sound effects only. When I first started radio acting, I was all for doing it in a very naturalistic way, which is fine if the listener is wearing headphones or sitting in a quiet room and listening on DAB, but if someone is bowling down the motorway with the window open and listening on a tinny radio on medium wave, you won't be heard, so it has to be a cross between the two. Naturalistic, but not completely realistic.

Christchurch has wonderfully different acoustics. Because it used to be a church, the main studio room is vast and echoey. Then there are smaller rooms for intimate-sounding spaces, and a state-of-the-art 'dead room', where all outside scenes are recorded because it is acoustically 'dead' and there's no reverberation, no matter how loudly you shout.

There, I learned about the three-dimensionality of radio drama. In those days we still recorded in mono, but there was close to the microphone and far away, there was up and down too. I also learned to engage with props – one of the first things I ever had to do was chop logs while speaking, timing my grunt of effort with the spot-effects person whacking an axe into a wooden block. It's one of the most important things and so often done wrong. I hate it when I hear an actor saying his lines, with the sound of the activity he's involved in going on in a seemingly totally detached space – especially if that actor is me!

Performing at Broadcasting House in London was so exciting. My father took me around as though it were his alma mater – he'd been a talks producer there before going into advertising, and worked with Jack de Manio and others on the *Today* programme. I felt a tradition being passed on and still feel ridiculously attached to 'Auntie' all these years later. There were no security passes or gates in those days, just a doorman who either knew you or didn't, and if he didn't, you didn't get in. There was the famous canteen up on the top floor – dreadful food but cheap and filling and always full of famous names and faces, and Miriam Margolyes telling dirty jokes.

I did a vast array of work with the Radio Rep, ranging from *Vanity Fair* and *Moby Dick* to *Brighton Rock* and contemporary plays. I could be playing a lead in one play and then fourth policeman from the left in the next. I worked with many well-known actors and would watch and listen to their performances, learning all the while. As has been said, you can always tell a radio actor because he reads the newspaper silently. Different actors have varied ways of turning the pages of the script in silence. It's a terrible give-away if an actor is nervous because the pages will rattle uncontrollably and they might suffer the ignominy of being asked to put the script on a music stand and separate the pages. This should be done only as a last resort, because holding the script gives you the freedom to walk around, use your body and give a more dynamic performance. The trick is to try to keep the page taut as you turn it – loose paper is what makes the noise.

I once found myself in the actors' green room with Norman Shelley. Now there was a familiar name; a part of my childhood was being serenaded by his renditions of *The Hums of Pooh* on World Record Club 45 discs. When I asked him if he was indeed the same Norman Shelley, he replied, 'Oh dear me yes, in fact A.A. said that I was the *definitive* Pooh. Let me tell you about it…' at which point about eight actors suddenly got up as they all immediately had Sudden and Important Things To Do Elsewhere. Norman was known for going on, and on, and this young actor was fresh meat!

The recording studios were in the basement, and the tube trains on the Bakerloo line beneath shook the building. Quiet scenes had to be recorded between train departures and period pieces couldn't get away with too many distant rumblings of thunder, or earth tremors. The old iconic BBC ribbon microphones weren't as sensitive as modern stereo ones, though, so you could get away with a certain amount of outside noise, and they also gave a wonderfully rich, analogue feel to recordings, which is rather lost today. The other great advantage to recording in mono was that the actors could face each other across the mike, which gives greater eye contact. The downside, of course, was that you never got to kiss your leading lady, having to employ the old back-of-the-hand trick instead!

So much has changed. Firstly, the production team was almost exclusively male, from director to spot effects – the only women, apart from actresses, were secretaries. The directors also had a tendency to be hugely intolerant and often downright rude. Lateness was inexcusable, fluffing was a capital offence, and smoking almost compulsory. The older actors would be formally dressed in suit and tie, and the place was run with an almost military strictness. In the early days of radio, plays were recorded in one go straight onto disc, so that if you fluffed a line at the end of a half-hour recording, you all had to go back and record it again. This, combined with the poor quality of the broadcast, led to that familiar old style of 'Mr Cholmondeley-Warner' acting that now seems over-enunciated and artificial. By the time I started doing radio plays in the seventies, of course, recording was on tape, but it was still a palaver to edit – there aren't many engineers left now who remember the days of chalk pencil and razor blade. There was much more a feeling of doing it like a stage performance then, as though it were live, and to carry on through any slips or disasters regardless. Today, we just stop and go back to the beginning of the phrase, and the edit is usually done by the engineer there and then. Not nerve-wracking at all – unless you're doing just one day on *The Archers*.

Homebuilding

During this time, we stayed living in Bristol because Judy was the wardrobe mistress of the Theatre School. When she'd come down to live with me, she'd got a job as wardrobe assistant, but when the head of department left she was promoted, so at least one of us had a proper job. I was driving trucks and doing the occasional radio play and fringe theatre in Bath before I went up to London for the six months with the Radio Rep, staying at my sister Anna's house in Tufnell Park.

We once had a 'Terrorist Party' at our basement flat in Clifton. I realise how tasteless that sounds these days, but then the connotations weren't quite so bad as they are now. When Adam Wide, an old friend from UEA, arrived, he kicked down the door and sprayed the room with toy machine-gun fire, to the shock of the elderly couple next door whose flat he had mistaken for ours. Dan Day-Lewis knocked on the door, and when I opened it to find him dressed quite casually, he rubbed his knuckles up and down on the brickwork until they were bleeding. 'This all right?' he asked, and sauntered in.

Homebuilding

My friend Peter Ackerman turned up driving his BMW motorbike sidecar, with Nick Farrell tied up and blindfolded in the
passenger side. Pete added to the effect by being tied up and blindfolded himself. He was without doubt the funniest actor of our year
at Bristol, but tragically died of a brain tumour not long after we all
left – the comedy award at the Theatre School is named in memory
of him.

I've always been one for a scheme. I'm not a businessman, and I
don't have the interest or the killer instinct that seems to be required
to be a successful one, but I've always tried to come up with ways of
making money on the side. I'm sixty-three now and I haven't managed
it yet. My brainwave at that time was buying Type 2 Jaguars and
exporting them to California. Apart from anything else, it would
involve driving Jags, which was almost enough in itself. Meanwhile,
Judy had a better idea. She'd worked out that buying a house on the
other side of Bristol would be a cheaper mortgage than the rent we
were paying in Clifton, so she went to her parents to ask if they could
lend her something towards the deposit. They were not wealthy
people; Jack was an engineer who had lost three fingers in an industrial
accident, and worked for Russell Hobbs where, among other things,
he was involved with the design of their classic electric kettle. Did they
think it was a good idea? she asked. They said yes, but are you going
to get married? No, Judy replied. Consequently they agreed to give her
the £1000 they had raised over many years to pay for her wedding.

Hence, the rather shoestring wedding we did subsequently have.
But we were on the property ladder. The lovely three-bedroom
terraced house in Stevens Crescent, Totterdown, cost a princely
£8000.

I hate the term DIY as it sounds like something someone does in
their spare time as a kind of hobby. My DIY has always been on fairly

major works that I have undertaken myself, firstly, because I could never afford to get anyone else to do it, and secondly, because when I could, I'd find that they'd done a bad job and I'd have to redo it all myself. I've taken on rewiring whole houses from scratch, knocking down walls and fitting steel beams, plumbing, plastering, joinery, painting, hanging wallpaper, laying concrete floors and building kitchens out of brick and oak. I love it. One of the best feelings in the world is sitting at the end of the day with a beer in hand, bruised and aching from hard work, covered in dirt and rain, surveying what you've just created. I'd already been doing this for years for other people, and here was a house of our own – like a new toy!

That mistrust of others doing the work pretty much started there, with an Irish builder. Don't get me wrong, I've got nothing against Irish builders; in fact the best plasterer I've ever known was a fella from Cork called Billy Curtin, who was great company, good value and a real craftsman. This guy though was letting the side down. In Bristol, I was knocking through the two downstairs rooms so I jacked the ceilings up with Acro props, knocked down the brick wall and had everything ready for the builder to fit the steel joist, which essentially would take the weight of the whole house. He turned up with a wooden beam. Dismissing my worries with a cheery wave and a cloud of dope smoke, he explained knowingly that the wall above was tied into the side walls. 'Think of it like Lego,' he assured me. I very dubiously accepted and he put in the wooden joist. After the concrete under the supports had set, I gingerly let down the props, and the beam seemed to be holding. We went to sleep that night, our bed directly above the beam. In the morning, I saw to my horror that the floorboards in the bedroom now had a two-inch gap to the skirting board. I raced down the stairs and saw that the whole beam had a massive bow in it. I then did something that I really don't recommend: I jacked our whole house back up again. The Irish may pride themselves on their flowery use of the old Anglo-Saxon, but someone once described David Archer as 'having a good shout on him', and that comes from me. By the end of the day, we had a rolled steel joist in place, and the house is still standing today.

During the building, Judy saw that the Methodist church at the bottom of the road was being gutted prior to demolition. She asked if we could have any of the beautiful wood panelling that was lying on the pavement. 'The skip's coming in an hour,' said the builder. 'Whatever you can take before then is yours.' We helped ourselves to enough wood to panel both the downstairs rooms and build two alcove cupboards and shelves. Scrap yards and reclamation sites were, and really still are, some of my favourite places.

Meanwhile . . . I was in a movie! *North Sea Hijack* with Roger Moore as 'Rufus Excalibur ffolkes', a maverick marine counterterrorism consultant who loves cats and hates women. I'd landed the part of Harris, ffolkes's right-hand man. Roger wasn't behaving like Bond. He had a thick beard to prove it and was quite wonderfully Roger Moore-ish, just as you'd hope he'd be, very funny, kind, easygoing, and totally in charge.

For the audition, I had been summoned to the Park Lane Hotel to meet Hollywood movie director Andrew V. McLaglen, son of the actor Victor McLaglen, and casting director Allan Foenander.

McLaglen was standing. He was six foot seven. I stood before him, six foot three. I felt like a child.

'Tell me something, kid, can you do a Scotch accent?'

I hadn't been told the character was Scottish.

'Mm, yes, I've spent a lot of Christmases in Scotland actually and . . . I mean . . . och right, aye, whellll, yeeees, I've Scoottish blud

actually [which is true but a long way back], so that's no' a prooblem.'
Blagging it here . . .

'Can you swim?'

Also not forewarned but, hey, result . . .

'Yes, I'm a good swimmer, I was captain of swimming at school . . .'

He walked towards me until his chin was an inch from my nose. Then he put his feet heavily on my shoes.

To this day I have no idea why he did that. A power thing? To see how I'd react? A fetish of some sort?

So I stared him out, what else could I do? Laugh? Nut him?

He stepped back, and then he said, 'Kid, I think you just got yourself a part.'

Those were the very words; they are burned upon my soul.

We filmed in Galway. I'd never been to Ireland before. It was a bit of a dream; I'd just come out of drama school and I was in a Hollywood film, not only with bloody *James Bond*, but also Anthony Perkins and James Mason for heaven's sake! This was it, I was a movie actor. It could only go stratospheric from here. I was the trusty lieutenant, promotion awaited, Tinseltown watch out!

As it turned out, that was almost it, Hollywood-wise. But it was great fun while it lasted.

Every time the film is on telly in the afternoon, which is about once a month, I rue the fact that it was a buy-out. The fit young man in the film hasn't the faintest idea what he's doing, is by no stretch of the imagination a hard military man, has never com-manded troops in his life, and is running around a ship and scuba diving in the open sea and Galway harbour, completely over-whelmed and totally bowled over at being surrounded by some of the hardest, most experienced stuntmen in the business. He is also having the most fantastic craic with the crew every evening in the bars of Galway, glugging water after a dive and finding it was pot-cheen, and being paid more money in cash per diems (as the daily allowances for expenses are known) than he had ever earned as wages before in his life. We spent one night at sea and I found myself in a mess room with Roger Moore, Anthony Perkins and James Mason, and we were all telling gags, and these movie stars were laughing at my schoolboy jokes! Roger was a wonderful raconteur, and filthy with it. One joke he told ended with him swatting a fly on the wall, but his hand was bandaged from a bad and painful cut. BANG! 'FUUUUUUUUCKING SHIIIIIT!'

Said James Bond.

I was in heaven.

We had to climb on board the ship using ropes from grappling irons that had been thrown up, so we rehearsed in the woods with two ropes hanging from a wide branch, tied there by Roger's personal stuntman, Martin Grace. Everyone else had a go but no one could do it. 'Never mind', said Greg Powell, son of the famous stuntman Nosher, 'we'll climb up the fucking anchor chain.' Then someone said, 'Oi, better let Tim have a go, eh? Come all this way, Tim, wanna go?' with the clear meaning of 'Yeah, come on then, posh boy, show us what you can do.'

Well it's difficult in those situations when you know you can do something, and one thing I could do after about ten years of enforced school gymnastics was shin up a couple of ropes; it was like walking. So, should I do that, and show them up in their eyes, or fail and be one of the gang? I shinned straight up the ropes and sat astride the bough. What the hell.

I got on a lot better with the stuntmen after that, and then I pulled one of the guys back from out in the bay one filming afternoon when he'd got breathless and inflated his life jacket. I used the old life-saving technique, and that was when I drank the potcheen afterwards. I choked, but from then on it was delicious.

There was a night scene where we scuba divers had to surface near a large ship in Galway harbour and begin to climb up the anchor chain. We were all kitted up. I was with a group of three other frogmen. Before take one, the word went out, 'Remember, fuck up the first two takes.'

Take one, someone comes up too early, 'Nooo!' from the loud hailer. 'On action, you descend, count to ten, then surface.'

The water was almost opaque with harbour pollution. I had encountered a very large turd on the surface and later developed a severe ear infection. 'Take two, and, action!'

Go down five feet. Wait. Come up looking menacing . . . start to swim purposefully towards the ship . . .

'Cut!' Now what? 'One of you is swimming the wrong fucking way!'

Not me, thank God. Take three.

In the bag. Nailed it. Moving on.

It turned out that the stunt team were on £100 *per take!* And I found out later they'd made sure that I was paid, too. It was really nice to feel a little bit accepted by such a bunch of seriously hard nuts.

At the end of the shoot, I was invited to apply to be a stuntman and asked to the annual Stuntmen's Ball at Pinewood. After seeing that half of them there were bandaged and quite a few were in wheelchairs, I settled for the pansy-actor option. I was tempted, though.

Spliced

Judy and I were married on 8 September 1979 at Marylebone Register Office in London. It was a very low-key affair with parents only at the ceremony, which unintentionally upset my sisters. Also, the very informal invitation, 'Tim and Judy are getting married', was sneered at by some. The small party of family and close friends afterwards is recorded by a single photo, since our official photographer, old chum Bill Butt, was going out with Greta Scacchi at the time and he used up most of the film stock on her. It didn't matter, it was the best day of our lives.

Best man Jamie Borthwick provided his flat for the do, and then – a huge surprise – the bridal suite at the Ritz for the wedding night. When I came to return the compliment a few years later, I thought it would be funny to put up my Etonian pal and his beautiful bride Peng at the best hotel in Harrow – which sadly turned out to be a flea-infested dump and unsurprisingly closed down soon after.

We honeymooned in Spain, where the rain happened not to be staying mainly on the plain but directly overhead. Such was my frustration after four days of torrential downpour that I strode into the local police station and demanded to know when the bloody sun was going to appear. I think I had gone very slightly bonkers at that point.

I do worry sometimes when couples have weddings that cost the earth and take months to plan. Absolutely everything has to happen without a hitch, and the pressure for the relationship to succeed because of the amount invested in it can become intolerable. Our thinking at the time was that we'd publicly tell our nearest and dearest that we loved each other and were making it official, and then we'd see how it went. Two children and thirty-seven years later, it's just got better and better, so in our case at least that lack of pressure worked fine.

Tales of the Unexpected

For my first telly part, I got to drive a Rolls – *and* I had a bedroom scene.

For an episode of *Tales of the Unexpected*, I played 'Meech', Joss Ackland's chauffeur who is having an affair with the wife of 'Stinker Tinker', played by the incomparable Denholm Elliot. 'Stinker' was his character's nickname at school, where the Ackland character had bullied him remorselessly. The Rolls was a nightmare to drive as it was a chauffeur's vehicle with an almost solid bench seat; Joss, poor man, was beset by personal tragedies and hardly spoke; Denholm was just intent on getting almost anyone to sleep with him, including me; and I spent a lot of time in bed with Patricia Quinn. This led to a great moment many years later, when filming *By the Sword Divided*, when I asked the unshockable Robert Stephens who was the wife 'Pat' he kept referring to.

'Pat Quinn,' he replied.

'Oh,' I piped up. 'I've been to bed with her.' Cue look of brutal antagonism from the wild Sir Robert. 'On screen, old boy, on screen,' I hurriedly explained. Much relief all round. He once drew blood from me in a swordfight and I wouldn't have liked to have crossed him for real.

Being David Archer: The audition

My agent rang.

'Do you want to be in *The Archers*?'

'I've never heard it, what's it like?'

'It's about farming.'

'I know a bit about farming.'

'Not required, it's a radio soap. Wanna go for it or not?'

'Where's the casting?'

'Birmingham.'

'Why Birmingham?'

'That's where they record it.'

'Oh blimey. All right, then.'

We were what you might call a 'dum-di-dum-di-click' family – the moment my mother heard *The Archers* theme tune she turned off the radio, so I had never heard an episode of the programme before I auditioned for it.

At the BBC studios at Pebble Mill in Birmingham, I met a charming man called Peter Windows, one of the producers, and a more enigmatic one, William Smethurst, the editor. The scene I was reading for the audition was a dialogue between David and Eddie Grundy. Trevor Harrison (Eddie) couldn't make it that day so I was asked to play both parts.

'Okay,' I said, 'what does Eddie Grundy sound like?'

A pause.

'Have you ever heard the programme?'

Gulp.

'Oh yeah, lots of times but I sometimes get confused which character's which . . . you know . . .'

'Sure,' said Peter. 'Well, it's not an impersonation. For this just do all-purpose rural, you know, put a lot of arrs into it.'

Well, I honestly thought he said, 'Put a lot of *arse* into it', so I made Eddie rural and a bit bolshie, and by complete chance landed on a pretty close impression of Trevor's brilliant and inimitable Eddie. I hardly even thought about the voice for David, so I guess he must have sounded a lot like me, which in many ways he still does!

So, I got the part. I started recording almost immediately. By this time, I'd been a pirate for quite some time on screen and on stage, so my first appearance in *The Archers* green room was met by some raised eyebrows from the long-serving cast. I had long hair, my mouse-brown locks highlighted with great streaks of peroxide, I wore a thick gold earring in my right ear, and had a habit of wearing a bum bag and leg warmers with pale blue Levi's and a faux-leather jacket. Pretty normal for the 1980s but Ambridge wasn't used to it.

Paddy Greene, who has played my mother Jill all these years, said I had the girls all aflutter, but all I remember is the terror of my first episode. Although I'd been doing radio for a while by then, a stray comment from a friend had got me into a bit of a state. She had told me that she – and all of her friends – listened to *The Archers* omnibus in the bath on Sundays (although presumably not the same bath). I combined this with another piece of information: that there were five million *Archers* listeners. So even if half the women were bone dry, that still made 1.25 million wet, naked women listening to my first words as David Archer, transmitted on 12 August 1982.

'Evening all.'

Shaking script? Thank God I didn't have to turn a page.

1982

Having met Judy and entered the world of radio drama, almost all the other major things that determined what my future was to hold occurred in 1982. I had been in *The Pirates of Penzance* movie, and was now ensconced in the Theatre Royal Drury Lane, giving my nightly pirate; I was still doing a lot of radio and voiceovers and I got the part in *The Archers* – and then we bought a house in London.

In *The Diary of a Nobody* by George and Weedon Grossmith, Mr Pooter's house is a semi-detached villa 'in a crescent in Holloway with the garden leading down to the railway line'. Well, that's our house. Nearly. The ones next to the railway are further round the crescent, but we have the iconic foot scraper, and I painted the bath red as an homage. When my sister Anna had got married and left home in the sixties, she'd settled in Islington, and so all my experiences of the capital had been in the north. South London is about as familiar and friendly a place as Beirut on a bad day, and I know the Southies feel the same about us. So, when we were house-hunting, we focused on the north, although Islington itself was too expensive, so it was Stoke Newington, Holloway, Hackney or Crouch End for us – basically anywhere with a prison near it.

Having sold the house in Bristol for nearly twice the amount we'd bought it for, the most we could afford was £28,000. We saw a photograph in the estate agent's window for a house in Holloway that looked lovely. It had a sitting tenant on a peppercorn rent, which meant it was cheaper, but £32,000 was too much. However, we toddled along to look, and just fell in love with it. Built in 1852, it had a large garden, two wonderful picture windows in the rear reception room, enough room for a family and half an hour by tube to the West End. It was divided into three flats. The basement contained the tenant, a Mr Crook, and his severely brain-damaged daughter. The other two flats hadn't been maintained or decorated for decades, so absolutely everything needed doing: new roof, new electrics, new plumbing, stripping out bathrooms and kitchens and building new ones, hardboard laid onto the floorboards and the whole house carpeted; every wall was lath and plaster, which would collapse when you tore off the woodchip wallpaper so would have to be plasterboarded, skim plastered, painted, new skirting boards added and picture rails fitted. And the rest. For me, it was pure heaven.

We managed to get a mortgage for it through a dodgy dealer at the Woolwich.

'See all these questions? Just answer no to all of them.'

'Erm, but that's not strictly true.'

'Look, do you want this pile of bricks or not?'

We reckoned we needed another £5000 to get going so we started off in London with a £37,000 mortgage, Judy working part-time in costume, and me a jobbing actor. We were an optimistic couple, and we needed to be. Those figures sound absurd today, but it was a huge amount to find every month.

Mr Crook was a diabetic and was finding it impossible to look after his poor daughter, who was also incontinent, and then one day she was taken into care. His diabetes got worse and he finally had to have a leg amputated. One of the stipulations from the mortgage company was that we had to put in a damp-proof course, treat the timbers for dry rot and put in a concrete floor in the basement. Amazingly, we got all this done while he was in hospital. When he got back he moaned about the new carpet and the smell. It was a different smell; previously it had just stunk of damp, rot, toadstools and urine. We thought it was an improvement, but you can't please everyone.

Every now and then we'd hear 'Help!' from downstairs and have to get him out of the bath or clear up the Meals on Wheels dinner that he'd spilled on the floor. The poor man was in a terrible way and eventually an ambulance pulled up outside the house and took him away too. That was when I started turning three flats into a family home. I've spent thirty-five years working on it, and it's still not finished.

Along with a perfectly preserved dead rat that could have been a hundred years old, we found things under the floorboards that told tales of the previous inhabitants, rather like archaeology. They included a letter written in Swiss German, that when translated was found to be a legal document transferring ownership of a carpenter's studio in Berne. Two extraordinary coincidences convinced us we were destined to live there. Firstly, this letter had been wrapped in a copy of *The Times* in which there was a long article about a certain Army captain called John Emerson – Judy's brother's name. Strangest of all was that, when we got the deeds, we saw that the original document from 1852 had been witnessed by Lord Henry Bentinck, a distant cousin, whose signature, just *Henry Bentinck*, was almost identical to my father's writing (also Henry). That knocked me for six.

Being David Archer: Early days

My first day on *The Archers* was a shock. I imagine it is for most new cast members, but in those days it wasn't the easy bunch of modern actors it is today. On 30 June 1982, I entered a strange new world. These days the programme is recorded at the BBC studios in the Mailbox in the centre of Birmingham, but when I started we were out at Pebble Mill in Edgbaston, a building now sadly demolished, with a character all its own.

The drama studio was on the ground floor at the end of a long corridor. The cast didn't have a green room to wait in but lounged around in a large open area just outside the studio. The first thing that struck me was the clear separation between the assembled cast. They were divided into two factions: the actors, who sat on sofas on the right side and talked about agents and money; and the older characters, some of whom had come to the programme from a different route – genuine 'country folk' who had started in local radio and somehow made the jump to drama. They sat on hard chairs on the left and talked about agricultural shows and silage.

The older men wore suits, smoked pipes at the microphone and had fought in the war. Characters like Bob Arnold, a folk singer and teller of country tales, who was cast as Tom Forrest three months after *The Archers* began in 1951; he sat in a padded chair and would sing 'The Village Pump' at the drop of a hat – and, unless you were very careful, *all* the verses. There was George Hart, whose genuine accent was exactly the same as that of his radio character, Jethro Larkin – until the Worcestershire tones were sadly terminated by a swinging branch care of yours truly, David Archer; Mollie Harris (Martha Woodford) who proved her Gloucester credentials by writing a fascinating and comprehensive guide to outside toilets called *Cotswold Privies*; and Chris Gittins, who, before Ruth's 'Ooooh Noooo', had the original and best catchphrase, Walter Gabriel's 'Me old pals me old beauties', uttered in an accent utterly unlike any other heard in these islands, all the stranger as the character's son Nelson sounded like a duke.

I thought I'd entered a madhouse when I started on the programme, as I was wholly unfamiliar with these voices that were the most famed in the country, and witnessed interchanges like:

'D'oh, dere yoo are Nell son me awd pal me awd bayooty!'

'Oh, for heaven's sake, do go away, Dyaad.'

The two factions never intermingled and woe betide a newcomer or guest actor who sat in one of the old hands' chairs. Almost the only time Bob Arnold ever spoke to me was after my character David had called off his engagement to the ditzy Sophie Barlow. He hobbled up to me with his walking stick and said, 'Now look here, David.' (He never knew my real name.) 'Nice girl an' everythin' but that Sophie would never 'ave made a Mrs Archer!'

The old country characters may not have been trained actors, but boy did they know what they were doing. Chris Gittins ended up in a wheelchair for the last year or so of his career in *The Archers*, and I'll never forget watching him do an 'approach' to the microphone. The dead room used to create the impression of outdoors at Pebble Mill wasn't anything like as acoustically efficient as the new one at the Mailbox, and if you shouted too loudly, you would hear your voice bounce off the walls, which it doesn't do in the open air. I watched as Chris wheeled himself forward with one hand, the other holding the script, and turned away from the mike, directing his voice into one of the soundproof tiles. He executed the trick, which is difficult to master, of sounding like you're shouting while not actually projecting that much, the opposite of what you have to do in the theatre. Then, as he wheeled closer, he brought his head round, slowly, until he was facing the mike, all the time putting an effortful quaver in his voice to suggest movement. When I heard the broadcast, there quite clearly was a fit old man, walking towards us across a ploughed field, hailing us with a cheery, 'Well hello there, me old pals me old beauties!'

By the Sword Divided

When I was still strutting my Pirate Kingly stuff at Drury Lane, writer John Hawkesworth and director Henry Herbert came to see the show. They were casting a new twenty-part BBC series about the English Civil War, and one of the lead roles was the young Cavalier hero, Tom Lacey. As a result, I found myself sitting in a room on the first floor of the BBC offices on Shepherd's Bush Green, wondering if leg warmers were a bit over the top, sight-reading stuff about battles and horses. It all seemed like an impossible dream, but amazingly I got the part, and therewith two more years of earning my living with a sword around my waist and an earring in my ear. Obviously, I took the sword off to record *The Archers*, but only just.

We rehearsed at the 'Acton Hilton', the ten-storey BBC rehearsal rooms off the A40, now sadly demolished – Miriam Margolyes was there too, still telling dirty stories – and the interiors were recorded at BBC Television Centre. All the locations were filmed at Rockingham Castle in Northamptonshire over the two blissfully hot summers of 1983 and 1984. In those days, British drama was shot in two formats, multi-camera video interiors, shot in a purpose-built set in a studio, then with 16mm film outside. You got used to it but the jump from inside to outside was always deeply peculiar. Also, everything was shot out of order, so a character would exit the wooden set of the main hall of 'Arnescote Castle', shot in a studio in White City on video in freezing February, and continue their walk, now shot on low-grade film, into the blazing sunshine of the castle yard of Rockingham in July.

It's such a shame that the TV Centre studios are no more. So much classic drama was filmed there and everyone who worked in the place has tales of getting completely lost due to the circular nature of the building. The studios were divided into colour zones so if you mistook your Green for your Blue, you could find yourself, as I once did, dressed in full Cavalier rig (an amazing creation made by Judy, who was employed to make all my costumes), jangling in thigh boots with stack heels and spurs, and huge black hat which increased my six foot three by another seven inches, striding confidently into a live recording of *Only Fools and Horses*.

We were a happy company, led by Julian Glover as Sir Martin Lacey, royalist father of twins Tom (me) and Anne, played by the ethereal Sharon Maughan, and sweet, pretty younger sister Lucinda – Lucy Aston. When Anne marries a Cromwellian, the Laceys become divided, hence the title, which reflected the true stories of so many families at that time.

I became obsessed by the period, reading Antonia Fraser's *Cromwell, Our Chief of Men* and anything else I could on the subject. I was like a kid in a toyshop, riding horses, doing major swordfights, defending the castle from sieges and working with some of the finest actors in Britain. My only issue was I was just a bit *too* keen, giving it the full 'My liege!' bravura period welly that we'd been taught at Bristol. The problem was nobody had told me that acting for the screen is completely different from acting on stage. The whole point about the theatre is you're a long way from the back of the auditorium, and you have to project your words, your thoughts and your emotions over a long distance. In *North Sea Hijack* and *Tales of the Unexpected*, I'd only had small parts in contemporary stories, so I got away with it, but here was my chance to shine, so Rudi's warning of 'watch out, actor about' was horribly appropriate for what I thought was youthful energy. The whole point about the camera is that it sees *everything*, so in total contrast to the stage, all you have to do is think, and the camera will see it. If only I'd thought about it more, and remembered that acting is about *being* and not about *pretending*.

In my defence, I wasn't entirely alone. The style at the time was much more mannered, but I was trying too hard. My enthusiastic gaucheness also led to a moment of acute embarrassment. One of the guest stars was the peerless Peter Jeffrey who was a magnificent Oliver Cromwell. Before I met him, I was reading the script of his first scene and the stage directions described a child being frightened by his 'warty face and bulbous nose'. Later that day, I saw him in full costume and went to introduce myself.

'My word,' I said, 'make-up have done a brilliant job on the warts haven't they?'

'No, no, old darling,' he replied with a tired smile, 'they come with the face, no make-up required.'

They were hot summers. Togged up to the hilt in a linen shirt, thick leather jacket and thigh boots, with a hairpiece that felt like a dead cat kirby-gripped on to the back of my head, topped off with the wide-brimmed black hat, I thought that I would cook, but after initially sweating profusely, the soaked linen shirt acted like a coolant while we rode into the castle on horses, had swordfights and ran meaningfully from place to place. Nevertheless, I smelled, the horses smelled, the straw and the sun and the hot stones smelled just as they did in the past. The Sealed Knot, members of the public dedicated to the re-enactments of battles, were our army and they smelled even worse – and drank all our beer.

One of the pitched battles featuring the Sealed Knot was a mounted attack on the castle, the defences of which had been reinforced with ditches and stakes. I'm pretty happy on a horse, having done gymkhanas when younger, so I'd been honest when they asked me up front if I could ride. Some actors, unwisely, lie about it, thinking, *How hard can it be?* The answer to that is that it's not hard to sit on a stationary nag, but galloping and jumping can be extremely dangerous if you don't know what you're doing. This shot needed about twenty horses, the steeds provided by the horse master, Dave Goody, and the riders were volunteers from the Sealed Knot. They were led by Mark Burns, a real horseman who had left the King's Royal Hussars to become an actor, notably featuring as a cavalryman in *The Charge of the Light Brigade*.

Having gone off to check on the quality of the riders, Mark had a word with that episode's director, Brian Farnham.

'How many cameras have you got on this shot, Brian?'

'Four.'

'Right, well make sure they're all working because there'll be no rehearsal and you'll only get one take.'

Sure enough, on action, a salvo of cannons erupted and the horses shot off, most of them bolting completely out of control, their panicking riders providing spectacular falls that no stuntman would have even attempted. One was dragged along by his stirrups with shards of fibre-glass 'armour' sticking out of him, leaving a trail of blood. One of the cameras caught this in close-up. It looked like the most brilliantly dangerous stunt, which it was, because the silly idiot nearly died from it.

I got to do three major swordfights! Two rough and tumbles indoors and a formal duel in a field. The fight director on all of them was Malcolm Ranson and my three opponents were Malcolm Stoddard, Andrew Bicknell and Gareth Thomas. This was more like it. Having spent the best part of a year doing the same cod musical-type bish-bash stage fight, here was the real, choreographed, messy, brutal stuff of the movies. You can usually tell a Malcolm Ranson fight because he loves his signature 'moody' at the beginning, when the blades touch in close up, just a little 'ting' before the action begins. I'd watched *The Duellists* with Harvey Keitel, and so had Malcolm. We wanted the duel with Gareth Thomas to look like that, and in a lot of ways it does. It took all day to shoot, so if you watch carefully you'll see that it goes from a wonderfully misty, moody dawn shot at the beginning, to bright afternoon sunshine by the end. A few years later *The Princess Bride* came out, and Cary Elwes and Mandy Patinkin blew all previous screen duels out of the water, but still, it's for jobs like those that you put up with the insecurity, the ignominy and the rejection.

I recently worked with Gareth again after a gap of some thirty years. We were doing a *Doctor Who* audio play for Big Finish, and we talked about our epic duel. I was surprised when said he'd never seen it, so I got out the iPad and we sat together, two old geezers watching our younger selves. 'We weren't bad, were we?' he smiled. Tragically Gareth died about a year later, but I'm glad he saw himself in his gladiatorial pomp before the end.

The fight against Andrew Bicknell, though, led to one of my life's most mortifying moments, which has lived with me ever since.

Whereas I had done stage fighting at drama school and pretend stuff as a pirate, Andrew is a real fencer, and a good one. He was wickedly quick, and the swords were real. We trained for days, getting faster and faster, my skill at leaping down whole flights of stairs learned from my fagging days at school coming in handy. When we came to record it, the adrenaline levels went up and we got even quicker. On the first take, he cut me just above the eye, but we carried on, figuring it would look authentic.

A year or two later, when Kevin Kline the movie star flew to London for a red-carpet premiere, he came to our home. A massive limo pulled up outside Mr Pooter's house in Holloway, and remained, engine running and double-parked, while British Tea was taken.

Kevin's just lovely, bright, easy, not up himself – a mensch. So, he asks me what I've been doing since *The Pirates of Penzance*, and I tell him about *By the Sword Divided* and he's so happy for me that he asks if can he see any of it. Well, I've been recording it on videotape.

'Show me!'

'Okay, there's a fight scene you might like.' I wind it forward to the beginning of the fight, but he says, no, let's see the build-up.

Hmm. In the scene, I'm challenging Andrew's character to a fight while, for convoluted reasons, pretending that I don't know that the woman who is sitting on his bed is my twin sister, so I'm doing awkward, trying-not-to-give-it-away acting on top of the already mentioned overdoing-it-somewhat style. The fight ensues, which is pretty impressive I think, and then I stop the tape. There's a silence. It's clear that to the eye of one of our greatest Hollywood screen actors, my acting looks like total amateur shit.

He left pretty soon after that. I haven't seen him since.

Being David Archer: History

I soon realised that I was involved in a series with iconic status, so I got to grips with some background research on the show. BBC Radio 4's *The Archers*, it turned out, was first broadcast nationally on the Home Service on 1 January 1951, and it isn't just a long-running radio series. It's the longest-running drama series in the world, ever.

It was conceived as a sort of 'farming *Dick Barton*' (*Dick Barton – Special Agent* was the adventure series that preceded it) and part of its remit was to educate farmers in the most efficient modern farming techniques for a post-war population that was struggling to feed itself. Rationing didn't finish until 1954, and so the content was part drama, part Ministry of Agriculture propaganda. Although today there is no government directive to that end, the sense of responsibility to the farming community endures, so one of the permanent jobs on the programme has always been that of agricultural advisor, whose task it is to keep up with the reality of farming and, as much as possible, to be ahead of the game.

I play farmer David Archer, and while I've had real farmers telling me I saved their harvest or helped rid their cows of warble-fly, it's not just about country matters. Over the years, the programme has covered so many difficult subjects: rape, arson, rural drug addiction, divorce, floods, dementia, cancer, family feuds, as well as addressing the changing values and attitudes of society. In recent times, as a result of the compelling story of Rob Titchener's controlling treatment of his wife, nearly £170,000 has been donated to Refuge's 'Helen Titchener Rescue Fund' for victims of domestic abuse. For a while, 'An Everyday Story of Country Folk' became 'A Disturbing Story of Emotional Abuse'.

One of the things that people complain about regarding *The Archers* is that there's not enough drama. The other thing that people complain about regarding *The Archers* is that there's too much drama. It is an unchanging certainty that pleasing every single listener is an impossibility. Listeners shout at the radio, they 'can't stand that man', they 'wish that woman would just stop moaning and get a grip', they engage, they argue with their friends, they *care*. I've heard people say that they want the programme to be 'nice', that their lives are full of conflict and nastiness and they want thirteen minutes of cotton wool every evening to soothe them and remind them that there is a calm, safe, friendly, bucolic world that they can dream about and, if not live, then live by proxy. *The Archers* tries to provide that. However, people wouldn't shout, get cross, argue at dinner parties and *care* about the programme if it were always so comfortable. Drama is about conflict, and story is about wanting to know what happens next. A balance has to be struck.

I can remember times in the past when three really serious, depressing storylines were going on at the same time, often in the same episode. That was a mistake, and acknowledged as such; it's better to temper heavy plots with levity – for every scene about marital strife you need a Grundy scheme about turkeys or Lynda finding Scruff after a year's absence. I'm told I once said that *The Archers* is 'life with the heat turned down' – maybe that's true as a general rule, but it would get awfully dull if it were always like that. You need to threaten that safe world occasionally in order to have the satisfying scene where it's all right again, when Elizabeth finally forgives David for inheriting the farm or causing Nigel's death, when Phil finally gets over his grief and marries again, when Ruth abandons Sam, or New Zealand, and comes back to the family – the two-timing hussy!

Musical auditions

One consequence of playing the Pirate King was that my agent then kept putting me up for musicals. I wasn't really cut out for musical theatre. I'd already auditioned for *Cats* in 1981 and gone through the equivalent of that scene in *A Chorus Line* where all the dancers are lined up on stage ready to strut their stuff, adjusting leotards and leg warmers and looking bitchily at the competition. I'd never done a *jeté* in my life. The choreographer's assistant, all pert bum and flounce, announced, 'Okay everyone, so we'll start off with a simple sequence, and *lunge* to the left, *pas de bourrée*, kick and step dig seven eight. Attitude round, three and four and step, ball, change, flick *jeté*, up and here and kick pa pa, finish with a double pirouette, shimmy and a tah.' I was still trying to work out what a lunge was when the rest of the company was on the other side of the stage halfway through the sequence, so I wasn't surprised that I was the among first to leave.

It had all started so well. I'd got through to this round because my agent had told me they weren't looking for dancers, but 'characters'.

'What does that mean?' I'd asked.

'No idea, darling, just do something original.'

So I wrote a song. I turned up at Drury Lane for my audition with my guitar, and there were Trevor Nunn, Andrew Lloyd Webber and the choreographer, Gillian Lynne. My song was a ballad about preparing for the audition and included the verse:

> So I had Kit-e-Kat and cream for breakfast
> I yowled on the wall all night
> I purred when I heard the chirp of a bird
> And I pissed in the pale moonlight
> I got me some T. S. Elocution, I read about
> Skimbleshanks and Bustopher Jones
> I read all about Cats
> Somethin' like that
> In a feline baritone

I may not have got the part in the end, but at least I made an impact. Many years later, when I was in *Arcadia*, Trevor Nunn told me he remembered it. So did Gillian Lynne when she was directing her first television play, a strange piece about interracial love and racism called *Easy Money*. I got a call from her asking me if I'd write the music for it. I was amazed, but coincidentally had been working on a lovers' rock reggae riff that went perfectly with the story. I sang it with a light West Indian accent, something that would be anathema today. We recorded it in the same studio where, two months earlier, I had auditioned for *The Archers*.

After my brief stardom in *Pirates*, I was no longer going for parts in the chorus, but for leading roles. Sky Masterson in *Guys and Dolls* is a wonderful part. It was produced at the National in 1982 and I found myself on stage in front of Richard Eyre *et al.*, giving it plenty in 'Luck Be a Lady Tonight'. They had been impressed with my Brooklyn accent and everything seemed to be going well right up until the very last line, where you have to hold the final 'To-niiiiiiiiiight' for about eight bars with gusto, vibrato and strength. As the agonising seconds passed and my increasingly obvious lack of technique became apparent, I saw the faces in the stalls go from smiling approval to regretful dismay. My musical career was officially over.

Being David Archer: Behind the lines

There are thousands of words written online every week arguing about *The Archers* plotlines, but those discussions are really for the listener. I have no control over or input to the story, I just do the acting! Over the years, though, I've grown to love the programme and I'm honoured to be a part of a team that takes its responsibility to the listener very seriously indeed. I care about David, his family, Brookfield, Ambridge and its residents, because I care about my own family, my home, my environment and the countryside, so I want the programme to have that same reality. Sometimes we'll finish recording a scene and say, 'That'll have them shouting at the radio' – it's not by accident that people get outraged or frustrated or weep for joy or laugh out loud: it was planned and produced that way on purpose.

I have been playing David Archer for thirty-five years. During that time he's gone from being the youngest child of a farming family, through marriage, children, inheriting the farm, marital crises, foot-and-mouth, TB, floods, nearly moving Oop North, being partly responsible for the deaths of Jethro, Nigel (only I know what really happened on that roof!) and the badger (okay, he shot the badger), and had countless other adventures amidst an endless backdrop of milking, drenching, dagging, fencing and fixing everything with baler twine, duct tape and WD-40. Now the tale has come full circle, with his own children having the same conversations about the future of the farm that David, Shula and Kenton had with Phil, and that Phil had with his own father, Dan. There is no other form of storytelling in the world that has this kind of longevity because even *War and Peace* doesn't happen in real time.

In all those years, David has never blasphemed or uttered an oath worse that the occasional 'damn' or 'for God's sake'. We *Archers* farmers are the only ones in the country who don't turn the air blue when they drop a hammer on their toe. I wrote a song once about Ambridge being a real village where once a day microphones descend from the sky and record fifteen minutes of random chat that the characters then have to repeat word for word the following day at lunchtime. The song had the line, 'watch out, they're listening in . . .' when everyone had to mind their p's and q's while the mikes were listening but could then carry on being rude, having sex and generally getting wasted once they had gone.

Equally, although the good denizens of Ambridge are exceptionally clean-minded, the actors behind them are certainly not. If the listeners ever hear a double-entendre concerning the size of someone's equipment or length of their prize marrow, they can be absolutely certain that the actors have had a field day with it in rehearsal. I hope it doesn't ruin the illusion to mention that at the read-through of the scene where David ejects Rob from the Bull, his parting words to the Controlling One were not as restrained as the ones in the script, but an earthy exhortation containing the words, 'Now', 'Just' and 'Off'.

Young parents

William Jack Henry Bentinck was born on 19 May 1984. We wanted to call him Willem, after my ancestor Hans Willem and to keep up the Dutch connection, but when he went to kindergarten, they pronounced it Will-EMM, so at his primary school we changed the spelling to Willam. They then called him Will-AMM, so at prep school we gave him an apostrophe, Will'm, which has stuck to this day, although he's usually a good old English Will. The Jack was after Judy's father and the Henry after my father.

I was surprised to find that Pa was furious that we hadn't included 'Noel' in his grandson's name. He was Henry Noel Bentinck, I'm Timothy Charles Robert Noel Bentinck (thanks, Pa) and it was his mother's surname, from the Gainsboroughs, the side of his lineage with which he had most empathy. I thought that, three generations later, we could probably ditch it and imagined he'd be flattered to have his own name in there, but there's no pleasing some people. Will is Will and could now never be any other name, but in retrospect it was probably a confusing choice, as almost every Bentinck in history is either William, Henry, Robert or Charles. I'm the only

Timothy Bentinck and it's better for Google having unique nomen-clature, so I'm sorry Will, you are more unique than The Unique Person of Unique-town, but please don't go calling your son Ziggy or Moon-Breath by way of contrast!

So, the building site in which we lived was now a family home. The house still looked like a squat inside, but we didn't care, we'd had central heating installed, we had hot water and the roof didn't leak any more. We bought a second-hand cot, some nappies and went off to ante-natal courses at the National Childbirth Trust. I was well up for sitting on the floor holding Judy's tummy while she was taught how to breathe properly. I was astonished to learn that the agony of childbirth – a natural but dangerous function that, without modern medical intervention, has historically regularly killed both mother and child – could be obviated by small regular puffs of breath and the loving support of your partner. Nevertheless, I was proud to be one of the 'new men' who would play a full role in the whole process, and be there at the birth, unlike our forebears whose only role had been to smoke furiously while the screams of their loved ones were silenced by ferocious midwives behind locked hospital doors.

Some mothers supposedly give birth in a serene and happy way, puffing fast to blow away those pesky contractions. That's not how it went with us. 'GAS AND AIR!' went the cry within a few minutes of the first serious contractions, and after two hours that included the full repertoire of Judy's gutter vocab list delivered at a volume that would have silenced Henry V at Agincourt, the epidural was administered.

Some memories are seared on the brain, and Will's eventual arrival is one of those, a moment of pure joy and love. I shot projectile tears across the bed onto the midwife as my child's head appeared, and more when I saw the size of his tackle. A worse memory was about ten hours before that, watching the junior doctor's hands shaking uncontrollably as he administered his first ever epidural – an injection into the spine, which, if done incorrectly, can paralyse permanently. The extreme contrast between my fear and Judy's agony one minute, and the delirious peace and joy the next, is extraordinary, and something that no one can ever prepare you for.

And it really was a life changer. One minute life was all about me, and us, then suddenly it was entirely about something else, that I loved beyond words and was the most beautiful thing in the world, and that I needed to protect and nurture – and I changed my attitude to poo, completely.

We didn't get much sleep. For the first six months, Will'm woke crying regularly throughout the night, and it's true that lack of sleep does send you a bit bonkers. It's extraordinary how fast you wake at the very first part of your baby's cry. I'm ashamed to admit I occasionally followed the cliché of male insensitivity and delayed my 'waking' by just a few milliseconds that ensured Judy was awake too before mumbling helpfully, 'Shall I go?'

She got wise to that pretty quickly, and then I'd go into his room at four in the morning and pick him up, rock him on my shoulder, and sing Helpful Sleeping Songs about Willo and Bilbo Baggins-oh, and after twenty minutes put him back in his cot fast asleep and tuck him up, and creep back to our bed . . .

'Waaaaah!'

We've carried on loving Will'm in the same house, until he was thirty, when we all agreed it was time to move on – to Hornsey. He got a first in Philosophy and was a professional croupier. He works in advanced computer training in Shoreditch, has a big beard and has sometimes been known to wear red trousers. He's also one of the cleverest people I know, so he's allowed to.

Walnut was the son we never had, he popped out two years later, but five months too early, though who's to say that if he'd lived, then Jasper would never have been born, and how could you have a world without Jasper?

I held Walnut in my hand. Above the kitchen sink. The doctor hadn't cleared up properly in our bedroom after attending Judy's miscarriage and, after he left, there was a bundle of towels on the bed. I found our son, about five inches long. I took him downstairs and washed him at the kitchen sink, I wrapped him gently in aluminium foil, then called the doctor. I don't know what I said to him. It probably wasn't very pleasant.

Two years later, when Judy went into labour six weeks early, I feared the worst. We had been talking about names, and we'd sort of decided on Jasper (a favourite name ever since I was a child and had a sheep-chasing beagle of that name) if it was a boy, and Lily for a girl (my suggestion of Tallulah was quashed). Judy was rushed in an ambulance to University College Hospital and I was to pack overnight clothes, change of underwear and washbag, then follow in the car. I was worrying about Judy and the baby, where was I going to park, and which knickers should I bring, all at the same time.

When I got there, parking badly on the pavement, I rushed into the hospital with the overnight bag, ready to endure together the agony of another lost child. I came into Judy's room to see her sitting up in bed, looking beautiful, but without a baby.

'It's a boy,' she said, 'it's Jasper.'

I actually said, 'What's a boy?'

'He's alive, he's Jasper, but they've taken him away for tests.'

Quite soon they brought him back and he was beautiful – small, a bit shrivelled, but perfect. The test results, though, were not so good.

Jasper was born with Listeria meningitis, was in intensive care for another six weeks, and developed septicaemia and hydrocephalus. Entirely due to the fantastic care of University College Hospital and in particular his doctor, Mark Rosenthal, he survived to become the indomitable man that he is today. I always reckoned that if you're born with the worst headache imaginable, then when it goes away everything else is just a bonus, and that's Jasp.

When he finished school, I asked him what he really wanted to do with his life. 'I want to be the lead singer in a rock band,' he replied, a quite reasonable aspiration, but one fraught with insecurity, as his jobbing actor father well knew. We finally agreed that he should get a degree first, and I couldn't really argue when he found a BA course at Cheltenham in 'Popular Music'. It sounded marvellous, but had little rigour (at the time at least) and, graduating three years later, he found himself lost and on the dole in Bristol. He had been doing temporary work teaching a Saturday singing class and really enjoyed it. When Judy discovered a week-long introductory course in TEFL (Teaching English as a Foreign Language), she booked it for him and he took to it like a duck to water, the teacher telling him that he was a natural. He then did a three-month Certificate in English Language Teaching to Adults course and got his teaching qualification. Days after getting his certificate, he applied for a teaching job in Tokyo and was offered it. Weeks later, we stood with our lovely boy at Heathrow as he set off for the other side of the world, to a totally different culture, where he spoke not a word of the language, to begin a job he had never done before. He's now been there nearly three years and is an enormously well-liked and respected '*Sensei*'. We simply couldn't be more impressed and proud, of both our wonderful boys.

TV commercials

Having been brought up on TV-commercial film sets, my first time on one as an actor was hugely exciting, and oddly familiar. In the very first commercial I did I wasn't yet an actor – I was still the producer's son. Michael Portillo made a fleeting appearance in a 1961 advert for Ribena, but I was the first 'Ribena Boy', in 1962, aged nine, when it was still promoted as a healthy drink: 'it does you so much good, we've known that since we read about all the Vitamin C in blackcurrants, that's what helps to keep you so sturdy and fit . . .'

I had to cycle through a water splash and we did take after take because I kept closing my eyes against the water. After about take five, my new corduroy trousers were so wet they split when I went to straddle the bike. I was scared my ripped crotch would show on camera, so I forgot about the eyes and instinctively closed them again.

'CUT! Eyes OPEN Timothy, please!' My first director's note, and one that I should have applied better to my whole life. They never did get me to keep my eyes open.

As an adult, I discovered that advertising castings are a cattle market where you abase yourself utterly for the possibility of a big pay packet. In the waiting area, there are usually six other blokes much better-looking than you, and then you are finally seen and have to give your all to the line you've learned, with a Welsh accent: 'Mm! Brain's Faggots! Crackin'!' More usually, there are no lines and you just have to stand there looking like a dick.

For some reason, I've done a lot of beer commercials. The main thing about these is that you have to be able to hold your drink, as industry rules decree that you have to use the real product when promoting it. One day, I found myself at Bray Studios to shoot a Guinness advert at some ungodly hour of the morning, feeling dreadful as I'd just gone down with flu. As our central heating hadn't yet been installed, I'd washed my hair under freezing cold water in the kitchen sink. This was when I really understood the best place to be on a film set – in make-up, as you can come in looking like death warmed up and emerge, after much pampering and mothering, like a screen idol – well, you feel like one anyway.

Then, around 8 a.m., I was required to drink copious amounts of Guinness for the closing scene, as the ad was being shot out of sequence. I was one of the 'Guinnless' and Angus Deayton was the doctor dispensing our 'cure'. My problem was that every time I savoured the delicious white Guinness head, I'd do what all Guinness drinkers do and suck the froth from my top lip, which apparently I wasn't supposed to. Like closing your eyes against water, it's an instinctive thing, and the more takes I did, the drunker I got and the less able I was to remember things like the director's note about not sucking my lip. By midday, I was tanked and feeling really ill.

After lunch, which didn't stay down long, we then had to film the first half of the ad, with me sitting nervously with my girlfriend in the 'waiting room' of the pub and then presenting my pint of lager to Angus for him to diagnose me as 'Guinnless' and hand me a prescription. I could hardly stand up. The first time I shoved my glass towards him, half of it went in his lap. After Angus's conclusion that I had 'Monotonous Pinticus', I was supposed to ask, 'Is that serious?' Which, after many takes, came out as, 'Issatsheeeriush?' Surprisingly, given that Guinness commercials have a great reputation in the industry, I wasn't edited out, so my slurring forms part of that iconic canon of films.

Terry's Logger Bar was a classic, too. The only photo I have of it looks like the set of a porn movie, with me as a lumberjack, holding an axe and lying on a log while surrounded by a bevy of adoring women – so eighties!

Will had been born the day before shooting and the producer turned up in the morning with an enormous box of Terry's chocolates for Judy as a thank you for her timing. There is a noticeable discrepancy in my hair. I still had long, highlighted hair from filming *By the Sword Divided*, but immediately after filming the Terry's ad I had it cut for my next job - playing a colonial diplomat in India in 1890, so I'd had a short back and sides for the first time since schooldays. Then they changed the design of the chocolate bar and I had to come back to re-shoot the end of the ad.

'Sorry, I've had my hair cut,' was met with a grumpy, 'Oh, we'll have to make you a wig then.' This would have been fine if the wig-maker hadn't taken for reference a photo of me heavily back-lit so that my hair appeared to be peroxide blonde – which is why, in the final cut, I look like a moustached lumberjack with a tranny wig. It was supposed to be a spoof of Python's Lumberjack song, but the line, 'I put on women's clothing and hang around in bars' was disturbingly apt.

* * *

One of the things you always hope for as an actor is the chance to go filming abroad. I was cast in *Man-eaters of India* with Freddie Treves, had all my jabs done and was about to fly off to the subcontinent when at the last minute it was decided that my scenes could be shot in Wales. I was enormously disappointed as I was due to have a week in a hill station in the foothills of the Himalayas. When I found that every single member of the cast and crew had gone down with serious dysentery on day one (waiters had refilled mineral-water bottles from the tap), I realised I'd had a lucky escape.

Since then I've done *Sharpe* in Crimea and other jobs in Europe but the two long-haul jobs were both commercials – one for the Australian Tourist Board and one for Wall's Feast ice-cream bar. The latter involved a week in the Maasai Mara National Reserve in Kenya and I was the Big White Hunter: 'You shouldn't be out here alone, Virginia, big cats are always ready for a feast!' It was an adventure.

Arriving in Nairobi, I went for a walk and was immediately taken in by a group of charming and incredibly persuasive Ugandan con artists, to whom I willingly gave all my recently acquired per diems for the whole shoot. I believed them when they said they would send me the money when they finally wrestled their savings from Idi Amin's clutches. It took me months to realise I'd been done.

Then we flew in an old silver DC3 Dakota into the middle of the Maasai Mara where an enormous camp had been built for us by Abercrombie & Kent. It was like experiencing the Raj. I had my own tent with separate bedroom, a manservant, and a hot shower – the water was carried from an enormous tank over a fire in the middle of the wooded encampment and poured into a canvas header tank over my shower. Unbelievable. We all ate together in a huge tent where the evening's entertainment consisted of massive liar-dice competitions. Armed guards patrolled the site, defending us from lion and elephant. It was impossibly exciting. However, that first night it rained, and the next day it was cloudy – too cloudy to film. Same the next day, and the next, and the liar-dice started to get boring, and I finished my book, and suddenly it wasn't exciting at all. All we did all day was listen to Paul Simon's *Graceland* and watch the skies.

When, four days later, the sun finally came out, we had to rush. The first shot was a close-up of me eating the Feast ice cream lasciviously next to my girl, played by the lovely Emma Harbour, with an acacia tree and the setting sun in the background. At the equator, the sun sets incredibly quickly, so we only had once chance at it that day. The Feast bars were kept in a cooler chest with bars of dry ice to keep them frozen, but it was so hot that only the bars right next to the ice were frozen. Having rehearsed with a soft one, on action, with the sun falling rapidly out of the sky behind me, I took a hunk out of the bar with erotic intent, expecting to bite through its soft deliciousness with one hearty crunch – and hit solid ice. So the take where I go, 'Ow! Christ, I think I've cracked a tooth!' didn't make it to the final cut and we had to do it again the next day.

The crew went on to shoot another commercial by the sea in Mombasa, so I got a couple of days R & R on the beach and took a photo of me on a sun lounger reading the *Daily Telegraph* with front-page headline 'Worst Winter for Thirty Years' above a photo of a snowbound London.

When I got home, full of sunshine and stories, I was greeted by three very dour and serious women: Judy, my sister Anna and my stepmother Jenny. Will had been in hospital for a week with suspected juvenile chronic arthritis, or Still's disease. While I was doling out presents, they were looking through catalogues for callipers and leg braces. I later wrote a radio play about it – it wasn't funny. Luckily, it turned out to have been an appalling piece of misdiagnosis – he'd put his neck out falling off a table, and got a temperature at the same time. Shyam Singha was again the one who got it right, but not before the doctors had given Will a massive dose of steroids, which did him no good whatsoever and took months to get out of his system.

Another weather-cursed TV advert adventure followed a few months later, but this time in the Arctic. I'd been cast in a Carlsberg commercial to be a David Attenborough type walking across a mountain while talking to camera.

'I'm just over the rim now. To the west, Gustav Holm, but in front of me the spectacular Mount Forel Glacier. Since the Ice Age this mighty glacier has gouged its unstoppable path to the Straits of Denmark, where it breaks off into the sea to form massive Carlsbergs.'

'Cut!' says the director, and the caption comes up:

'Probably the easiest mistake in the world. Carlsberg. Brewed in the UK by Danes.'

Getting there was an adventure in itself. On the plane to Norway we were given some cash by the production company to each buy two bottles of spirits, as the price of alcohol in the country was prohibitive. I was already enjoying this job. I also made a new friend in Michael Percival, playing the director, a delightful, clever and funny man who tragically died recently. We took a coach north on snow-packed roads for the best part of a day, then transferred to a military half-track troop carrier with no windows, and set off across frozen lakes and mountain foothills until we reached the most remote hotel imaginable. Utterly beautiful, with each one of us assigned our own log cabin. The first thing we did was pool our alcohol resources, which resulted in a large dining table groaning under the weight of dozens of bottles of hard liquor, thenceforth free to anyone in the company. We were then encouraged to use the huge communal sauna to warm up after our long, cold journey. Stark naked was a great way to meet the gorgeous Norwegian make-up and costume girls – oh and the Ski-doo riders in whose hopefully expert hands our lives were to be held the next day as they drove us to the top of the mountain. A hearty meal and far too much whisky later, we trudged off to our cabins for a blissful night of deep arctic sleep.

The costume call in the morning was the first one I'd ever had that was far more practical than cosmetic, as not getting frostbite was more important than looking good. First, a layer of silk long johns, then cotton fleece, then wool, then the outer waterproofs, then boots and gloves and Norwegian hat. Onto a Ski-doo and hang on tight to the driver as he takes 'route one' up the mountain – just vertical. Halfway up, we enter a fog bank. We keep driving through the fog. We stop at the summit – in thick fog. Optimistically the film crew unload all their kit, the camera is set up, we rehearse the scene, but can't shoot because of the fog. We wait, and wait, and wait. Someone has the bright idea of building an igloo. Well, there is little else to keep us occupied on the top of a fogbound Norwegian mountain, so that's what we do.

Suddenly the fog lifts and we realise why we had come all this way – the view is incredible, just magnificent, a vista of arctic beauty, mountain behind mountain behind glacier, and a bright blue sky. Panic. The camera is loaded, my radio mike pack is attached, I have to run the long way around to my start position so they can't see any footprints. I have a walkie-talkie with me. I stand ready. I wait . . . then,

'Okay, ready Tim?'

'Yes, standing by.'

'Okay, turn over . . .'

'Sound speed.'

'Okay, Tim, and . . . ACTION!'

I start walking towards camera.

'I'm just over the rim now. To my west, Gustav Holm, but in front of me . . .'

'CUT!'

I look up the mountain to find that the camera crew has completely disappeared again . . . The fog rolls down. I return to the igloo.

But now, instead of playing Eskimos with my new-found friends, I had to wait alone about fifty yards away in my start position, ready to go the moment the fog lifted again. Luckily, I had a book. So I sat on a rubber mat for the next five hours with three Mars bars while the fog didn't lift in the slightest.

At the end of the day, one of the Ski-doo drivers asked me if I'd ever done cross-country skiing, which I hadn't, only downhill, but he lent me a pair of langlauf skis anyway and I skied, fell, slid and bounced my way down the slope into the welcoming and warm embrace of steak, whisky and the sauna.

The next day we did it all over again, except this time there wasn't even a single break in the fog. And the next day too. If ever a production was going to turn me into a smooth-skinned alcoholic it would be this one. Finally, on day four, it broke and we got the shot. One-take wonders the pair of us, wide shot, mid-shot and close-ups. But in commercials you always do multiple takes, so there was a lot of crunching through snow.

TV commercials

The director asked us to improvise some dialogue at the end for them to fade out on, which we did. When I came to see it on TV a while later, they hadn't faded our dialogue at all, but kept it all in, so the thirty-second commercial ends with this:

ME   . . . to form massive Carlsbergs.
PERCIVAL   Cut!
ME   Sorry. Are the footprints a problem?
PERCIVAL   Just wait at the bottom, there's a good chap.
ME   I feel a complete amateur.
PERCIVAL   No, honestly you mustn't . . .

Which did make it a lot funnier.

Years later, I was waiting in reception at the advertising agency who had produced it and saw that it had won some copywriting award. Did Percival or I get a mention? Nah, mate, you're just the actors! And the real irony of it all was that once the fog had lifted, the bright sunshine and blue sky looked far too pleasant for the story, so in post-production they had to add wind noise and fake snow, which ultimately made it look as though it was shot in a studio.

I have danced with the Bolshoi Ballet. Yes, in another exercise in 'unusual ways of earning a living', that particular bucket-list entry got ticked in the late eighties when I landed a part as a travelling businessman for Austrian Airlines. In a dream sequence, he finds himself in a line-up with the Bolshoi doing Cossack dancing. It was a night shoot in a cold barn just outside Vienna, the dancers had just flown in from Moscow, and, never having done any such dancing before, they had to bring me up to speed in about half an hour. They promised they would send me a tape of the finished advert but never did, and despite recently writing to Austrian

Airlines to try and find it, this classic still eludes me. There is, however, a lasting legacy from this job – one evening when I was in my mid-fifties, Judy and I were out to dinner with friends and I related this story.

'Go on then, Tim, show us your Cossack dancing!' said the ever-daring actor Rupert Farley.

Three glasses of wine told me I was up to this challenge, despite my age and weight being quite significantly different to the fitter, younger Tim who had no trouble with it twenty years earlier. So, down on my haunches, stuck my leg out . . . and snapped an anterior cruciate ligament. I was on crutches for six months and will never ski again. Quit while you're ahead.

My favourite ad though is the commercial for Herte Frankfurters that I did with my son Jasper. My character is a Dad teaching his son to ride a bike and making them both a meal of frankfurters. At the casting they said they were looking for a young child who could just ride a bike, and I mentioned that I had the perfect candidate, so the next day I brought Jasper in, and he got the part. I've got the tape of the casting, and as posh put-downs go it doesn't get any better than when the director asked Jasper if he'd seen the film *The Aristocats*', which he pronounced 'Ar*i*stocats'. With just one word, Jasp nearly lost himself the gig, but it would have been worth it. '*A*ristocats,' he corrected, completely dead-pan, aged four. We shot it on a lovely summer's day in a wood and a pretty English cottage, and all day people were telling Jasper he was a star. At the end he was given the bicycle. When he got back to school and was asked about it by his teacher, he said, 'I'm a star, and I got a bike,' neatly summing up the entire acting profession.

Being David Archer: Contractual obligation

When I started following my sister Anna's path into the acting world, she gave me a great piece of advice, 'Keep your mouth shut and never be late.' With the former I try, honestly I do, but I'm not very good at it. With the latter I'm better, because I'm aware of what's at stake – after all, if you're late for the theatre, a show with no understudies can't go on; if you're late for filming, it can cost millions; and if you don't turn up for an interview, you won't get the job.

When, fairly early on in my *Archers* career, I answered the phone at 9.05 a.m. on a Monday morning, in bed at home in London, and Jane, the *Archers*' P.A. in Birmingham said, 'Tim?' and I said, 'Yes?' and she said, 'Oh God,' and I realised I wasn't there for the nine o'clock episode, it did not go down at all well.

When I joined the programme, echoes of the last war still permeated an old-school-tie BBC, and the male-dominated hierarchy ran it like the Army, either because they'd been in the services themselves or, probably more often, because they hadn't and were trying to make up for it. So, something as horrendous as not just being late but actually not getting there at all was Bateman-cartoonish in its horror. As a result of my one lapse, I developed a reputation for being late that was entirely unjustified but lasted until Ian Pepperell (Roy Tucker) did something similar in the late 1990s and had to take a taxi to the studio from London. Consequently, he took over as the protagonist in the 'Worst Late Story Ever'. He has just been usurped by James Cartwright (Harrison Burns) who was in Leeds at the time of his episode. The thing is, these more recent diary failures are treated with banter, jokes and teasing. When I did it, it was akin to murder. I nearly lost my job.

Another hairy moment was when I was offered a very high-paying TV commercial for the Australian Tourist Board – four weeks in Oz being filmed in all the most exotic locations in the country. Not only was it a dream job but I was spectacularly broke at the time, so much so that we were thinking that we would have to sell the house – this job would rescue us. The problem was I had one *Archers* episode to record slap bang in the middle of the shoot dates. When I asked if I could get out of it, I was told no 'because someone has to be at Brookfield for Christmas'.

'Where's everyone else?' I asked.

'They're all doing panto.'

So, after a lot of thought, I did something I'd never done before and have never done since – I broke my contract. I was off to the land of my birth. If I lost my part in *The Archers*, then so be it. In hindsight, it was an incredibly risky call.

When we arrived in Sydney they let us lie by the pool for five days to recover from jet-lag and get a bit of a tan – not a bad way of earning money. It was around Christmas time and I remember lying in the sun, listening to 'Jingle Bells', watching kids the same age as my boys play in the pool and missing them like mad, wondering whether I'd have a job when I got back. For the next three weeks, myself and the actress pretending to be the love of my life were flown everywhere, diving on the Great Barrier Reef, flying a seaplane, driving a four-wheel drive across the Northern Territory, canyoning, joining in an aboriginal corroboree, kissing on the sand as the sun set behind us, and bedroom scenes in five-star hotels – basically everything I dreamed of when I joined up.

While I was there, I received the *Archers* bookings for the following month – eight episodes! Well, I thought, either they're killing David off, they're recasting or they've forgiven me. When I got back, along with Paddy and Arnold Peters (Jack Woolley) I was interviewed on the *Wogan* chat show, and in the hospitality room afterwards I was handed a letter. I feared the worst, but luckily it was an official rap over the knuckles, full of phrases like, 'we reserve our position', which I didn't understand. When I asked what that meant, I was told, 'Do that again and you're out.' Thought so. I still owe our then temporary editor, Neil Fraser, a bottle of vodka – apparently that was what it took to persuade the powers that be not to sack me.

The coda to that tale is that when I arrived for said recordings, Peter Windows, who was directing that month, asked me to come into the studio to listen to something that had just been recorded. This had never happened before. Again, I was worried. I stood in the studio with Felicity (Ruth) and Graeme Kirk (Kenton) as they played the following scene over the speakers:

KENTON   Hi Ruth, how's the honeymoon going?
            I bet Spain is a lot warmer than it is here!
RUTH   (ON PHONE, DISTRESSED) Oh Kenton,
            something terrible's happened, we were on
            the coach travelling to the hotel and it crashed,
            and . . . and David . . .
KENTON   What? What's happened? Is Dave okay?

As the scene was playing I was getting progressively more concerned. Felicity and Graeme were looking at their feet, while behind the glass Peter and the crew had their backs turned; I knew I was done for.

RUTH   Well he's alive, but when it crashed he was
            drinking a can of Coke, and the can has sort of
            got stuck in his throat, and the Spanish doctors
            say that even if he gets his voice back, he may
            never sound the same again!
KENTON   Oh shit, Ruth, that's terrible!

Only when Kenton said 'shit' – a word which has never been used in *The Archers* – did it finally dawn on me that it was a wind-up. This was confirmed by my colleagues and, up until this time, my friends, collapsing on the floor with laughter. When he'd recovered, Peter finally came on the talkback and said, 'Just remember, Tim, it's that easy.'

Point well made.

Sitcoms

After *By the Sword Divided*, I continued to work in TV and theatre, playing Archer (ha ha) in *The Beaux' Stratagem* at Southampton, which involved more sword fighting and my first male-to-male full-on kiss, and an episode of *Boon* with Michael Elphick and Anthony Head – playing an arrogant toff property developer with a shotgun. Was I becoming typecast? When I got my next part, the answer appeared to be 'yes'.

In a new sitcom series for LWT called *Square Deal*, filmed in 1988–9, Nigel Barrington was a young, posh, heartless estate agent married to the Sloaney Emma (gorgeous, Irish, Lise-Ann McLaughlin) and next-door neighbour to oiky but annoyingly good-looking Sean (naughty, funny, Brett Fancy). Brilliantly written by the ever-youthful Richard Ommanney, and directed by similarly young at heart and follically challenged genius Nic Phillips, once more I thought that fame and fortune beckoned. Quite what it is that determines whether a new comedy series becomes a hit or languishes on a 'Forgotten Sitcoms' website is a mystery. Rich had a great track record, having written four series of *Three Up, Two Down* with

Elphick and Angela Thorne, and Nic is a wonderful and experienced director. It did all right at the time and ran to a second series, but hasn't gone down as one of the icons of British comedy.

It was my first sitcom and the format takes some getting used to. The problem is the studio audience. It's like doing theatre, but not, and like recording telly, but not either: it's halfway between the two. In the theatre, you wait in the wings and when you emerge on stage you are in character, which provides a kind of carapace of security because whatever you do isn't really you, so if anything goes wrong you can cover it up as the person you are playing. As long as you don't corpse, you'll usually get away with it. In a sitcom, you're waiting in the wings as the warm-up man goes through his shtick, then get introduced to the audience, one by one, as yourself.

'Ladies and gentlemen, playing Nigel Barrington, TIMOTHEEEE BENTINCK!'

Big round of applause but, of course, we were all unknowns so unlike David Jason in *Only Fools . . .* where the audience knows that everything Del Boy says is going to be funny, we had to earn their laughter from scratch. The public buy into the fact that they are a part of the production and kindly laugh at anything that sounds vaguely like it's meant to be a gag, but problems arise when you have to do another take. If it's an actor's fault, like they get a line wrong, or corpse, or dry up completely, the audience love it, as they become complicit with the unseen workings of the show and know that it will probably appear in an out-takes programme. But if the problem is technical, like a wrong camera angle or a sound boom in shot, their patience starts to wear thin and they stop laughing dutifully at the same weak gag. By the time they've heard it eight times, you can hear the tumbleweed.

The other problem is that the technicalities of acting on stage and acting for camera are two very different things. One is big and the other is tiny. When filming, there is always 'quiet on set' and you're utterly immersed in your own reality. On stage, the audience becomes another performer, particularly in a comedy where you have to ride the laughter (or deathly quiet) and time your performance to something that will vary every night. When doing a sitcom, you're acting small for the camera, but timing it like you would on stage. All of us were new to it, so we had to find out the hard way, and made plenty of mistakes in doing so. After a while, just by the sheer volume of scenes and episodes, we got used to it and not so frightened, but later in my career when I had the odd guest part in a long-running series, I realised why successful, experienced actors who came into our show for the odd scene or few lines were in a blue funk of terror and would very often totally dry, speak in tongues or spend most of the recording on the loo.

Nigel's partner at 'Barrington and Grout' was the kind face of estate agencies, Max, played by the late, great, Jeremy Sinden. In one scene, Nigel is flipping through *The Times* obituary column, looking up the widows of the recently deceased in the phone book, then ringing them and offering to sell their houses. In 2013, we nearly sold our house in London, with a mind to do what my pa had done and start a new life in the country. It didn't work out but on the way we had to deal with the extraordinary world of enormously plausible and entertaining estate agents, who all turned out to treat the truth with cavalier abandon. I mentioned to one of them what Nigel had tried and showed him the clip. Far from laughing at the immorality of it, he was hugely impressed and assured me he would try it out.

The series climaxed with Nigel challenging Sean to a boxing

match, which given that he had been fisticuffs champ at Marlborough and Sean very much hadn't, he was cockily sure of winning. Neither Brett nor I had ever been in a ring in our lives, so LWT sent us down to the Henry Cooper Gym on the Old Kent Road to learn. Our teacher was a former British cruiserweight champ called Billy who didn't really get the idea that this was for telly, and who's teaching technique was to shout, 'Go on, 'it 'im . . . just fuckin' 'it 'im in the face, will ya?'

Stage fighting, and fighting on screen, is all about making it look like you're beating the living daylights out of someone, without ever touching – unless of course you're Mickey Rourke or Robert De Niro or Sly Stallone in which case you train for a year and get your nose busted and become good enough to win real boxing matches. That wasn't us, and when Billy asked me if I'd like to spar with him, and I said, 'What, actually hit each other?', you should have seen his look of utter disdain.

Not wanting to come across as a complete wuss, I agreed and got togged up with head guard, groin guard and mouth shield. I was pretty fit at the time, I worked out, did weights and bicycled to work, so I thought I was ready. The first thing I did was incredibly stupid. I let my jaw drop in what I thought was a boxer-ish look of casual aggression – so he hit it. I honestly thought he'd broken it, first punch. So I hit him back. I realised I'd never actually hit anyone in the face before in my life, so when his head snapped back (apparently I've got a very fast jab!) we were both pleasantly surprised, me because I'd made contact, and Billy because clearly his sophisticated teaching methods had paid off.

In the story, Sean is being totally trounced by Nigel right up to the end, when he distracts him by shouting 'Don't shoot, Emma!' Nigel turns in panic and Sean knocks him out. So, we were rehearsing doing very bad boxing, not actually hitting each other, and we were watched by a group of young boxers who were waiting impatiently to use the ring. Sitting in the sauna afterwards, one of these bad boys came in and sat next to us with a towel over his head and a look of glowering contempt on his face.

'You two looked terrible up there, man, you know? Really amateur.'

Well, I wasn't having it.

'Yeah, well that was the point, mate, we're actors and it was meant to look crap. I mean if I asked you to stand up on stage and play *Hamlet* you'd look a bit of a twat wouldn't you?'

I turned for confirmation to Brett, who was staring at me with a look of 'What. Have You. Done?'

After a long and extremely scary pause, I was relieved when instead of driving my nose into my brain, the boxer replied, 'Yeah, fair enough, good point.'

Phew.

Actors are an easy target. The common perception is that our only conversations revolve around agents, money, and jealousy. While that's often perfectly true, I've also had the most interesting political, artistic and philosophical debates with my fellow thesps, and laughed long and loud with some of the funniest people in the world. If I had to describe my class – rather than upper, middle or working – I'd say I have most in common with other actors, in that your class is really the kind of people you feel most comfortable with, and with whom you have a common life experience, a common language – an understanding without having to explain. My father called it 'ping' – when a few words are enough. We come from all walks of life – education, accent, family or income all count for nothing when everything about you is exposed on stage and you are utterly dependent on your fellow actor saying the right words at the right time. That trust and shared terror is the unspoken link that binds us all together, and, along with a shallowness that enables us quickly to forget the brotherly love for the person with whom we've just shared months of 'shouting in the evenings', is why we all call each other 'love' and 'darling' – it *is* genuine affection, but it's usually because we can't remember their ruddy name!

I may feel a sense of kinship with my fellow actors, but I can't stand divas. There are a few famous people in the business who have a reputation for being up themselves, rude, arrogant and generally unpleasant. One of the things I've always loved about coming into long-running series like *EastEnders*, *Casualty*, *The Bill* or *Born and Bred* is how welcoming, respectful and polite the major characters usually are, and in *The Archers* we always go out of our way to make guest actors welcome, as we all know what it's like guesting on something where you don't know anyone. Of course, if someone turns up being a bit grand they'll soon get the silent treatment, especially if they're crap, and the two do tend to go hand in hand.

There's a silly game that is sometimes played in bored moments in the green room called 'Arse or Angel' (or words to that effect). Someone says the name of an actor and everyone else has to reply immediately with either 'Arse' or 'Angel'. The fun is hearing five actors instantly saying 'Arse' in unison when [redacted] is suggested. There's also something very special when you find yourself working with people who are huge stars and who you admire enormously, and find that they're charming, generous, selfless and interested in others. I was so sad when John Hurt died – I'd worked with him on a Doctor Who audio drama only a few months before. I told him he'd once been to a party at our house in the sixties. 'Oh no, did I misbehave?' he asked wretchedly. I hadn't the heart to tell him the dampers on the piano he spilled a bottle of wine into still produce what became known as 'the Hurt octave'. Now there was a man who would always get a 'Lovely' from everyone.

Sometimes, in the heat of the moment, we can all let ourselves down and have a 'Christian Bale meltdown', even on a happy set like *Square Deal*. In one scene, Nigel is seen belting a punch bag in an uncontrolled fury in preparation for the boxing match. Takes one to three didn't work for technical reasons and I was getting a bit tired. On take four, I got a note from Nic up in the control room, delivered by the floor manager, to lift my head. Take four, he asked me to hit the bag harder. Take five, he told me to keep my guard up. Take six, I'd had enough. Pouring with sweat, with bruised hands and in a fury of antagonism, I yelled out, 'All right! You come here and show me how you bloody want it done!' Deathly silence from the audience. The floor manager came up and whispered, 'Nic's coming down.' Long embarrassed pause as the director came down the spiral stairs from the control room and took me round the back of the set. Ego massaged, profuse apologies from me for having lost it. Thirty years later, while having a lovely dinner with Nic and the series writer Richard Ommanney, I asked if they remembered the episode. 'Remember?' Nic spluttered. 'I thought you were going to kill me!'

To publicise the first series of *Square Deal*, we were taken on a jolly to the Montreux Film Festival and paraded before the press for photos and interviews. Lying in my bed in the five-star hotel, looking out onto Lake Geneva, I really thought my time had come. I was getting used to this press interview lark I thought, so when I got home and was asked to do a centre spread for the *Daily Mirror*, I jumped at the chance. So then came the reason why you should never believe what you read in the papers, in the form of an article by a seasoned *Mirror* hack by the name of Sharon Feinstein.

'BABY ANGUISH SENT ME MAD SAYS SQUARE DEAL STAR'

Well, as I'd been at pains to point out, it hadn't. Jasper's birth had been a very worrying time, but the brunt of it was borne by Judy as I was down in Southampton doing *The Beaux' Stratagem*, but Sharon was having none of it. We sat in the garden, she was as nice as pie, and I spoke to her in an entirely unguarded way, as you would to a friend. I happened to mention Jasper and how he'd nearly died, and from then on that subject monopolised the conversation.

'Surely you must have been worried sick. Weren't you angry or frustrated? Did your relationship suffer?'

'Not really, by the time I was doing the play he was out of immediate danger, but Judy had to cope with it all as I could only get home at weekends.'

'Did you take it out on inanimate objects at all?'

'I don't think so. Well, there was one funny moment when I was coming downstairs with a full tray of coffee cups and the cat nearly tripped me up, almost had me crashing all the way down the stairs!'

The *Mirror*'s translation: 'KICKED his cat around in wild temper fits.'

'And I guess I got a bit forgetful. I once locked the keys in the car and went a bit Basil Fawlty on it . . .'

The *Mirror*'s translation: 'SMASHED in the roof of his car . . .'

It went on like that. I really should have learned the lesson but I'm a trusting soul and journalists are generally extremely good at finding an 'angle' if you don't provide them with one. Since then people have advised me that you should always come ready with your own 'angle', as it's a lot easier for the writer than them having to invent one, but I'm still pretty bad at it, I'm far too truthful. And saying things like, 'this is off the record' doesn't work at all – nothing is, ever.

Just recently Felicity Finch (Ruth Archer) and I were interviewed about *The Archers* for the *Observer* and right at the end, after the journalist had packed away her recording device, she asked me, 'Why is David always out of breath?' This is a rather sore point. Ninety per cent of the time he's not, but when engaging in hard work, in order to let the listener know there is physical activity going on, then effort in the voice is required! I can't stand hearing actors who are meant to be belting seven kinds of crap out of a ploughshare sounding like they're having tea with the vicar, so with an exasperated smile I said, 'Well, he's out of breath when he needs to be. I mean, you try digging a four-foot hole for a fence post without breathing, fucking hell!' So, of course, that got printed verbatim.

I rang Sean, our editor, to apologise for saying 'fucking' to the *Observer* but he was entirely supportive – 'It was you swearing, Tim, wasn't it? Not David.' Exactly.

After *Square Deal*, I was in three episodes of *Three Up, Two Down*, my first casting against type as the heavily moustachioed and cockney George the barman, but my next regular part in a sitcom wasn't until ten years later, with Chris Barrie in *A Prince Among Men*.

Written by old chums from the *Pirates* film, the 'Sitcom Boot Boys' Tony Millan and Mike Walling, this was the tale of retired footballer Gary Prince, a Scouser with more money than business sense and a childish love of expensive gadgets. I played his posh accountant, Mark Fitzherbert. Coming on the back of the hugely successful *The Brittas Empire*, this was clearly going to be massive and we would all become huge telly stars. How many times have I thought that over the years?

It's hard playing a comedy character who is completely obnoxious. Having been a posh, selfish, opinionated, ruthless landlord and estate agent with no real redeeming features in *Square Deal*, I tried to make Mark – a posh, selfish, opinionated, ruthless accountant – a bit more likeable, but it wasn't easy. Twelve episodes later, Mark had spent most of the time sneering at the working class and doing barely legal business deals that relied for humour on his utter lack of morality. I was talking to Martin Clunes recently about how his Doc Martin, despite being completely ghastly to everyone, nevertheless manages to remain such a sympathetic character. Part of it is down to Clunes's subtlety as a performer, but also because the character has a vulnerability that comes from being cruelly abused as a child. When you're trying to get laughs from ringing up old chum Tubby McKinnon to arrange a Vicars and Tarts party, any vulnerability from being abused at Marlborough is hard to reveal.

Chris Barrie was my second encounter with a *Red Dwarf* actor, but my meeting with Craig Charles was not as an actor, and the blows exchanged were not stage fighting or choreographed. The blood was real. I'd been travelling down by train from recording *The Archers* in Birmingham and was sitting with Charles Collingwood, June Spencer and Moir Leslie who was in her first *Archers* incarnation as David's fiancée, Sophie. We were in a non-smoking carriage, and when the loud, drunk pair at the far end lit up their third fags, Muggins here decided it was time to ask them to cease and desist. This was a couple of years before *Red Dwarf* and I had no idea who Craig Charles was. It turned out later that he too had just been at Pebble Mill, doing a TV appearance as a 'Punk Poet', but faced with his aggression – 'Oh, here comes the rugby club!' – I was lined up for my first ever fight.

Remembering that Lord Byron was renowned at Harrow for fighting dirty, and figuring that this coiled spring of Liverpudlian aggression probably had more pugilistic experience than me, I decided to get my defence in early and kicked him in the balls and under the chin. The problem was my stage-fight training: I pulled both the blows and delivered a soft kick to his inner thigh and a light tap to his chin (although that did crack a tooth). My intention was that he should now be incapacitated, but his immediate response was to nut me twice on the nose, causing blood to gush over us both and it was only Charles Collingwood's timely intervention that stopped it developing into a brawl. Luckily, the visual anonymity of being a radio actor and Craig only being on the cusp of stardom meant that few people realised that David Archer and David Lister were having a scrap.

We then stopped at Coventry where, bizarrely, we were joined by another actor friend, Daniel Hill, who also knew Craig, and politely introduced us. I spent the rest of the journey trying to apologise to him, with that strange sense of fellowship one gets with people you've had a fight with. As we got off at Euston, far from leaving me with a sneering Parthian shot, Craig's last words were, 'Blessed is the peacemaker.'

One of the strangest aspects of recording sitcoms is that as well as doing the indoor stuff in front of a live audience, you also have to shoot all the exterior and location shots beforehand, and these get played in the studio during the recording so the audience can understand the story, and to record their laughs. This means that you must anticipate the response and leave a suitable pause so your next line doesn't get drowned out by the gales of hilarity. This is fine when the script is funny but deeply eggy if you leave a long pause and there's stony silence in the studio.

A first for me on *A Prince Among Men* was acting while driving. I'd done a parking sequence in *Square Deal* but that was just talking to myself. This was a long, involved scene with Susie Blake, made harder because they rigged the camera on the driver's side door, started the camera, clapper board, 'Action!' and we drove off, with only the sound guy on board lying on the back seat and no director monitoring it. I then had to drive around a council estate with a car that had thousands of pounds' worth of camera equipment sticking out about four feet from the right side of the car. The dialogue ensued, leaving appropriate pauses for laughs, and when we got back to the crew, the director rewound the tape and decided if it was any good. Looking at it now, all I can see is my eyes frantically checking whether I was about to wipe out the camera on a passing car.

Sometimes we *Archers* actors get to work with each other outside of Ambridge – I do a lot of additional dialogue replacement (ADR) with Alison Dowling (Elizabeth Pargetter), Becky Wright (Nic Grundy) and Roger May (James Bellamy), and I keep getting brutally murdered by Andrew Wincott (Adam Macy) in a strange German audio drama series in which I'm a vampire. We record on separate days so disappointingly I never get to bite him. I once sang and played my banjo on a gig featuring a couple of my songs with John Telfer's band, the Bushido Brothers, at the Tobacco Factory in Bristol – when John sings he is a rock god, and totally unrecognisable as the Ambridge vicar, Alan Franks.

The Archers cast sometimes find ourselves doing other voice work together, including ELT (English Language Teaching) recordings with the aforementioned plus Carole Boyd (Lynda Snell). I once did a hysterical re-enactment of *Dick Barton* onstage, in costume, with original BBC microphones and sound effects, with me as Dick and Terry Molloy (Mike Tucker) as 'Snowy'. Ironic really, as that programme was axed to make way for *The Archers* in 1951.

However, *A Prince Among Men* was the first time I'd ever done a long scene in vision with any of *The Archers* cast. My character Mark Fitzherbert had been sent to a factory that Gary Prince had just bought, with information for the long-time owner that we were closing it down. The factory owner was played by Arnold Peters, Ambridge's own Jack Woolley. You get very used to radio actors gurning, contorting themselves, doing anything that will make their voice sound right with no attention whatsoever to how they look. It was so strange to see Arnold without a script, proving why his final scenes as Jack with Alzheimer's, when he too was suffering the early symptoms of the disease, were so rightly praised and won the programme the Mental Health Media Award in 2007. In vision, he was a lovely, subtle actor, the master of baffled incomprehension, and when I told him I was closing his factory, he nearly had me in tears.

Being David Archer: Phil and Jill

On the actors' side of the room at *The Archers* there were my 'parents', Norman Painting as Phil and Paddy Greene as Jill. By an extraordinary coincidence, Norman, who was also a writer on *The Archers* from 1966 to 1982, had used 'Bentinck' as a nom de plume. He wrote hundreds of episodes as 'Bruno Milna' but for some reason he also used 'Norman Bentinck'.

Painting and Bentinck are slightly homophonic – but it was a pretty amazing chance that the actor playing your son would turn up with that very name.

Although Norman was nothing like my real father physically, or in almost any other way, the one thing they did have in common was a love of pontificating, authoritatively, on almost any given subject. Norman had been a postgraduate research student at Oxford and was extremely well read, and liked to show it. I was brought up to challenge or at least query everything, which he might easily have taken agin in one so callow, but it was only because I was genuinely interested. We used to have wonderful long talks on so many subjects, notably the Civil War – because I was filming *By the Sword Divided* and he lived about a mile from the site of the Battle of Edge Hill.

Thank goodness the eating-averse Twitterati weren't around when he was at his on-mike eating prime; these days they give us a hard time if we so much as crunch a piece of toast, so they'd have got their knickers well and truly twisted to hear him talking while eating a full English – an imaginary one, mind you, as he was always proud of his munching technique with nary a BBC biccy in sight. I also learned two other radio techniques from him: the art of slowing a scene if the episode is running too short, which he used to do by stroking his chin a lot, and the end-of-episode, pre-music rallentando. I used to call him the *rallentando-meister*:

> PHIL   I don't like the look of that marrow Jethro,
>   I don't . . . like it . . . at all.
> (MUSIC)

One of Norman's claims to fame was that, as the longest-running character in a drama series, he had once been invited to the *Guinness Book of Records* annual dinner. He had been seated between a Russian air stewardess who had survived the longest fall from an aircraft without a parachute, and who spoke no English, and the fattest woman in Britain, who needed two chairs and preferred eating to speaking. Loquaciousness being Norman's best thing, he suffered the whole dinner in tortured silence.

Once Paddy had got over my streaked hair and earring, she soon started being more to me than just a radio mum. She called me 'Timlet' and took me under her wing. You can hear her beautiful dry wit in her impeccable acting. When the script calls for this:

JILL Yes.

Or this:

JILL I see.

– in Paddy's hands those words can have limitless meanings. She describes the role of Jill as essentially cooking and agreeing with the men, which she endured with the patience of a saint until Norman's death, when Jill was finally allowed to blossom and reveal gravitas and wisdom – though never abandoning the ability to imbue the words 'fruit cake' with innuendo, sexual or otherwise. Paddy gave a wonderful speech on the day we all left Pebble Mill, talking about Margot Boyd (who played 'the dog woman' – Marjorie Antrobus) giving her dress size on the phone – 'Forty-two, forty-two, forty-two!' She also told us that when Jack May (the inimitable Nelson Gabriel) came back to the programme after a few years' absence, and was told by the producer Tony Shryane that 'We now do the read-through in the narrator's room,' he replied, 'My God, you've made enormous progress in the last ten years.'

Her comic timing is impeccable. After Norman died, she was in many episodes to record the passing of Phil, her radio husband of over forty years. I asked her what it was like doing her scenes without Norman. When she replied, 'It's strange, very strange . . .' I thought I understood. When she added, '. . . nice though,' I was in bits.

The dangers of mucking around . . .

Most of my contemporaries started their careers doing rep theatre and tours. Apart from *Joseph and the Amazing Technicolor Dreamcoat* in Plymouth, *Henry IV* and panto at Coventry, *Charley's Aunt* in Watford and *The Beaux' Stratagem* at Southampton, my theatre experience has been a lot of fringe in Bristol, Bath and London, or in the London West End. Having been in the RAF TV drama *Winter Flight* in 1984, I continued the military theme, playing a young National Service conscript called Tone in the play *Reluctant Heroes* by Colin Morris at the Churchill Theatre, Bromley, directed by John Alderton.

We were all hugely impressed to have such a big telly star directing us, but although he's a wonderful comedy actor and all-round nice bloke, he had never directed anything before and had the unnerving habit of showing you how to do it. Since he was extremely good at pratfalls, double-takes and baffled innocence, it just showed up the fact that I wasn't.

The play had been a huge hit for Brian Rix in 1950, when the entire audience had been through the war and the younger ones were still doing National Service. The French's Acting Edition of the play had stars in the script that marked where the laughs would come. They didn't. By 1985, the topicality had worn off somewhat. The play also starred the lovely Jeff Rawle, who recently reminded me that once it had opened, John and his wife Pauline Collins sloped off on holiday to Portugal, leaving us to cope alone for the three-week run which he, mistakenly, believed would be transferring to the West End. So we started misbehaving.

In one scene, as the gruff sergeant, played perfectly by ex-Grenadier sergeant Shaun Curry, is leaving our barracks, he says, 'Any questions? No? Lights out in five minutes,' and exits. One empty matinee, I decided it would be a good idea, when he said, 'Any questions?' to say, 'Yes Sarn't.'

A wicked smile playing around his moustachioed lips, Shaun said, 'What is it, Tone?'

'I need to report a terrible case of piles, Sarn't.'

'Piles?' He was now about to corpse. 'Piles of what, Tone?'

'Piles of haemorrhoids, Sarn't.'

He had now lost it but managed to utter, 'Report to the medical orderly in the morning. Lights out!' And off he went.

I thought that was the end of it. No such luck. The next scene was set in the morning with us recruits in vest and underpants lined up for inspection. In marched Shaun.

'Tone, touch your toes!'

Five years of school cadet force and three weeks playing an obedient recruit meant that I immediately did as ordered.

'Medical orderly, got that syringe? Man here with a bad case of piles.'

I shot upright. 'It's all right, Sarn't. All cured now, Sarn't, thank you. I'm fine.'

Appallingly childish and unprofessional I know, but you can get bored doing long runs, and the house was half empty – or so I thought . . .

Ten or fifteen years later, I was auditioning for a TV part and the casting director mentioned that she saw me in 'some play in Bromley about the Army'.

'Oh yes, *Reluctant Heroes*. Did you enjoy it?'

'Not much, there was a long sequence about piles that I simply didn't understand.'

Whoops. Lesson to us all – you never know who's in!

Being David Archer: Bristol Court Hotel

I retain happy, and some not so happy, memories of Pebble Mill. The thing that's changed most from those days is the sense of togetherness that *The Archers* actors had as a company. For one thing, everyone ate lunch in the staff canteen on the top floor, and this was where the gossip, stories and intrigue would be traded, until the producer came to join us, when, depending on who it was, mouths would be zipped and careers protected.

Another thing we miss about Pebble Mill is that in the evening we would all troop round to the BBC club, which was in a separate building, and for staff and performers only. You could eat there too, which was preferable to the hotel, where the term 'food' was stretching the definition of the word.

These days the cast stay in many different hotels and eat at a huge choice of bistros and restaurants in central Birmingham, but back then there was really only the famed Bristol Court Hotel, or 'Fawlty Towers' as we called it. Jack May loved it because the bar served Bell's whisky, and since it seemed that was all he ever consumed, he had no truck with his fellow cast members moaning about cold rooms that stank of stale smoke, the damp, the nylon sheets, the single beds with a thirty-degree slope from decades of overweight travelling salesmen trying in vain to reach their socks, the tiny televisions with lousy reception, or the blue or pink plastic shower cubicles with tepid water dribbling through limescale-encrusted shower heads. The heating was turned off during the day, and one winter afternoon between recordings stands out in my memory – watching daytime TV in black and white, lying in bed fully clothed under the polyester duvet (TOG rating minus twelve), running a hair dryer to raise the ambient temperature above freezing, wondering seriously if I'd made the right choice of career.

The owner was a friendly chap called Don, far more affable than Fawlty, but otherwise the place was almost identical to the éponymous 'Towers', right down to the actual 'Major' in the form of Ballard Berkeley (Colonel Danby), joining Jack and Margot Boyd for a post-prandial Bell's or three in the bar. So much has changed in just one generation; Margot was never seen without her 'face' on, her hair perfectly coiffured, an impeccable wool skirt suit and sensible shoes, and in the evening a cigarette in one hand, a whisky in the other, telling filthy stories – she was one of the funniest women I've ever met.

At her funeral, Charles Collingwood told the story of how, in her later years, she decided to change agent. The new agent's office was on the fifth floor of a building in Soho. Her large frame and weakened knees and hips made the climb excruciating. Entering the room and gasping for breath, she announced imperiously, 'I have two things to say . . . [wheeze] . . . firstly, you will never see me again . . . [gasp] . . . and secondly, [massive inhale] I don't want to work.'

Swordless

Aside from commercials and sitcoms, I was offered a healthy range of roles on stage and television following *By the Sword Divided*. After the excitement of playing the lead in a twelve-part costume drama, and effectively earning my living with sword and earring for the past four years, by contrast my next TV job was about as unglamorous as you could imagine.

Winter Flight was the story of a young RAF serviceman (Reece Dinsdale) and his waitress girlfriend, with the Falklands War in the background. I, my flowing locks shorn to a short back and sides, was a flight controller who makes the mistake of going to bed with Sean Bean's girlfriend, played by Shelagh Stephenson. In revenge, he picks my sports car up with a JCB and smashes it into my barracks bedroom as I and said girlfriend are on the job. Simulating sex with a total stranger while an MGB GT comes through the window isn't something you get taught in drama school. With no read-through it was literally, 'Tim, this is Shelagh, Shelagh, this is Tim. Okay, here's the bed. On action have sex.'

We filmed it in a deserted barracks that was about to be knocked down, so the room was ruinous, freezing and damp. It had been dressed to look lived-in but the single bed had starched sheets and just one regulation RAF blanket. We were alone in the room because the first shot was a POV, or point-of-view shot, from outside, as Sean peeps through the window and sees us making love. On take one, we didn't hear the director shout 'action' so a runner was sent to put a walkie-talkie in the room. We waited, frozen and silent, lying side by side in a single bed in an empty room, for the thing to be delivered. Then, absurdly, there was a knock on the door. 'Come in?' In crept the runner, averting his eyes from the bed, saying, 'Sorry, sorry,' put the walkie-talkie on the floor and shot out again. I've often wondered what on earth he thought we were doing. Well, at least it broke the ice, not the real ice that was forming on the bed, but at least we laughed, which made what happened next slightly easier.

Naked from the waist up but with underwear just hidden by the blanket, trying not to actually touch each other at all, a wonderfully British scene evolved. The walkie-talkie crackled into life.

'Okay, turn over.' 'Sound speed.' 'Aaaand, ACTION!'

Snog snog, writhe writhe, move on top, bump bump, grind grind, moan moan, quiver quiver, please God can we stop . . .

'CUT!'

Instantly roll off, maintain distance. 'Sorry, you okay?' 'Yes, fine, no, sorry, you all right?' 'Yes, well at least we're a bit warmer now!' Silence. Oh shit, too much information.

Crackle crackle.

'Okay, we're going again. Guys, can you try and make it look like you're enjoying it? In fact, I think it would be good if you were actually both climaxing, it'll give Sean more motivation. Okay, so on action you're both about to come. Thank you. Okay turn over.' 'Sound speed.' 'Aaaaand, ACTION!'

'Aaaah, aaaah, ohmygod, mmm, mmm, aaaah, aaaah, AAAAAAA
HHHHHHHHH!'

'CUT! Great. Okay, moving on. Let's get the JCB in . . .'

We then had to do it again, many times, but now with the whole
crew in the room, while dust and rubble were thrown on us to
simulate the car smashing through the window. When all the
reaction shots were finished, we then came to the bit we'd all been
waiting to see. With a remote camera in the room in case the entire
building collapsed, and another two outside, there was only going
to be one take of this. The stunt driver fired up the JCB, picked up
the MG in its bucket, drove towards the building, where the
brickwork around the window had been weakened, and smashed
it . . . and smashed it again . . . and made no impression on the wall
whatsoever. RAF barracks are built with bombs in mind, and even
the mighty Sean Bean couldn't get through that.

Being David Archer: Ruth

For a moment, Shelagh Stephenson, having barely survived
simulated sex with me in *Winter Flight*, was in danger of
becoming my wife.

David Archer is six years younger than I am, so when I
joined he was only twenty-three, single, handsome and deeply
eligible. Older actors kept telling me, 'Don't let them marry you
off, darling, you won't get any episodes.' David went through a
succession of girlfriends: before I took over the part from Nigel
Carrivick, he'd lost his cherry to a Kiwi sheep-shearer called
Michele Brown; in my time he fell first for Jackie Woodstock,
then Virginia Derwent the ice-maiden, had a brief fling with a
divorcee called Frances, then there was Sophie Barlow the

fashion designer to whom he got engaged, and a Ford Escort XR3 (seriously, he loved that car).

One day in 1987 I was asked to come up to the studio to help audition for David's new squeeze. I suspected at the time that this might mean wedding bells, so I was in the difficult position of choosing a wife from a list that I hadn't made – like an arranged marriage. Very odd. It came down to a choice between two great actresses who both, for me, had the same disadvantage – they were tiny. I'm six-foot-three and, to address the microphone at the same level as anyone around the five-foot mark, I have to adopt a less than dignified splayed-leg posture, which I have now been doing with the girl who got the part, Felicity Finch, ever since. Who knows if the other applicant – the equally tiny Shelagh Stephenson – would have still gone on to be a hugely successful playwright had she got the part.

Ruth Pritchard was from the north-east and was on a year's work experience before going to Harper Adams Agricultural College. When she arrived at Brookfield it was as a farmhand, and her modern farming views and feisty attitude instantly got up David's nose. He was completely sexist, reckoning that no woman could possibly do his job. However, in the familiar path trodden by buddy movies and love stories since time immemorial, sure enough opposites attracted and within a few months they were rolling in the hay, or at least our spot-effects person was rolling in discarded recording tape while we were snogging the backs of our own hands. 'Ooooh noooo' didn't happen till later; then it was 'Ooooh yes please' – as often as possible.

Since Ruth's arrival, Felicity – Flick – and I have been through some amazing stories, have become enormously fond of each other, and can sometimes be heard bickering like a real husband-and-wife team. For instance, she insists that the meal you eat in the evening at Brookfield is called 'tea', whereas for me that's a mug of builder's and biccies around four-ish. She can't travel anywhere without at least three suitcases, assorted carrier bags and the last three days' newspapers, but, once she's taken about a week to discuss the menu with the waiter, we've had some great evenings together, happily disagreeing about almost everything. In all this time, apart from the occasional very small toy being tossed out of the pram, we have never fallen out.

She's a great actor and an extraordinary person. Wearing her journalist hat she's travelled, usually alone, to make radio features in Rwanda, Albania, Pakistan, Cambodia and, most recently, Afghanistan, for which she had to undergo a 'hostile environment training course'. And they say Ruth is plucky.

Made in Heaven

In 1985, stardom beckoned yet again. On paper, it sounded superb: a pilot episode of a new long-running series that was billed as the 'British *Dallas*', which was the biggest thing on TV at the time. This UK pilot was called *Griffins* and revolved around a high-class health resort set in a country-house estate and catering to the rich and famous. I was the sports instructor and was there to get everyone fit, including all the beautiful female inmates who I would get to exercise in bed. I wondered how to play him, and asked Judy what I should do to come across as smoulderingly sexy.

'Play him Irish,' she suggested.

The opening credits are hysterical. Over throbbing music, the major characters are shown in a montage, doing their thing, then turning to camera with a cheesy grin. I was rowing a boat in a shell suit. It went downhill from there.

My first 'conquest' was the delightful and beautiful Debbie Arnold. The opening scene was me teaching her how to shoot a bow and arrow (the producer was an *Archers* fan and this was his little joke); we then graduated to the indoor pool where I was teaching her to swim (we both got ear infections). Next was the bedroom scene. Debbie is splendidly endowed but, not wanting the entire crew to cop a look, she stuck circular Band Aids on her nipples to stay decent (albeit with eyelashes painted on!). There is really only one memory I have of that show: Debbie and me in helpless fits of laughter.

When it came to the cast and crew showing we knew it was doomed. One of the main problems was the sound – filmed in the cavernously large rooms of the stately home, every footstep, movement and line was accompanied by a booming echo. You couldn't hear a word. At least you couldn't tell how unconvincing my Irish accent was. 'Sure, an' you'll need-need-need some extra-tra-tra tuition-shun-shun in my room later-later-later so you will-will-will . . .'

It didn't go to series. Indeed, so much of a death did it die that you can't even find it on the internet. I probably own the only copy in existence.

How I landed my next leading TV role I've no idea. I was in the middle of doing *Hedda Gabler* at the King's Head in Islington and had quite a thick beard. I was up to play the role of Steve, a once famous Man United and England football player, who, having damaged his knees, was now running a wedding agency called 'Made in Heaven' – the title of the series. It consisted of four two-hour episodes with two weddings in each, and well-known names coming in as guest stars: Keith Barron, Kenneth Connor, Julie Covington, Colin Welland, Maggie O'Neill and the like.

I don't look like a footballer, I don't sound like a footballer, I had a thick beard (not a footballer look in 1990) and had last played soccer, badly, when I was twelve.

I got the part.

We filmed in Manchester. While the rest of the cast stayed in a hotel, I booked myself into what used to be the stables of a pub called the Rampant Lion. Set at the bottom of the pub's garden, it was like a tart's boudoir with a four-poster bed and lush chinoiserie. It was summer and the noise from the garden was intense until exactly eleven o'clock every night, after which it was wonderfully peaceful. I loved it. Meanwhile Louisa Rix, who played my wife, was fending off the attentions of one of said 'names' at the hotel, whose bravura chat-up line was, 'Would you like to come upstairs and see the size of my room?'

It was all going swimmingly until the read-through of the third episode when the guest writer, a well-known grittily northern playwright who cannot be named, clearly saw through this southern wuss and decided to cut nearly half my lines, which when you're playing the lead is a bit off. She then took her name off the end credits – did she really hate me that much just from a reading? I think maybe she couldn't tune in to the appropriately estuarine footballer accent I was using, and just saw me as posh boy.

Louisa's character and mine were married but separated and I was having an affair with the equally gorgeous Maggie O'Neill. The day came when we had a bedroom scene, although unlike the freezing RAF fiasco, this involved leaping out of bed mid-howsyerfather stark naked to check my diary. My first 'closed set' – where only necessary crew were allowed. We rehearsed the scene. I leapt out of bed, grabbed my diary and stood there starkers madly checking appointments. I looked down to find the continuity girl sitting on the floor making notes. The only continuity she could possibly have been recording was the tumescence, or otherwise, of John Thomas, but thankfully he had remained well behaved under all that scrutiny.

After we'd finished filming and were back in London, Judy and I asked Louisa round for dinner. She was going through a rather difficult divorce at the time, and, needing another singleton, we also asked old chum Richard Ommanney, the writer of *Square Deal*, as he too was in the aftermath of a separation. At first, we thought the evening was a disaster as they hardly spoke to each other, Rich and I talked computers all night, while Louisa and Judy became firm chums. Around midnight, Rich mumbled something about him possibly driving back in Louisa's direction and would she maybe like a lift, sort of thing, or not. She grudgingly sort of accepted, a bit. It turned out they'd fallen madly in love with each other at first sight and had both been struck dumb. They're still blissfully happily married. A wonderful coda to a television series called *Made in Heaven*.

Being David Archer: Sound effects

'Rolling in discarded recording tape while we were snogging the backs of our own hands'? I should explain. Kissing the back of your hand started in the days of mono recording when you were physically separated by the microphone. It's also slightly easier to control as the real thing runs the risk of scripts clashing, and you've also got lines to read. The fake often sounds better than the real in radio.

An ironing board, old quarter-inch tape and a pot of yoghurt are all handy for sound effects. In thirty-five years of being in *The Archers*, it's always been the same ironing board – old and rattly, and it's used for all the metal gates and cattle crushes. The yoghurt is used for all the squelchy farming sounds, like calves and lambs being born, and the recording tape sounds much more like straw than real straw – also it doesn't smell or rot, so is perfect for a recording studio.

Lambing is a good example of the teamwork required to make the 'picture' of a radio scene. On one side of the sound-proofed glass is the recording team – the director who runs the show and makes the final decisions, getting good performances out of the actors and, eyes closed, listening to the mix and balance of the various ingredients, which are all recorded in real time. Next to the director is the production coordinator who times the scenes and writes down everything about the process. Then there's the sound recordist at the panel, who 'drives' the whole thing, sat at a huge desk of faders, twiddling and tweaking to get the sounds just right. Behind them all are 'grams' – what used to be turntables with vinyl records of sound effects, then CDs, are now MP3s which play at the touch of a button.

On the other side of the glass are the actors and the 'spot-effects' person – in effect an actor who never speaks but makes all the live sounds, like teacups, opening Aga doors and digging fence posts, and who sometimes rolls around on the recording tape, simulating cows in distress. So, for instance, a lambing needs the distressed baa-ing of the ewe (grams track 1), other ewes in the background (track 2) and the atmosphere of the barn (track 3). Then you need the actor cajoling the beast,

> DAVID Come on girl, you can do it, (squelch) that's it,
> (squelch) just a bit more, nearly there
> (big squelch) . . . and . . . there we are . . .

while the spot person is squelching yoghurt with rubber-gloved hands. At the moment of birth a large towel soaked in water is dropped from high onto a pile of recording tape, at the same time as which the grams play the lamb's bleating entry to the world (track 4). *Voilà* – one new addition to the farm!

Regular listeners to the programme will have heard David and others getting down from the tractor. You may be surprised to hear that this is done with a bucket. It's an old, metal bucket filled with a manky pillow to deaden the sound and I can remember my first encounter with it. I hadn't been in the programme long when I walked into the dead room at Pebble Mill to find a very wobbly Chris Gittins standing on top of it.

'Hello, Chris, why are you standing on a bucket?' I asked naively.

'D'oh, this ain't a bucket, David,' he scoffed, 'thism's me tractor!'

The explanation is that you need something to sound like the steps down from the cab. Obsessive listeners will have noticed that the single step of a petrol Ferguson in the 1950s and the enormous flight of stairs required to get out of a modern Fordson behemoth have exactly the same sound.

Year of the Comet

So many false dawns.

Another Hollywood movie! Not only that but written by probably the most successful screenwriter ever, William Goldman, he of *Adventures in the Screen Trade*, the bible of movie wisdom, containing the famous line, 'Nobody knows anything.' Coming on the back of his *Butch Cassidy and the Sundance Kid*, *All the President's Men*, *Marathon Man*, *Magic* and *The Princess Bride*, *Year of the Comet* was bound to launch me into the stratosphere, we'd have to move to LA and the boys would grow up as Americans and say 'was like' instead of 'said'.

I wore a three-piece pinstripe suit for the audition with famed English director Peter Yates to play the spoiled, arrogant, upper-class, stuffy Brit half-brother of American star Penelope Ann Miller in a film about a Europe-wide chase for the most expensive bottle of wine in history – they told me later it was the suit that clinched it. At the read-through I was one of the first to arrive. There was a friendly American there called Bill. I asked him how he was involved with the movie. 'Oh, I'm the writer,' he answered shyly.

I only had a few scenes, but they were all indoors, while most of the filming was on location, so I spent weeks in Skye and the south of France on 'weather cover'. This means that if it's pouring with rain, they've always got a set built for other scenes and actors on standby to shoot inside if necessary. My father was played by Robert Hardy – the most wonderful company for a young actor, he taught me so much and was hugely generous. We used to go for dinner in Nice and he'd order lobster, always picking up the tab. I once offered to pay – 'Dear boy, don't be ridiculous, I earn *far* more than you do.' Sadly, his availability ran out before we ever got to our scenes and the part was taken by the equally fascinating, but more serious, Ian Richardson.

It was the French actor Louis Jourdan's last film role before retiring – what style that man had. While in Scotland, we actors were put up in a three-star hotel in Fort William. As we gathered in the bar after checking in, M. Jourdan's chauffeur-driven Rolls pulled up outside, the driver got out and opened the rear door. Louis, coat draped French style over his shoulders, Gitane dangling from his lips, sauntered into the lobby, ignored us completely, looked around for a moment, turned to the driver, sighed, said quietly, 'Non,' and sashayed out to the Rolls again. He ended up in a massive suite in a nearby castle.

A week later we were introduced to the best restaurant in Skye by fine actor and gourmand Ian McNeice. Louis was sitting alone in the bay window overlooking the loch. He acknowledged acquaintanceship but didn't ask us to join him. When we looked at the handwritten menu, we noticed a recent addition in different ink – 'Haricots Verts à la Jourdan' – he had obviously had a word with the chef.

After weeks of touring Europe in wonderful locations but never even turning over, we eventually filmed my scenes in the Electricity Board's offices in Islington – about two miles from home. I was enormously flattered when Peter Yates asked me to be sure to let him know next time I was appearing on stage. It wasn't until many years later that I had a light bulb moment and realised it was a very English, polite way of suggesting to me that I was overdoing it – again!

Tim Daly, who played the dashing male lead, and Penelope were pretty good and quite friendly but, still, American actors need to be careful working with British film crews. Tim was a bit short with one of the crew once, which resulted in a classic wind-up routine one morning.

Tim arrived on set. A passing grip said, 'Oh 'ello, Tim. Are you still . . . ?'

'What?'

'No, sorry, we thought you'd been . . .'

'What?'

'No, no, never mind . . .'

Tim walked on. The gaffer walked by. 'Tim! Oh. Are you . . . ?'

'What?'

'No nothing, we just heard that . . .'

'WHAT?'

'No, it's fine, just surprised to see you that's all . . .'

How to get an actor completely paranoid.

The film, which was released in 1992, was William Goldman's only ever flop. He wrote: 'There was nothing we could do because no matter how we fussed this was a movie about red wine and the movie-going audience today has zero interest in red wine.'

Tim Daly summed up my experience too, in an interview with the A.V. Club in 2014: 'What a bummer, man. I loved that movie,

On the old Ferguson tractor in Tasmania with my father. *(author's collection)*

In 'Folksie' – the VW Beetle that got us to Scotland and back. *(author's collection)*

My first job –
Ribena Boy.
(author's collection)

The house in Hertfordshire where I was brought up. *(author's collection)*

Swimming at Harrow. *(author's collection)*

Weighing a sheep at Wigham. *(author's collection)*

Pa ploughing with the Fergie. *(author's collection)*

Judy when I first met her. *(author's collection)*

My father, Henry.

My mother, Pauline.

Nimble balloon with the tiny banner. *(author's collection)*

Me and Judy at Bristol Old Vic Theatre School. *(author's collection)*

BOVTS with me, Dan Day-Lewis, Peter Ackerman, Nicholas Farrell, Kim Wright, Jenny Seagrove and Russell Roberts. *(author's collection)*

North Sea Hijack with James Mason and Roger Moore *(Cinema Seven Prods)*

Terry's Logger Bar commercial. *(author's collection)*

The Pirate King. *(Drury Lane Productions)*

The real Colin the Campervan, with Jasper, Will and Judy. *(author's collection)*

The young Ruth and David. *(BBC Photo Sales)*

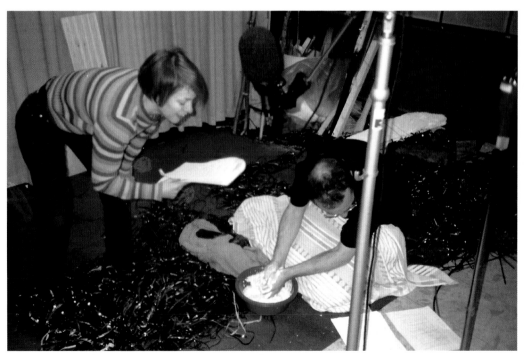

Using yoghourt for lambing, with Felicity and Andy Partington. *(author's collection)*

All the kitchens in Ambridge. *(author's collection)*

Felicity and me.
(BBC Photo Sales)

With Graham Seed, just after the death of Nigel. *(author's collection)*

Recording the Great Flood, with Trevor Harrison (Eddie). *(author's collection)*

Paddy Greene and Ysanne Churchman, Jill and Grace together! *(author's collection)*

By The Sword Divided with Lucy Aston and Julian Glover. *(BBC Photo Sales)*

The Hippo.
(author's collection)

Re-building our house. *(author's collection)*

Wall's Feast advert. *(author's collection)*

Square Deal with Lise-Ann McLaughlin and Brett Fancy. *(ITV)*

Made in Heaven with Louisa Rix and Moira Brooker. *(ITV/REX/Shutterstock)*

Carlsberg commercial. *(screen capture)*

Captain Murray in *Sharpe's Rifles*.
(author's collection)

Wg Cdr Raikes in
Strike Force.
(Yorkshire TV)

Mark Fitzherbert in *Prince Among Men*.
(BBC Photo Sales)

The article in *The Jamaica Gleaner*.
(Jamaica Gleaner)

– Contributed

■ The Earl of Portland, an accomplished guitarist, sings reggae for a happy gathering in the cottage restored to 18th century condition in Port Antonio by the Portland Heritage Foundation. From left, Eric Aarons, the 90-year-old parish organist and Minister of Tourism, Portia Simpson Miller, Viscount Woodstock, Lord Portland's elder son; Yvonne Ridguard, member of the Portland Heritage Foundation; Earl Levy, chairman, and Jasper Bentinck, younger son of the Earl and Countess of Portland, who are patrons of the Foundation.

Generalleutnant Speidel in *D-Day*.
(author's collection)

U-Boat commander in *Enigma*.
(author's collection)

University Challenge – The Professionals with Charles Collingwood, Felicity Finch and Louiza Patikas.
(BBC Photo Sales)

Prof Bryant in *Educating Rita* at the Watermill Theatre, with Claire Lams.
(Watermill photographer)

Our 30th wedding Anniversary, with cut-out of our wedding day.
(author's collection)

The eponymous Wade Ellison! *(© Eoin McLoughlin)*

Judy and me on board
HMS Portland.
(author's collection)

With Tim Roth in *Reg*. *(author's collection)*

On the set of *Fantastic Beasts and Where to
Find Them*. *(author's collection)*

Jasper and Will'm playing at William Tell! *(author's collection)*

Me today.
(Mark Dolman)

Then and now. *(author's collection)*

I loved doing it. It was just a great part for me! And that was my shot, right? That was my shot to be a movie star. I mean, on paper, it was a William Goldman script, Peter Yates directing, it was a Castle Rock production, it had a good budget – and the movie just did not work.'

Year of the Comet proved to be one of the biggest flops in Castle Rock's history. It was released in the United States on the weekend of the Rodney King riots and no one was going to the cinema, so Tim didn't blame himself for its failure.

I wasn't in it enough to think it was my fault either!

Sharpe's Rifles

One of the great attractions for becoming an actor, beyond the cerebral art of it all, is the idea that you'll travel the world and be paid huge sums of money to be filmed entwined with beautiful women in exotic locations, shoot guns, drive fast cars and scream 'Land ahoy!' from the crow's nest of a pirate ship. Maybe that's just us men, or just me – well, anyway, they were on my bucket list. I'd ticked the box on the exotic entwining front with the Australia ad, but flying out to Russia shortly after the fall of the Berlin Wall to face a massed cavalry charge of Cossacks and, with my dying speech, bequeathing my sword to Sean Bean, was altogether another kind of adventure.

I actually died twice, once in a manger with Paul McGann and once with Sean. I'd read all the Sharpe books, and when I got the part of Captain Murray in the first of the new Sharpe series, filming in the Crimea, I couldn't have been more thrilled. The British Airways flight to Moscow was fairly uneventful, then we changed to a different airport – and a Russian charter plane.

The Ilyushin, parked on the far side of the Moscow air base of the

Russian Air Force, smelled strongly of damp. The hold wasn't big enough to fit all the camera equipment so they simply piled it up in the aisle and across the seats at the back. This created a kind of private cabinette that contained assorted newly met chosen men and other ne'er-do-wells. The Pathfinders of episode one were on their way.

When I say 'on their way', it took about an hour to get the engines started, and when they finally caught, huge clouds of smoke belched from the jets under the wings and the whole plane shook violently. Vodka seemed the only sensible option and the cabinette turned into the bar.

Three hours later, we started our descent into Simferopol. Within thirty seconds, we had landed. Apparently the captain was a military jet pilot whose technique for landing a plane was almost identical to that for vertical dive-bombing. Jason Salkey (Trooper Harris) used the plummeting plane to demonstrate his skateboarding skills. The rest of us curled up and prayed – even the atheists.

We were transported by minibus to Simferopol town centre, immediately dubbed 'Simply Awful'. A faceless hotel looking out onto washing lines. Welcome to Crimea.

The adventures that followed made up for it. I was soon facing a cavalry charge of twenty Cossacks dressed up as French Hussars, swords drawn, coming at me at full gallop, led by the guy who was supposed to slash me across the chest – he was a Scot on horseback, and I imagined therefore spurred on by acts of woad-painted, Sassenach-hating frenzy. The camera crew were safely tucked behind strongly built wooden barriers, and I was in front of them, alone, with a sword. No acting required here then. Having been sliced (he actually missed me by about six inches), I had to stagger midst the onrushing cavalry and collapse on the hill, whence to be carried off to die by Jason, who has very muscular but bony shoulders.

I remember sitting with Jason in the back of a Lada in a forest, with two Russian mafiosi in the front seat trying to sell us tank helmets with attached infra-red night sights. In order to prove it worked, one of the Russians got out and hid in a bush. I then put the helmet on and they plugged me into the cigarette lighter. Wow, green binocular night-vision, lit by an eerie glow, which turned out to be the cigarette the guy in the bush was smoking. I bought four and Jason equipped the entire cast and crew.

The reason for this was that our daily per diems were more than anyone there earned in a year, and it took us a while for that to sink in and to respect it. But we did buy a lot of caviar and fur hats. I think Jason just bought weapons.

We took a day trip to Balaclava and Sebastopol and saw the 'Valley of Death' of Light Brigade fame. An ancestor of mine, General Sir Henry Bentinck, had led the Coldstream across the Alma, and here was I with a video camera in a Russian Army encampment in the Crimea pretending to be a soldier, about five miles from where that battle had taken place.

I was filming the pack of nuclear submarines in the harbour at Balaclava from the steep hill that guards its entrance, when my view was blocked by a Russian sailor with a Kalashnikov pointing idly at me. This was an area that had only just come out of fifty or more years of military control. I explained that I was an English actor, pointed at the submarines, said 'Glasnost' a lot and gave him ten dollars. Everything was smiles and joy.

Julian Fellowes, who was playing my commanding officer, entertained us with lectures on the relative architectural merits of Soviet bus shelters, and we lunched on the ridge where Raglan saw the Russian dispersion of guns and troops that he so tragically failed to convey to Lucan and Cardigan. To see the view is to understand everything about what happened. Earlier, we had driven to the head of the valley where the Light Brigade were formed up, and the misunderstanding is so clear.

Meanwhile, everything with the filming was going wrong. There was no stunt coordinator, so people started to get injured. The food really was appalling and those uninjured became ill. There was no way to phone home so everyone got frustrated and homesick, Then in an episode of almost suicidal bad judgement, one of the producers, playing football on the beach, tackled Paul McGann (the original Sharpe) hard and buggered his knee. The following day, Paul had to lead an attack up a steep hill under fire from the 'French', who were in fact all Russian conscripts who delighted in shooting us capitalist running dogs and fired their blank cartridges straight in our faces if they possibly could. Paul soldiered bravely on but it soon became apparent that his leg was too bad to continue, and eventually the production was pulled under an insurance contingency called 'force majeure' and, after a month of really quite dangerous work, we all came home.

Julian and I are cousins by marriage, but we had never met before. We had a wonderful dinner on the return journey in a brand-new hotel just outside Moscow airport. This was 1992 and Russia was like the Wild West in the days of the gold rush. Driving past puttering Ladas and ancient ZiL limousines on roads that hadn't changed since the war, we saw an enormous petrol tanker billowing smoke and flames in a field with no one paying the least attention, then turned a corner to find this brand new, state-of-the-art European hotel. In the lobby, prostitutes in mink coats flashed their nakedness at you as you checked in; then caviar and champagne in the bar with businessmen from all over the world, there to rape a country that was on its knees and utterly ignorant of the scheming ways of the West. How quickly did they pick it up? Well, who owns Kensington and Chelsea now?

Paul was replaced by Sean Bean, and after a few weeks of sitting at home on full salary, we flew back out to do it all over again. This time we were on the coast in Yalta, in an enormous sanatorium complex usually occupied by the KGB. One night we were playing the Risk boardgame and the table in my room wasn't big enough, so we borrowed the enormous desk that was manned by the two soldiers in the lobby.

'Hope you don't mind, Boris, we need this to play a capitalist game of world domination – a game it seems you have recently lost.'

The contrasts were so great, and really sobering. I had never seen such poverty. I went out one day to buy toothpaste, *zubnaya pasta* but there was none to be had; no shops stocked it. I eventually bought a half-used tube that was sitting next to a single AA battery and a comb on a table of other paltry offerings in the flea market. Roubles were worthless, our US dollars were far too much, so we paid with coupons: 100 coupons represented about one US cent. The toothpaste was five coupons.

Jason Salkey is a professional Frisbee player and we made friends with inquisitive students and others as we played in the park. What struck me most, when talking life and politics with these fellow humans who had been raised and educated in such a radically different system, was how, looking westwards at my privileged life, it seemed so shallow, so preoccupied with earning money, a raison d'être built entirely around the need to get work in order to survive. I'm no communist, but what was so apparent was that these young students had absolutely no idea what we were talking about when we tried to explain. Their lives were financially poor but they had no opportunity to change anything, so for them life was about learning, about art, philosophy, theatre and literature, with an engagement that was different to ours. For us, those things are, in a sense, luxuries to be studied at leisure and for pleasure. For them, it *was* their life. For all our money, they pitied us. It was an eye-opener.

The contrast really hit me one night in the hotel bar when, fuelled with local vodka, the Russians started singing – beautiful, achingly sad, three-part-harmony folk songs, every note an expression of suffering and oppression, and they wept as they sang. We were invited to sing in response. The only thing we could think of was 'The Hokey Cokey'.

Being David Archer: High drama

There are two episodes that Felicity and I agree were unforgettable.

We usually receive our scripts about four days before recording, but sometimes, if we're away when they arrive or there's a delay, it has happened that we only see the lines just before we record, but there's always a read-through beforehand so we get to know what it's about. In one case, though, I'd been off filming, hadn't got the script and we had to hurriedly record a scene that I hadn't even looked at. We went straight for a take without a rehearsal, so I was sight-reading.

The green light came on and an actress whom we had barely met sat across a table from me and Flick, and nervously told us that Ruth had breast cancer. I hadn't seen it coming and nor had my character David, so in the words of Robert Mitchum, there was 'No acting required' – we were both really struggling to hold back tears. And it saved someone's life. Felicity received a letter from a woman who, but for the storyline about Ruth's breast cancer, would not have noticed a lump that then got treated just in the nick of time.

I prepare the scripts with a pencil, underlining DAVID and then a vertical line by the side of each speech. We all do it differently, some use highlighters, some biros, some scribble all over the page, others leave it almost pristine – whatever works. I usually do it at home, but sometimes on the train or in a hotel. Having done that, I read the scene and think about what David's train of thought is, whether he means what he says, what is the time of day, whether it's outside and raining and he's digging a ditch, or inside curled up with the missus. They all sound different, and you need to be in the right place in your head. When I read the scene in which Ruth tells David she's in love with Sam the dairyman, I was in a hotel room in Birmingham, and I remember it making me nervous for the first time since I'd started in the programme. Written by the longest-running of our team of wonderful writers, Mary Cutler, it twisted David's mind like nothing had ever done before. This was a turning point, a *Wendepunkt*, and it had to be done well.

Now here I need to give you David's side of the story. There have been suggestions that his attentions to Sophie blew Ruth into Sam's arms. This is palpable nonsense. The whole point about David Archer is his integrity. In the years I've been playing him, I've portrayed that integrity being tested, over and over. Usually he wins, but when he falters, it's like a morality play – he stumbles, is tempted by the Devil, nearly succumbs to temptation, then pulls back from the brink at the last minute.

In this case, he didn't even come close. His own wife was behaving extremely oddly and he became convinced that her cancer had returned and she wasn't telling him. His ex-fiancée Sophie turns up and is friendly and funny and listens to his worries. The idea of having an affair with her *doesn't even cross his mind*! His wife meanwhile, without his knowledge, has become hopelessly sexually attracted to Sam and, having lied to David for months and treated him like an irrelevant idiot, has planned to go to a nearby hotel to have sex with a hunky stranger while her husband is cooking spaghetti bolognese at home for their children. Get real people, there is no comparison. And give it up for spag bol – it saved their marriage!

So, there we were recording this scene. Ruth is in floods of tears in the bedroom, David is comforting her: what is it love, tell me, what is it? Oh David . . . What, please tell me, I've been so worried (it's the cancer come back isn't it?). Oh David . . . Yes? . . . I . . . I . . . Aaaaaaaaaah! (tears of desperation) . . . What Ruth, darling, please tell me . . . I . . . Yes, say it . . . I'm . . . I'm in love with Sam and I nearly had sex with him in a hotel last night (or words to that effect) – (MASSIVELY LONG PAUSE) You. Did. What? Cue David losing it big time and Flick generating extraordinarily committed amounts of mucus to the reality of the situation. Finally, it ends. It's been a long, very emotional scene. We're drained. One take. Nailed it. A seminal radio moment.

Our director Kate Oates comes onto the talkback,

'That was great, guys. I'd like to do it again. Tim, page 12 line 4, can you pull back on "lied" – I think it'd be stronger quieter. And Flick, a bit less snot, darling. Okay, green light coming . . .' So we did it all over again.

Back to school

Back home from Russia and back in the theatre. I was cast as Torvald Helmer in a fringe production of Ibsen's *A Doll's House* at the Bridge Lane Theatre, Battersea, directed by Polly Irvin, produced by Adjoa Andoh and with Sophie Thursfield as Nora. This was a fascinating example of how a lack of preconceptions can help to create something original and new. We were in our thirties, traditionally too young to play the main parts, where the controlling Torvald demeans and patronises his 'doll' of a wife, using diminutives and pet phrases that belittle and dehumanise her. One of the things we were taught at drama school was 'text study' – the only thing you have as source material is the text, not how the play has been done before, or what has been written about it by critics, academics or even the writer himself. Acting is an interpretative art, and as long as you're true to the words, plays can be done in so many different ways. In our case, we started with the idea that Torvald and Nora had a very active sex life, and fancied each other madly. If you start like that, the rest of the play changes quite radically, and the diminutives become endearments, his protestations

160

of love and loyalty, which later sound like empty half-truths, we played as male weakness rather than chauvinist manipulation. Probably not what Ibsen intended, but it had a validity and was an original interpretation. We contrived to make Torvald a sympathetic character, and by the end the audience was torn as to who to feel sorry for when she left him. Judy brought Will, then aged eight, to see it one night and he felt sorry for his pa, and cried. The audience didn't know he was my son and were amazed to hear a child so moved.

We received a lovely review in the *Observer*, as a result of which we were invited to the annual Ibsen Stage Festival in Oslo, to put it on in the Nationaltheatret for a week's run. We were terrified that the Norwegians would think we were taking the mickey, and on the first night we took our bows to a slow handclap, facing serried ranks of dour academics with moustache-less beards, frowning intensely. We didn't know that this was the ultimate Norwegian accolade, and the reviews the next day were unanimously glowing. With wonderful performances from Sophie, Thane Bettany, Julia Barrie, Yvette Rees and Chris McHallem, this was the most rewarding play I'd ever been in.

A few years later, Yvette died and we went to her funeral. At the reception afterwards, I found myself talking to the amazing Ken Campbell, one of her oldest friends. I was telling him I'd once been in his first play, a fringe production in Bath of *You See the Thing Is This* and was being complimentary about his brilliant writing. After a pause, he looked me directly in the eye and said, 'Yeees. Actually, I think I'm going to go and find somebody more interesting to talk to,' and wandered off. It remains the most staggeringly rude thing anyone has ever said to me.

* * *

In the mid-1990s, I had a proper chance to work out how to do this screen-acting malarkey. I was cast as a running character in *Grange Hill* – Lucy Mitchell's father, Greg, whose wife had recently died. In shock and mourning, he then discovers the cause of death – AIDS. He goes mental, assuming she had been having an affair. It turns out they'd had a car crash in California, she'd had a blood transfusion and the blood was infected. A great storyline about father/daughter relationship, grief, guilt, blame and anger. After a while, he starts seeing someone new, so from Lucy's perspective the story was about step-parents too. I've always been a better actor when the part is very different from me, and after seventeen episodes of sounding like a proper geezer from Billericay, I finally learned the most fundamental lesson of all, that the camera doesn't lie, it sees the truth: you just have to immerse yourself in someone else's reality.

At the same time, I was playing a very different character, in Tom Stoppard's *Arcadia* at the Theatre Royal Haymarket, directed by Trevor Nunn. The contrastingly posh Captain Bryce has some funny lines in the first half and doesn't appear in the second, but I had made a bit of a mistake – I was understudying Roger Allam. That's Roger 'Never Off' Allam, as I discovered far too late. After *Pirates*, when understudying had changed my life, I thought I might get the chance to do it again, but hadn't reckoned on Roger.

'Roger's been shot!' came the cry down the narrow corridors of the Theatre Royal dressing rooms. My heart leapt in terror and anticipation. How had I allowed myself to get into this situation again? And this time in one of the most complex and difficult parts in Stoppard's oeuvre, but a triumph if you can pull it off.

'Shot?' I squealed.

'Someone's shot him in the head with an air rifle.'

'My God. Is he dead?'

'No, he's in his dressing room, putting on a plaster.'
'He's going on?'
'Of course he's going on. Roger's never off.'
Another day he twisted his ankle running for a bus – went on with a limp. Bastard.

At the end of the nine-month run, we understudies auditioned in front of Trevor to take over the main roles. I didn't get it. Win some lose some, but that really would have made a difference.

As a result of doing these two jobs at the same time, plus a load of *Archers* bookings, I was unable to go on a big family holiday, which is one of my life's greatest regrets. This was the whole family: my father, my stepmother, my sisters and their children, and Judy, Will and Jasper. They had rented a huge villa with a pool in Italy for two weeks, and it happened without me. Pa died three years later, and it was my last chance to spend some real quality time with him, and when I hear the stories about the adventures and fun they had, I feel a real pang. These are the perils of being an actor, though: you have to take the work when it comes along.

That work in the mid-1990s included the lead in *Strike Force*. I was very nearly a pilot. When I was at school, I imagined my future either doing what my pa did, advertising, or flying planes. I flew light aircraft with the Combined Cadet Force and got *Flight* magazine monthly. My favourite reading was about Spitfires and Hurricanes, and I seriously considered joining the RAF for a while. The appeal of flying never left, though, and when I landed this part, it was as though it had been written by my guardian angel.

Wing Commander Jonathan Raikes was 'awesome in the air', as one of my pilots put it. Bliss. I so nearly blew it. Having got the job, two weeks before filming I was meeting Judy in a pub in London for my birthday when someone smashed a pint glass full in my face.

I was millimetres away from being blinded in one eye and my face was cut to bits. I had to go up to Manchester to show the producers the damage. I remember standing in a hotel car park as the two executives peered at my lacerations.

'No, I don't think we'll have to recast.'

Phew, but it meant that I spent hours in make-up every morning and was the palest fast-jet pilot you've ever seen.

The 'Strike Force' was an elite group of Tornado pilots based in Cyprus and trained to instantly answer the call to scramble anywhere in Europe. This pilot episode (yes, we did that joke to death) was about the selection for the team. I was the boss. If the pilot episode was successful it would go to series – like *Soldier Soldier* in the air – so we were all very keen to make it work. We filmed it on location at RAF Leeming in Yorkshire, and we pilots met up on a train at King's Cross. We'd clearly all had the same idea – look butch. Leather jackets, shades, stubble and monosyllabic grunts failed to cover the fact that we were all like excited schoolchildren, let loose with millions of pounds' worth of toys.

We were '555 Squadron' and, amazingly, as we wandered around the base in uniform, the real RAF would fire off salutes and call us 'sir'. One day we were lounging in the mess room and one of our number, a delicate soul, came in flapping and saying, 'Oh my God, I've just been saluted!'

We, butch as hell and Ray-banned to the nines, said, 'Yes, and what did you do?'

'I went "Aaaaaaaaahhahaahahhaaaa!"'

'Nooooooo!'

We were filming in a stationary Tornado just off the main runway with me fully togged up in the pilot's seat, when the Queen's flight took off in formation for a fly-past over Buckingham Palace. The leading plane was hit by complete engine failure and, in order to miss him, the plane behind pulled up and to the left, heading straight for us. Someone was filming it on a camcorder and when we looked back at the footage, its wing can't have missed us by more than a foot. 'Not ideal,' as they say in the forces.

I was invited to follow the real Wing Commander around on his duties, to get the style of the man and see how it was really done. We went into the 'hard' bomb-proof shelter for a briefing and instead of introducing me as 'the actor prat who's pretending to be me', he said, 'This is Wing Commander Raikes, O.C. 555 Squadron.' I left the briefing walking on air. He offered to take me up for a flight but the insurance wouldn't cover it. I'd practised for hours at home on a Tornado computer game, but when it came to the simple matter of shooting down a Russian MiG with cannon on the training sim – a computer in an office – I was dead meat within seconds. However, I did get to land in the full-size simulator – real cockpit, full G-kit and helmet, communicating with the ops room as they talked me down – and I didn't crash, which made it easier to play the part.

The pilot didn't go to series. The problem with pilot episodes like these is they try to cram too much in. The RAF wanted it to be a recruiting film, and kept changing the lines to make it accurate but dull, and the writer wanted to fit everyone's back-story into an hour, so there were about four storylines going on at the same time. The result was laudable but messy. The flying shots were great and it would have got better – good actors and great potential. We heard that the caterers had been booked for Cyprus, but that was it, it was broadcast but never picked up.

Is there a pattern here? Am I jinxed?

Being David Archer:
'Shocking Ambridge to the Core'

They say that every cloud has a silver lining but I know that real farmers who went through the horror of foot-and-mouth disease in 2001 won't be in the slightest bit mollified to hear that the extra *Archers* episodes I was in when Brookfield was affected by the disease paid my tax that year.

From the production point of view, it's always a difficult decision to know what to reflect in the real world, and what to ignore. We sometimes have to rush up to Birmingham to record what are known as 'topical inserts' where a piece of important breaking news needs to be recorded on the day of broadcast – taking the place of a scene that had been laid down weeks before. In the case of foot-and-mouth, it was impossible to ignore as it was a terrifying crisis for all farmers. Far from the odd mention, the story took centre stage as our family, along with Bert Fry, were barricaded inside the farm for the duration. Over 2,000 cases of the disease were recorded across the country, leading to the slaughter and burning of more than ten million cows and sheep. The story was handled with accuracy and sensitivity, and received praise from reviewers and farmers alike for doing what *The Archers* does best, combining drama with much-needed information.

To mark our fiftieth year at around the same time, we were all invited to St James's Palace where we were feted by Prince Charles and an enormous number of celebrity fans (who would have thought that Phill Jupitus was a closet listener?). I was photographed with the heir to the throne beneath a massive painting of our common ancestor, William IV – although my lineage is not as respectable as his, as I'm descended from the

King's illicit liaison with Dorothy Jordan, the actress who trod the Drury Lane boards 200 years before I did.

The famous guests kept staring at us. It's different from being recognised from the telly: when *Archers* listeners finally put a face to the voice they've been listening to for so many years, they stare and stare. I've always wanted to do a play at the National Theatre, so when Richard Eyre locked onto my eyes with a probing gaze of fascination, I thought I'd be in his next five productions at least, if not a lifetime regular. Sadly, he's obviously typecast me as a farmer – I've never had the call.

So, when the sixtieth anniversary came around, we were all awaiting a party that would outdo that one. Instead, Nigel Pargetter fell to his death from the roof of Lower Loxley (I didn't push him, honest!) – a difficult and controversial decision that was taken hard by many listeners. The distinctive voice of Nigel lives on in the form of actor Graham Seed, so mourning *Archers* addicts can still get a dose of his tones in the theatre and on TV, along with appearances on *Saturday Live* and *Broadcasting House* on Radio 4. His one-off performance as the very un-Nigel-ish abattoir owner in the hour-long jury special at the end of Helen's trial showed what a good actor he is.

We had been told that one of our characters was going to die to mark the sixtieth with an event that would 'Shock Ambridge to the Core', but for weeks none of us knew which one. None of us that is except Graham, who had been told in advance but asked to keep it quiet, so the poor bloke had to sit with all his mates discussing who might be going, all the time knowing it was him. *The Killing of Sister George* for real. I think the intention was to balance the death with the birth of Henry Archer, and the subsequent reconciliation of Tony and Helen, and the celebrations continued into the year with the appearance on the programme of the Duchess of Cornwall, but the focus of course remained on Nigel.

We recorded his demise in the dead room, a horribly apt description. On the speakers we heard the wind whistling around the chimney pots. We edged carefully along the floor while John, the spot-effects artist, chinked bits of tile and brick together – it sounded pretty hairy (John had provided tiles from his own house, and they are now framed in his living room). When I listened to the broadcast, it was in the early days of Twitter and I was following this new thing called a Tweetalong. The moment David shamed Nigel into coming up with him to get the banner down – 'Are you a man or a mouse?' – someone tweeted, 'DON'T GO UP ON THE FUCKING ROOF!!' and I think from that moment there was an inevitability about what was going to happen. Graham and I discussed the length of the scream, imagining the height of Lower Loxley and figuring that the scream would be quite short. He slipped, yelled as he backed away from the mike (he didn't need the script for his last ever line), I screamed, 'NIGELLLLLLLL!' – and that was that.

I asked John to take a photo of us. I posed with what I thought was a face of sympathy, but in the picture I just look insufferably smug. They lengthened the scream in post-production to make it more dramatic, but the office was then flooded with letters and emails from people who had worked out that given the feet per second rate of acceleration of a human body at sea level, Lower Loxley must be the height of Salisbury Cathedral.

Night Must Fall

When an actor says, 'When I was doing *Charley's Aunt* at Watford . . .' you know they're the real deal. So, when I was offered *Charley's Aunt* at Watford, despite hating the play, not loving Watford and having a nasty chest infection, I felt I had to do it or I'd never be taken seriously by my peers.

Everything comes in handy. Five years of wearing a detached stiff collar at Harrow meant that I was in white tie and tails before the others in the dressing room had got their trousers on. That and getting my car broken into in the Watford multi-storey car park – after twenty-odd years of vandal-free parking in Holloway, for heaven's sake – are about my only memories of that box-ticking exercise.

Soon afterwards, in 1996, I had a nice part in Emlyn Williams's *Night Must Fall*. Jason Donovan is a lovely bloke but his Welsh accent is not as good as his singing. As he has admitted, he was also going through his cocaine period, which didn't help with the accuracy of his lines in *Night Must Fall*. I'm so glad he's cleaned up his act now, as I was genuinely fond of him and he was on the path to nowhere.

We opened in Leatherhead where the weaknesses of the production were forgiven by a ready audience of teen fans who were in thrall to the Antipodean blond one. When it came to the West End, though, the critics were unsparing. And I didn't escape either. David Benedict wrote in the *Independent*, '"This is all getting pretty terrible, isn't it?" That observation by the walking blue blazer masquerading as a character is both an understatement and the nearest you'll get to dramatic truth all night in this preposterous revival.' I was that blue blazer, with a stick-on moustache and a pipe. The moustache tended to flap off mid-speech and I hate pipes.

When it transferred to the West End, at the Theatre Royal Haymarket again, we were set for a long run, but about two weeks in, after the dreadful reviews that slayed everyone involved, our notice to quit was given. Sadly, it was on the night that Jason's dad Terence, himself an actor, had flown over from Oz to see his son. I was in Jason's dressing room, meeting his dad, when the company manager brought the bad news. Father and son greeted it with cheerful Aussie disdain – they do stiff upper lip even better than we do. I felt very sorry for him, he's a good actor and a lovely bloke, but sometimes you just get completely miscast.

He wasn't put off the stage – he has been in several successful musicals since – but it would be a long time until I trod the boards again.

I sought solace back in the television studio, and in the world of Robin Hood that had brought me so much joy as a child, but the unlucky streak continued. It's almost impossible to be good in something that's dreadful, especially when it's produced by American control freaks whose only criterion for success is the bottom line. *The New Adventures of Robin Hood* was one such production. It was like panto on telly – enormous fun to do, but quite mind-bogglingly execrable. It made Mel Brooks's *Men in Tights* look like a historical documentary. I was dreadful, and therefore fitted into it perfectly.

We filmed in the Lithuanian National Film Studios just outside Vilnius, so it was a bit of an adventure. I'd lost my glasses on day one so could be found sitting three inches away from my hotel TV watching the football – the European Championship – with prescription sunglasses on. In my episode, I was the evil Count Frederick who looked like Ming the Merciless with a hangover. Pouring sweat in wig, beard and heavy velvet in a boiling studio with massive brute lamps and no air conditioning, Frederick had to battle with an enchanted sword while it destroyed four banqueting tables laden with food. So, the brief was to swipe specific parts of the table settings but not others, all the time making it look like the sword was doing it, and I was trying to hold it back. Not easy.

It's at times like these, when you're draped on your throne, confronted by a Ninja warrior (in Sherwood?), and delivering lines like, 'Who do you think you are?' and worrying whether you should hit the 'who' or the 'do' that the will to live is to be glimpsed scuttling out the side door, never to return.

'I'm a grown man. What on earth am I doing?'

I often think this.

Being David Archer: Deaths and recasting

Although Richard Derrington had been told that his character Mark Hebden was going to die, he still found it a shock when he came to read his final script. He told me, 'I was just marking up the script as usual, I'm driving along in wet weather, I hit a bend, the car skids, I go off the road and hit a tree, I turn the page and there it is, I'm dead. Bit of a blow, I can tell you.'

At least David wasn't involved with that death, unlike Jethro, who David did for with a falling branch, or indeed the badger that he shot and then threw in the road pretending it was roadkill – and he was chairman of the Parish Council at the time! I play a lot of evil characters for computer games and the like, but as harbingers of doom go, David takes some beating.

Mary Wimbush (Julia Pargetter) died as most actors would like to go, at work. An old friend of my parents, we used to visit her idyllic cottage in Aldbury, Hertfordshire, that she shared with the poet Louis MacNeice, and in which, age twelve, I smoked my first cigarette in an upstairs bedroom with her son Charles, while the grown-ups partied below. Mary lived life to the full, and believed that taking the safe path was supremely dull and to be avoided at all costs. She finished recording an episode at the BBC recording studios at the Mailbox in Birmingham and, aged eighty-one, died on the stairs in the arms of her radio daughter-in-law, Alison Dowling (Elizabeth Pargetter).

When an older actor passes away their character usually dies with them – out of respect if nothing else. If the actor decides to retire, or is forced to by ill health, or, as can happen, is simply given the boot, then they might be recast, which can be quite a thing. It's asking a lot of the listener to believe that someone whose voice, mannerisms and style they have come to know intimately over a period of years can overnight turn into a completely different person. In a way, it's even more difficult than when it happens in vision, where you can at least see that it's palpably a different actor, but when it's just the voice, you're imagining the same body that you've always known, but the voice is suddenly someone else's.

Often, the new actor will do an impression of the previous one, and then gradually change it to something that they're more comfortable with. When Eric Allan took over the part of Bert Fry on the death of Roger Hume in 1996, his impression was uncannily accurate, and he has kept it up ever since. Heather Bell created the character of Clarrie Grundy, followed by Fiona Mathieson, who tragically took her own life after a very short time in the part. She in turn was replaced by Rosalind Adams who made the character her own over fifteen years. When Ros sadly decided to retire to spend more time with her family, we were thrilled to find Heather back again after all that time, but some new listeners of course complained that she sounded nothing like 'their' Clarrie – hugely ironic.

I'm a replacement myself. Baby David was actually Judy Bennett (who plays Shula), then as an adult he was first played by Nigel Carrivick, but David was sent to an agricultural college in Holland for a year, so by the time I turned up, I hoped that people had forgotten what he sounded like. I was never played a clip of the previous actor, and indeed I have never heard a recording, but when I met Peter Windows recently at William Smethurst's funeral, he told me that I was a shoo-in for the part, so I must have sounded pretty like him – unlike recent changes such as Pip, or Tom, or Tony, or Kate, or any number of characters over the years who have undergone a pretty radical vocal transplant.

When Tony Archer had a heart attack, listeners were not aware that the actor Colin Skipp also had one at about the same time. Life imitating art, like Jack Woolley getting Alzheimer's as Arnold Peters took the same sad journey, and continued portraying him with such poignancy until his own condition made it impossible. Colin was replaced by the distinguished Shakespearean actor David Troughton, who did sound very different. When Tom Graham was then replaced as his son Tom Archer, listeners complained that the new actor sounded nothing like 'Tony's son', which was odd because he actually is – William Troughton.

These cast changes are nothing new. Dan Archer was played by four different actors, as was John Tregorran. Until Annette Badland made the part her gloriously nasty own, Hazel Woolley tended to be played by whoever was available from the radio rep on the day. Nigel Pargetter was played by Graham Seed, then Nigel Carrington, then Graham again. When Sam Barriscale decided to leave the programme, he found out pretty soon that there was no coming back when his character, John Archer, was crushed beneath a Ferguson tractor – Colin Skipp's finest acting moment, but a closed door for Sam. I recently took a slightly surreal photograph of Ysanne Churchman and Paddy Greene – the long-dead Grace Archer with Phil's second wife, Jill.

In the past producers would cast radio actors with their eyes closed – after all, it was only the voice that was important. In these days of social media and the occasional big press story, it's helpful that Timothy Watson looks suitably handsome and dangerous as Rob, and Louiza Patikas as beautiful and vulnerable as the emotionally damaged Helen. Of course, from the actors' perspective we all look exactly the same as our radio characters, but in every case five million people would disagree.

Henry Noel Bentinck

In 1997, my father died. The cancer slowly wore him down. He had a morphine drip that would take him off to his 'other world' as he described it. One of the last things he said as he woke from a reverie was, 'You know, they used to walk more slowly in the nineteenth century.' I'm so happy his final thoughts were about gentle things like that. He died too young and I miss him still.

There wasn't much to inherit, just the proceeds of the house in Devon, split three ways with my sisters. After tax, there was just enough to buy a cottage somewhere. For years we'd been loading up the car and taking the family down to Devon for Christmas and summer holidays, and we wanted to buy somewhere near there to continue the tradition. Then it occurred to us that Devon would only have sad memories, and it was a five-hour drive, so why not look nearer to London?

When my mother had died in 1967, I used to get farmed out to stay with friends in Norfolk, and those chums, and my best man Jamie Borthwick, were still there. We started looking for somewhere in north Norfolk, and very soon we found the perfect place. We brought the boys up to see what they thought, and Will said, 'You must be mad!' It was a cold, unloved holiday cottage with lino, poky rooms, a minute kitchen, and it didn't do itself any favours by having a spectacularly ugly name – 'Preshute'. We ceremoniously burned the name and got to work. One thing Judy and I have always been good at is seeing potential in houses, and we knew what could be done.

In a quiet village by a large duck pond, the honking geese and quacky mallards kept us awake at first, but soon became a kind of lullaby to a rural idyll in what is now a lovely home. I knocked two rooms into one, built a new kitchen and enlarged it, and we stuck a conservatory on the back. I built a gazebo in the garden that looked odd for a bit but is now almost entirely grown over, and is where I sometimes write. Whether writing words or music, some places are like a muse; the ideas float in through the windows and the blank sheet of computer screen fills up as though the ideas were someone else's.

Norfolk locals have an unwarranted reputation for being rude to 'foreigners' – meaning people from London. I've never found that myself. They just have a perfectly justifiable dislike of people who are up themselves. Anyway, not only was my pa brought up in Heacham on the north Norfolk coast, but lots of things in King's Lynn, including roads, pubs and farms, are called 'Bentinck' because, without the efforts of one of my Dutch ancestors who knew a thing or two about drainage, large parts of East Anglia would still be under water. Consequently, it's one of the few places in the world where they spell my name right.

I lost one source of inspiration but gained another. My father's portrait looks down at me as I sit and write or play the guitar or piano, and his smile is an encouragement to be brave and original, like he was.

Armando Iannucci

Improvisation. The very word fills some actors with dread; to others it is what they thrive on. It's about quick thinking, having an imagination and going with the flow. If someone says, 'I love your hat,' the answer is not, 'I'm not wearing a hat,' but 'Thank you, it was my father's.' 'Deer-stalker?' 'No, pig-stalker, he used to stalk pigs. He got three years for porcine harassment.' Or some such. Rule number one is 'don't block' – always accept a situation that's being presented.

I was quite good at it at drama school but when I attended a workshop at the Donmar Warehouse for a thing called *Theatre Sports*, it got a lot harder because you had to be funny. This is stand-up comedy territory – one of the few things I've never tried because you have to know your limits. If you listen to Paul Merton on *Just a Minute*, riffing for a full sixty seconds on washing lines, you have to take your hat off and wonder at an imagination that can think that fast. You can improve with practice, and I have done, but when the *Theatre Sports* people asked me to be in their first performance, I was well outside my comfort zone.

In the first sketch, audience members were asked to pose us into a frozen tableau. I was positioned with clenched fists held up either side of my neck. I started with 'Javelin thrower's off target again,' and got a big laugh, and I have a memory that an improvised opera about a barber wasn't bad – 'I'm all alone, with my comb!' Although I got away with it, I knew it wasn't a strength, it takes practice. I've got that practice over the years and these days I'm pretty good, but watching the likes of *QI* and listening to radio panel shows, I know that there's a way that certain people's brains are wired to be on hand with the witty line all the time. I can be amusing, quick-witted and can always hold my own, but a laugh is not absolutely guaranteed. Merton once said that sometimes he puts his foot on the accelerator and there's nothing there. I know that feeling too.

So, when I went to meet Armando Iannucci for his series, *The Armando Iannucci Shows*, I didn't think I'd get the part as I probably wasn't funny enough. As it turned out, though, the brief was to be real in a funny situation, and I was asked to join a wonderful cast of talented oddballs, all of whom were as astonished as I was that they'd been picked, but who had in common an ease with being inventive in front of a camera, and being real.

The Armando Iannucci Shows were a series of absurd sketches that took the audience to the edge of their taste and comfort limits. Although scripted, we were encouraged to 'loosen it up' by Armando, which stopped us being script-bound and allowed for invention. On the day of filming, where I would be a Catholic priest whose congregation falls in love with him, Armando asked if I played guitar. I said yes. He said would you play a song from the pulpit? Okay, what song? Well, nothing that's copyrighted or we'll have to pay. Okay, shall I sing one of mine? Sure. Which is how 'Quangos in the Shelter', a song about how civil servants will be the only ones to survive a nuclear holocaust, came to have its one and only public performance.

That sketch has since become a bit of a classic. The congregation persuade the priest to take them back to the rectory for coffee and they all end up in bed together. Poking my head round the bedroom door in the morning to find a queue for the bathroom snaking down the stairs was extremely bizarre. The priest goes into a toy shop and comes out with twenty-five teddy bears. Kicking leaves, all holding hands, they romp through a park, full of the joys of new-found love, before going out to dinner with the parents, all fifty of them! Sitting in the restaurant with seventy-five cast and extras, I asked the producer, Adam Tandy, how they got the BBC to cough up for such an expensive production. His answer was revealing – 'Nobody said no.'

Armando is such an original talent, so off the wall while representing the new wave of alternative comedy, that the uncomprehending bosses at the BBC gave him an office and free rein to do whatever he wanted. Some of it wasn't funny in the laugh-out-loud sense, but all of it was wildly imaginative, absurd and totally original. I was an inmate in the 'Home for Men aged between 42 and 55' in which we were told that our life was basically over bar the certainty of incontinence and dancing to Abba tribute bands – 'You will never be astronauts.' And I was the Yorkshire mayor introducing a 'Knife Attack Reunion' party where attackers and heavily scarred middle-class victims chatted sociably about the violent events that had brought them together.

I thought that would be the end of working with Armando, but years later he asked me back to star in the opening fifteen minutes of *The Thick of It*.

Hailed as one of the best TV comedy series ever, *The Thick of It* showed the inner workings of government, allowing us to view the august corridors of power as teeming with power-hungry, foul-mouthed cynics. The political advisor was Martin Sixsmith, and when I once asked him how much of it was accurate, he replied, 'Oh, it's actually much worse.' The character of Malcolm Tucker, played with scary Glaswegian venom by Peter Capaldi, was based closely on Alastair Campbell. While Peter is the most charming and generous of actors, being sacked by Tucker from my post as Minister of Social Affairs was a terrifying experience.

Armando had a unique way of working. The cast met for the first time at the BBC rehearsal rooms in Acton, were presented with a script and did a read-through of the episode. Then Armando asked us to put the scripts down, move over to the other side of the room and go through what we remembered of the essence of the scene. The scriptwriter, Jesse Armstrong, sat in, and he and Armando took notes on our improvisation. We then went home. A while later, a new script arrived, which was a mixture of the original script and our improvised gems.

On the day, in order to get the fly-on-the-wall, faux-documentary feeling, the rooms had no film lighting, we did no rehearsal and didn't even block out our movements, and there were two hand-held cameras that just followed us around. Having filmed a scene a few times until Armando was happy with it, he then sprinkled the whole thing with his special stardust.

'Okay, so let's loosen it up a little,' he said as he handed me a sheet of A4. 'Here's some lines you might like to throw in, and I've given Peter some of his own, so it'll be a little different.'

And this is why the whole series was so unique: the actors really are reacting to something they have heard for the very first time. I have to say I did feel a bit awkward about saying, 'stuffing a cat up my arse and having a wank', but it was worth it for the flicker of a smile on Peter's face, particularly as he had just given me what one commentator describes as 'the first manifestation of the Malcolm Tucker Death Stare'.

In a later summer-special episode, 'Spinners and Losers', I'm in the back of a black cab driving round and round Parliament Square with another scary Glaswegian character, Jamie McDonald, played by Paul Higgins. The scene has developed a reputation, with its own internet meme. So much so that once, when I was performing my Earl of Portland duties on board HMS *Portland*, a Chief Petty Officer came up, introduced himself and said he had a message from the crew.

'Oh really,' I said, intrigued, 'what's that?'

'The message, my lord, is, "Are you a horse?"'

Working with Armando proved Rudi Shelly's adage at Bristol that 'acting is the art of reacting'. When Paul threw in a line about my horsey wife, which was a last-minute 'loosening' line from Armando, my reaction to hearing my wife insulted included a flash of anger in my eyes which is almost unactable. I was so shocked that all I could come up with was, 'Okay, leaving the wife aside for a second . . .', which I felt at the time wasn't witty or clever, but in fact was completely perfect for the character. That's Armando's genius, getting genuine reactions from his cast, along with writing biting political satire couched in glorious filth.

Being David Archer: Freelance

The listener might imagine that the *Archers* cast is up in Birmingham the whole time, and that we don't do anything else. This couldn't be further from the truth. The programme is recorded over eight days per month, each episode takes two and a quarter hours and we do four episodes per day. How much we're up there depends on how many episodes we're in, and we only get paid per episode – there is no retainer fee. We are also not paid per line – we could be in every scene or only one. Ted Kelsey holds the record for 'Fewest Lines Spoken' – he got a full fee for Joe Grundy's only line of an episode – the final one – which was:

JOE   Uuuugh!

So, one month I might get eight days' work, and get paid accordingly; the next month nothing at all, and not make a penny. When people say, 'I saw you moonlighting on *EastEnders* last week', I'm not taking time off from the farm: I'm just being a jobbing actor like the rest of my profession. Tamsin Greig continues to be a stage, film and TV star while Debbie Aldridge is in Hungary. Michael Cochrane is a regular telly performer while Oliver Sterling is in Italy. Josh Archer wasn't heard during the 'Are They Moving to Northumberland' marathon because Angus Imrie was in three plays at Shakespeare's Globe. Some actors' other work takes over to the exclusion of *The Archers*. Felicity Jones stopped playing Emma because she was getting too much work and ended up with Best Actress nominations across the board for *The Theory of Everything*. Lucy Davis was Hayley but after her bravura turn in *The Office* left in 2005 to work in Hollywood. Our previous Pip, Helen Monks, went on to be utterly brilliant in *Raised by Wolves*.

Some of us do loads of voice work, including voiceovers, computer games, narration and audiobooks, and still more are theatre and TV/film regulars. In a disturbing crossover, I was the voice of the helicopter pilot that wiped out most of *Emmerdale*!

After watching J. K. Rowling's *Fantastic Beasts and Where to Find Them*, in which I pretty much open the movie as

'Witness', who describes the magic force in a Bronx accent, someone tweeted, 'David Archer doesn't look like that!' It's hard to know where to begin with that one.

It's always great when actors and celebrities 'moonlight' in the other direction and appear as guest stars in the programme, for they are often as excited about being in *The Archers* as we are about meeting them. You would have thought that Sir Bradley Wiggins, having already won the Tour de France, four (now five) Olympic gold medals and been knighted, would think nothing of standing in front of a microphone and playing himself, but, great bloke that he is, he told us he was bricking it. Guest stars that I have met include Zandra Rhodes, Chris Moyles, Colin Dexter, Anita Dobson, the Duchess of Cornwall, Judi Dench, Terry Wogan and Victoria Wood. One guest was the Duke of Westminster, who I was at school with – 'Hi Tim'; 'Oh, hello Gerald.' I turned up in jeans and T-shirt when everyone else had togged up. I fondly recall the wonderful Richard Griffiths, who made the only ever appearance of Ruth's father, toilet-roll manufacturer Solly Pritchard.

Now we have the fun of working with new regulars Eleanor Bron and Simon Williams, but there were raised eyebrows among the cast when Bristol Old Vic School chum Alex Jennings, who had come in for an episode, was introduced as 'a proper actor' – dammit I've done *Charley's Aunt* at Watford, that's as 'proper' as it gets!

Going Deutsch

My father survived the war because, when lying wounded in a shell hole near the river Po in northern Italy, he understood the German for, 'What's in that shell hole, Günther?' 'I don't know, Hans, but shoot away,' and stood up and yelled, '*Freund!*' very loudly.

I've always loved languages and accents, so when I went to Harrow, beyond the simple attraction of doing Modern Languages, there was the thought that without Pa's smattering of Deutsch, I would never have been born. I took it up with his encouragement and it has served me well.

I've been employed a number of times to speak the language, but also to speak English with a German accent, which is harder than it seems. It's not the cliché 'Ve haff vays . . .' of *'Allo 'Allo* fame – the vowels are subtler and the rhythm is different. It really makes a difference if you can speak the language, and the point is that the speaker is trying to speak English as well as they can, so they're not putting on an accent, but trying hard to speak without one.

Going Deutsch

In 2000, I was cast to play the U-boat captain in the film *Enigma*. After the read-through, we were invited to go on a trip to Bletchley Park to see the huts where the real code-breakers had worked – it wasn't open to the public then, so, with my software programmer hat on, and always intrigued by codes and cyphers, I was fascinated to see it. The cast had already started to get into their roles so, although Jeremy Northam used to be our lodger and Kate Winslet lived opposite us in Holloway, everyone was slightly reserved with the bloke who was commanding the U-boat – they treated me as though I were a spy!

In the script my lines were written in English, and I was surprised to find that they trusted me to do the translation, which involved German naval commands and compass bearings – not something you can just busk. It took days of research to get right. We filmed it in the enormous outdoor tank at Pinewood, with the mock-up of the sub's conning tower in front of a vast green screen. The director, Michael Apted, handed me an enormous pair of completely opaque goggles with the words, 'Your agent's not going to like this.' It was a night shoot, and in the story the U-boat captain, looking through binoculars, sees a sentry on a British destroyer lighting a cigarette, at a distance of about a mile. I said, 'But Michael, these are for wearing down below to get your eyes accustomed to the dark. When we come up here, they're taken off, otherwise we can't see a thing.'

'Sorry, Tim, it's the military advisor. Have to do what he says.'

I didn't argue, mainly because it was Michael Apted, but I did think it was his movie and he was the boss, and it was quite obviously nonsense.

While we were chatting, he asked me what I'd been up to recently.

'You mean my U-boat captain is David Archer?' he asked, horrified.

My next German part was in 2003 in *Born and Bred* as a war veteran who comes to England, dying of his wounds, to make peace with the parents of the English soldier that he had shot, and who had shot him, and who died before the medics got to them. They were holed up together in a barn and had become friends at the last. It was a sweet story and a friendly and welcoming cast of regulars made it a joy to work on. One of my scenes was with John Henshaw, who played Wilf, the railway station master. John is a Mancunian and only started acting at forty having been a binman for ten years. This is what I love about being an actor, an ex-binman and an old Harrovian working together as equals.

I hated learning German, but the next gig was worth the whole five years of hell at school – mastering the grammar, three genders, umlauts – when I found myself teaching Claudia Schiffer how to perform her German lines for a movie.

'Claudia's overslept. She'll be with you in a minute,' her PA apologised as I arrived at her flat in Bayswater. She appeared a few minutes later, hair tousled, in pyjamas and robe, and curled up on the sofa for her 'lesson'. She was intelligent, funny, modest and quite jaw-droppingly beautiful. The part she was playing was in a film called *666: In Bed with the Devil*, and she had a cameo role when Mephisto turns first into Boris Becker, then into Claudia Schiffer. She has to whisper sweet nothings into Faust's ear, then kiss him passionately. So, I'm with a supermodel in her jimjams, she's looking at me adoringly and whispering '*Ich liebe dich, ich liebe dich so* . . . and then we go mwah mwah mwah . . .' and I'm trying to resist the temptation of saying that I'm a method actor and we really ought to do the kissing thing properly, and all the time thinking, *IT WAS ALL WORTH IT, EVERY BLOODY MINUTE!*

* * *

Going Deutsch

The sixth of June 2004 was the sixtieth anniversary of D-Day and a drama/documentary was made about it. At the audition for *D-Day 6.6.1944*, I read in English with a German accent. They then asked if I could speak German. I said yes. They passed me a photograph of a 1940s poster written in German *Schrift*, which is the old-fashioned, really difficult to read stuff. At school, half the books we'd studied had been written in *Schrift* and I'd always thought it was completely pointless – now it was getting me a part playing a Nazi general.

I was Rommel's second-in-command, Generalleutnant Hans Speidel. Rommel was played by another Englishman, Albert Welling. We met on the Eurostar and have remained close friends ever since. It was filmed at Château de la Roche-Guyon, the very same castle north of Paris that housed the real German High Command during the invasion, and on the walls were photos of our characters and of how the castle had looked at the time. One morning, I came out of costume in full Wehrmacht rig and frightened the life out of an elderly resident, who thought the Boche had returned. When I assured him in French that, 'non, non, n'ayez pas peur, je suis Anglais!' he was even more confused. 'Anglais? Mais non, c'est pas possible – les Anglais ont gagné!'

The other actors playing Germans were all real Deutschers and were mighty fed up that the two leads were being played by Englishmen, but having lost the war they felt they really couldn't complain too much and resorted to teasing and banter. I threatened to have anyone who complained shot at dawn, thus repeating the gag that the real German officers had played on my father.

I'd rung my cousin, Wilhelm von Ilsemann in Hamburg, to ask his advice on pronunciation, and when I asked if he'd ever heard of Speidel, he answered, 'Heard of him? I knew him!' – which was odd.

Albert's mother was German and between us we made a pretty good fist of it, and to an English ear it sounds fine. We were re-voiced for the German broadcast, though, because we're quite obviously English. It would have been like watching a German film in which Churchill says, 'Ve vill fight zem on ze bitches . . .'

The great spin-off to this job was that during the shoot, Albert and I came up with the idea for a book.

In the sixties there were two very popular books called *N'Heures Souris Rhames* and *Mots d'Heurres Gousses Rhames*, which, when read out loud, sound like *Nursery Rhymes* and *Mother Goose Rhymes*. They contained spoof French poetry which followed this conceit. 'Un petit d'un petit' was Humpty Dumpty. Albert had an idea to update this idea with modern pop and folk songs. I was amazed because I'd had a similar idea, called *Crises, Masques, Rôles* – Christmas Carols. We had just the best time inventing new poems after dinner in the hotel. We asked the friendly French waiter to audition them for us.

'But zis is nonsense!'

'Yes we know, but please read it out and see if these Brits understand.'

'Okay . . . *Et joue deux. Dans mais quitte bas de. Thé que ça de sang, animé quitte bête heure. Rime même beurre, toilette heur y ne tu Euro arte. Seine y ou Cannes ce tarte, tout mais quitte bête heure.*'

The crew were falling about because what they'd heard was *'Hey Jude, don't make it bad . . .'* etc. We knew then it was going to work. Over the next couple of years we wrote a lot of poems, because you can actually use this technique to write anything you want in English, using French words. When you translate them they are of course complete nonsense, but are not unlike the Dada poetry of the early 1900s. So we invented a 'lost' Dada poet called Paul

Déaveroin (pull the other one) and an Icelandic professor of Phonetics called Isskott Belsohn (it's got bells on) and called it *Avant Garde à Clue* – published it on Kindle and then went round touting it to literary agents and publishers. The idea was to make it like a real academic work and fool the experts, but the problems with copyright were insurmountable. 'Are you writing Beatles lyrics?' asked the lawyers. 'No, they are French words, but they sound like Beatles lyrics.' They couldn't give us the go-ahead because there was no precedent. So it sat idle for four years until the copyright law changed in 2015 allowing quotes of copyright lyrics if they are 'Caricature, Parody, or Pastiche' – which they are! So we're having another try - meanwhile you can read it on Kindle, or to put it another way, *Y où quand ris dit-ons qui ne d'Arles!*

Being David Archer: Editors

The recent cast changes in *The Archers* were all the doing of the man who took over as editor in 2013, Sean O'Connor. Because he had once edited *EastEnders*, he was accused by fans of bringing the ethics of Walford to the village – before he had even started the job. And now that he has gone back there, you can of course hear the cows mooing in Albert Square and everyone's comparing the size of their melons – although the latter is probably par for the course. The 'EastEnderisation' of Ambridge is nothing new; when John Yorke took over briefly in 2012, having once been the executive producer of *EastEnders* (besides being the Controller of all drama series – *Holby*, *Casualty*, etc.), knickers were manically twisted that he would bring Walford to Ambridge. No doubt because the latest boss,

189

Huw Kennair-Jones, was also once tainted by 'Enderness, the same mud will be slung at him.

Along with the cast changes, Sean's arrival brought a new perspective. His stated intention was to re-establish the values that had been the genesis of the programme – community, family and the land, more Thomas Hardy than Albert Square. While these had all been there to a greater or lesser extent under previous editors, he wanted to re-emphasise the core qualities. He gave more focus to Jill and the Brookfield Archers, looked at the long-term effects of soil erosion due to intensive farming with the flood story, the threat to the community with the long tale of the Route B bypass, and gave David and Ruth a tortuous choice between self-interest and land custodianship in the 'Moving North' story.

Hearing his father's voice during his near nervous breakdown brought home to David the responsibility he bore to carry on what previous generations of Archers had created through hard work and sacrifice. When we recorded that scene, so subtly written by Joanna Toye, I was alone in the studio with a pair of headphones and Norman's voice in my ears. It wasn't hard to get emotional, for I can hear my own father's voice giving words of advice in times of crisis. It was a blurring of fiction and reality, and an actor should always use their genuine emotion, experience and thoughts to create a believable performance. It's not pretending.

Every new editor comes with their ideas about the direction of the show, and consciously or not will always bring subtle, and sometimes noticeable, changes. The really challenging brief is to attract a new generation of listeners without losing the old one, a difficult and very fine line. When William Smethurst left in 1986 he was replaced by our first female editor, Liz Rigbey. Among other adjustments to the cast, it was she who decided that Sophie wasn't farmer's wife material, and brought in the Geordie Ruth, after successive Scottish characters, named variously Anne, Heather or Thistle (to suggest spikiness) were rejected.

Most of my *Archers* career, however, has been under the guiding hand of the longest-running editor, Vanessa Whitburn, who despite 'previous' on *Brookside*, for twenty-two years steered the ship through the hazardous waters of social and political change with enormous skill and professionalism. She modernised Ambridge in a way that often attracted traditionalist ire, but without which the show would slowly have started to lose any contemporary reality. Her performances on *Feedback*, dealing with the brickbats thrown by the presenter Roger Bolton and irate listeners, whether you agreed with her decisions or not, were masterclasses in diplomacy, worthy of the most experienced politician. She could have been a diplomat.

She lost her temper with me once, though, with very good reason. For a good many years, the actors used to receive all the scripts for the month, no matter whether they were in them or not. This meant I had huge piles of scripts that, when the boys were young, were perfect for drawing and painting on. As they got older, we used them less and the pile got bigger and bigger. One day when I was about to chuck them all out, I had a thought that for many people these scripts were gold dust, so I put it about that for a donation of £5 to the NSPCC I would send them an old script, signed by me if required. This went very well and I was soon spending hours each week filling the stamped addressed envelopes and making decent money for the charity. The only thing I had to be careful of was that the scripts I sent out were of episodes that had already been broadcast. One day I got it wrong and sent one off that wasn't due to be broadcast for another three weeks.

This would have been bad enough but it was compounded by a sequence of incredibly bad luck. Firstly, the people I'd sent it to ran a pub, the Cock Inn at Gamlingay in Cambridgeshire. They were amateur dramatics enthusiasts as well as *Archers* fans, so they thought it would be a great idea to cast some of their regulars as the characters and do a public performance of the episode for charity. As chance would have it, there was a reporter from the local paper in the audience, who ran the story the next day. This still might not have got back to Vanessa but for the other major problem. The episode was not about the Flower and Produce show, or the panto, or any number of everyday stories of farming folk, but the top secret and *massive* story of the death of Mark Hebden in a car crash. So, far from hiding on the inside pages of the local paper, it was subsequently splashed across the front page of the *Daily Telegraph*, which I happened to be reading, in shock, when the telephone call came from a furious Ms Whitburn. Thankfully the papers didn't reveal the storyline but, knuckles duly rapped, my stupidity unfortunately put an end to that charitable fundraising exercise.

Terror

Conquering fear is one thing but living with abject, self-imposed terror is quite another. When, in 2004, I was asked to play Frank, the Michael Caine part, in *Educating Rita* at the Watermill Theatre in Newbury, I hadn't been on stage for almost a decade. It was a daunting task. I hadn't had a lead in a play since drama school, it was a two-hander, I would never be off the stage for the full two hours, and it was scheduled for a six-week run with matinees on Wednesdays and Saturdays.

The Watermill is a lovely theatre, misleadingly intimate in that you feel the audience is close but the wooden construction absorbs the sound so you have to belt it out to reach the back. My Rita was the supremely talented Claire Lams and the director was Jamie Glover, the son of my *By the Sword Divided* father, Julian. It was like being on a small university campus and we lived in a little cottage on the site, which was bucolic but ultimately boring and lonely. Claire soon mastered both the Scouse and the lines, while I, very much out of practice, struggled to get fully on top of the learning – it's like a muscle, use it or lose it.

The night before the first producer's run, when you're off the book for the first time and watched by the heads of department, I didn't manage to sleep a wink. I couldn't remember that ever happening to me before and it worried me a lot. During the producer's run, I was in a state – not only was I still not word perfect, but the lack of sleep meant I was barely at the races at all. It was pretty disastrous, I kept calling for a prompt, mistimed the gags, forgot props, generally gave them hundreds of reasons to recast or cancel the show.

That evening I Skyped my close friend, actor Tony Armatrading in LA and gave vent to my fears. I really wondered if I hadn't bitten off more than I could chew. It was the first time in my life that I'd ever thought I actually couldn't do something. Tony got really angry with me and told me I was being a complete wimp and coward and of course I could do it, standing on my head if necessary. That's what friends are for and, even if I didn't necessarily believe him, the fact that a man who is only ever quite brutally honest about everything was certain I could do it made me gird my loins and plough on. I must add that, of course, Judy was saying the same thing, but sometimes you need the cold, hard appraisal of a fellow actor, which is more professionally bolstering than that welcome but unconditional loving support.

The day when you see the stage set for the first time and move out of the rehearsal room is always hugely exciting. Frank's office was surrounded on three sides by bookshelves. The books were real, gleaned from charity shops in the area – there must have been hundreds of them. As part of the action, I had to climb the library steps to reach a book on the top shelf, so, getting used to the space, I climbed them and reached out at random for the first book that came to hand. What was the book I was now holding in my hand?

Night Must Fall by Emlyn Williams, the last play I had done. Spooky or what!

The relief at the end of the first night was like a kind of ecstasy – I'd done it, it had gone down well, there was a great reaction from the audience and thunderous applause. It was only when I was wandering back to the cottage in a beer- and adrenaline-induced cloud of smug satisfaction that it occurred to me that I now had to do it another forty times, starting tomorrow. And so the fear returned.

I must have got used to the adrenaline, and perhaps I'd started to go cold turkey, because finding myself broke from having been away from the voice circuit for two months, I needed to drum up some work fast. Charles Collingwood had made a great success of a one-man show that he'd been doing on and off for years, so I reckoned I'd give it a go in 2010. I thought I'd combine the funny or interesting things that I'd done in my life with my inner geek, so I devised a PowerPoint presentation that allowed me to combine stories, live and pre-recorded music and the odd bit of stand-up.

I needed a title, and the ever-generous Collingwood came to the rescue. I'd once told him a story about meeting the vicar who was to conduct my father's funeral. As an atheist, Pa had never met the man, but he was enough of a sucker for tradition that he'd wanted a church service at the end, probably hedging his bets. I was worried that the vicar might pronounce Pa's name wrong on the day, so as we were having tea in the house in Devon, I checked with him that he was going to be able to get 'Bentinck' out okay, as most people get it wrong.

'Oh yes, absolutely,' he assured me, 'a well-known and familiar name.'

As he was leaving, he turned in the porch, looked me in the eye and said, 'Oh, and before I go, can I just say . . .' Usually when people start off with 'Can I just say . . .' they continue with, 'I've been listening to *The Archers* since it started and I've never missed an episode?' or words to that effect. Which is fine because I'm always more than happy to talk about the programme, I'm a great believer in *noblesse oblige* which, translated into the acting profession means that whatever success you've had in the public eye is only there *because* of the public eye – acting without an audience is spectacularly pointless, so being gracious to people who like what you do is a very pleasant and rewarding part of the job. I did think that in this case the timing was a bit off, what with my father being dead and all, but I smiled and waited for him to complete the sentence. 'Can I just say,' he repeated, 'that my wife and I *love* your chocolates? Bendicks Bittermints – our annual Christmas treat!'

'That's your title!' cried Charles.

And that's why I toured a show called *Love Your Chocolates* for the next three years.

'Bendick' is not the only misspelling or mispronunciation of our name. If it were spelled 'Bentink' people would pronounce it correctly, after all it's just 'Bent' and 'Ink'. It's the 'c' that throws them, and I've long since ceased correcting people who call me Mr Bentinick, but for a time I used to collect misspelled envelopes and stick them on the downstairs loo wall. Here are some:

Monsieur Beatnick	I now always use this in France
Tim Fenting	This is good for N. Ireland, where Bentinck is associated with King Billy and the Orangemen
Mester Tom Bentyick	Russia and Poland
Mr P. Bening	Annette's ex
Tim Bentwick	I wouldn't have survived this at school

Terror

M. S. J. Bertink	A Jamaican ring to this one
Mr T. C. Bestnick	Just plain ugly
Mr Bentlack	Starting to take the piss really
Mrs Cenpink	And this was a letter to me!
Time Bentinck	Yeah, man, hippy dude parents
Tom Benstink	Yes, I chose this name when I became an actor
Signore Timoteo Benedictine	I adore this, thinking of a deed poll job
The Right Honourable, The Earl of Bent	Just so wrong in every possible way!
Mr Bentdick	Again, what parent would have allowed their child to bear this name at school?
The County Inspector	This was actually addressed to my mother – the writer had misheard Countess Bentinck!

In creating my one-man show, I wrote down everything on yellow Post-it notes and stuck them on the bedroom door, whittling down the material to a satisfactory running order. In retrospect, I should have got a director, or at least an editor, to curb my excesses and *folie de grandeur*. The first time I rehearsed it, in the cottage in Norfolk in front of an open fire, it took just over three hours. Cut, cut, cut. Did it again, two hours forty. Cut, cut, cut. Two and a half. The problem was I wasn't sticking to the script, so I was waffling away ad lib and taking for ever. The fireplace was getting bored. Cut, cut, cut and just read what you've written – better, just over two hours.

My first performance was at the Westacre Theatre in Norfolk

197

and, as the days got closer, my terror increased. I'd never known anything like it. I'd wake up and immediately be hit by a shock of almost debilitating anxiety that would last all day. I knew that such nerves came from the fear of the unknown, and that rehearsal and preparation would cure it, but no matter how many times I went through it to the fireplace, and practised the songs on the guitar until my fingers were raw, I couldn't dispel it. Looking back, I think it must have been the lack of any support system – no director, no writer, no other actors, just me. I'd created the most enormous rod for my back and the decision to do ten songs was completely barking mad.

The Day of Reckoning dawned at last and, loading the car up with props, including yoghurt, audio tape and wet towel for the lambing sound effects, an old ironing board for the gates and cattle crush, I drove with increasing trepidation to the theatre. The only things I had no control over were the microphones, the projector and the RGB cable connecting it to my computer. I started setting up. Immediately there was a disaster. The RGB cable was displaying the Green and the Blue perfectly, but there was no Red, thus rendering all the carefully chosen photos and videos un-viewable. A helpful techie leapt into his van and shot off to Fakenham to get a new one but the seeds of doubt had now taken root and were growing into triffids of uncertainty.

Then the calm and unflappable theatre director, Clive Hadfield, came to the rescue. It was still early afternoon and he suggested I run through the whole show, on my own, to an empty auditorium. The cable arrived and the pictures looked fine. He closed the doors and I started from the beginning. Two hours later I knew it would be all right, I knew the songs, I had PowerPoint to prompt me, the theatre was intimate and the audience close to the stage, and one thing I'm perfectly happy with is nattering away to people, so that's what I did.

By the time I walked onto the stage at seven that evening, I was calm, happy and really looking forward to it. It went well. It was too long and I immediately set about cutting another half-hour from it, but the sense of achievement was massive. Alone in the cottage again that evening I swore I would never ever get that scared about anything again. Of course, I was wrong, and over the next three years every time I did the show I'd get the same build-up of tension and uncertainty, wondering why I'd volunteered to do it, until the end of the show when I'd feel on top of the world. What a ridiculous way to earn a living.

I was booked all over the country, in village halls, churches and theatres. I'd load the car up, 'Have Ironing Board Will Travel', and head off to a far-flung destination, sometimes for two or three consecutive nights. Generally, the more intimate venues were better and being able to see the audience meant more engagement. Sometimes, when you're downstage during a play and looking out, you can see the first few rows, all eyes on you and your own eyes on someone's groin or chair arm, anything but catching their eye. By contrast, the requirements for doing a show like mine meant that eye contact was beneficial. I found it strange that the moment I walked on stage I effectively became someone else, the nerves disappeared, I was ready to engage and the only thing I had to worry about was just droning on too long!

As with all theatrical tours, I had my good nights and my bad. Towards the end of the run, I had three nights in a row in Norfolk. The first two went really well, and then . . . well, I realised afterwards that up until then I'd been lucky. I had a huge advantage in that most of the people who'd come to see me were *Archers* fans who loved the programme, if not necessarily David, and I started on a wave of goodwill. On a cold evening in a desolate village hall in the fens my luck finally ran out.

It started the moment I arrived.

'Why are you here so early? You're not on till seven.'

'Oh, I just like to make sure everything's working, I've had problems in the past.'

'Are you suggesting we don't know what we're doing?'

'No, no, just need to check my own equipment.'

'Well, I have to tell you I don't listen to *The Archers* and nor does anyone else in the village.' Ah, *that* sort of village. A bit like Ambridge where, surprisingly, no one listens to *The Archers*!

'Right, well never mind, there's plenty of other stuff.'

'When was your publicity photo taken?'

'Oh, a couple of years ago, I think,'

'It's longer than that, you're much older.'

Right. Didn't realise there was an age limit.

His stage introduction continued the theme.

'You probably won't recognise him from the photo on the flyer, it must have been taken about ten years ago, but anyway please welcome Timothy Bent... Bentin . . . Benny . . . well, here he is.'

Ironic really considering that the very title of the show was about how no one could pronounce my name.

When the audience consists of about twenty farmers, their wives, their children and their dogs – all with their arms folded and that look of 'Come on then, entertain me', and the first few *Archers*-related gags are greeted with stony silence, you know it's going to be a long night.

At the interval I popped outside for a breath of fresh air – a Joe Grundy clone was there having a fag.

'Are you enjoying it?' I asked.

'Not really.'

The show started by explaining the title with the story of the vicar and 'love your chocolates', and it ended with David Frost saying the same thing when I was on *Through the Keyhole*. I'd got my son Will to do a clever bit of Photoshopping on the 'Bendicks' logo, so I was able to top and tail the whole thing with the line, 'Well, if you can't beat 'em, join 'em! Introducing *Bentinck's* Chocolate Mint Crisp!'

Desultory round of applause and everyone got stuck into the beer, which was obviously the only reason they were there. No questions, no queues for signed scripts, nothing.

As I was clearing away and loading the kit back into the car, Joe Grundy came up to me. *Ah*, I thought, *I've won him round!*

'Scuse me.'

'Yes, hello!'

'So, where is your chocolate factory then?'

All that effort.

Being David Archer: Fame

I do get recognised every now and then. 'Video Killed the Radio Star', of course, but occasionally the papers do a feature on *The Archers* and our photos crop up. Even though most people don't know my name, they have a nagging suspicion that they might know me from somewhere, and I've appeared on screen in their living rooms enough times that the face is vaguely recognisable.

I went to a Michael Jackson concert at Wembley once with my old chum Rena. Although wheelchair-bound, she still drives like a racing driver and I was pleased to have got there in one piece. We couldn't find the disabled entrance that had a lift so I ended up carrying her on my back up about ten flights of stairs. As we appeared in the Royal Box (Rena knew the tour manager), the whole of Wembley rose as one with a mighty cheer. For a brief moment I thought there was an extraordinary crossover between Michael Jackson fans and *Archers* addicts, until I looked to my left and saw that Charles and Diana had appeared at the other entrance at exactly the same time.

I sometimes find myself baffled at a party when a complete stranger admonishes me for the way I treat my son, until I realise they're talking about my *Archers* son, Josh.

'You'll drive him away, Tim, if you keep behaving like that.'

It's the 'Tim' bit that's the most confusing.

If I ever state an opinion on Twitter, or even a wry observation, some wag will ask me why I'm not milking. This blurring of reality and fiction goes with the territory and I completely accept it now. After all, it's only being teased and nothing like the real abuse and sometimes violence actors can endure if they play rapists or paedophiles. Now that's scary.

When I was younger and on TV a lot, particularly with my *By the Sword Divided* long hair and earring, I was recognised much more. At first, I was flattered and quite enjoyed the attention. After a while, though, I began to find it a bit intrusive, and realised that anonymity was something to be cherished and that privacy is a privilege. Radio celebrity is more enjoyable, and can sometimes surprise the hell out of people. Doing 'celebrity' quiz shows are enormous fun and I wouldn't have got all the wonderful travel articles without my *Archers* association.

But these are just perks. The real joy is when someone thanks me for all the pleasure I've given them over the years, reveals that *The Archers* has helped them through their life or taught them something they didn't know, says that by adding my name to the fundraising gig will earn more money for a charity, or is over the moon because I have recorded a birthday greeting or donated a signed script. Fame comes with a price, and nowadays it's a price that I'm all too happy to pay.

Shorts

I love doing short films, mainly because I get the leading role and often play characters very different to myself. When you start off in this business, you're required to be listed in *Spotlight*, a directory of every professional actor in the UK, containing photograph and contact details. It's divided into two categories, Leading and Character Actors. It's a misleading distinction really, but, aiming high when I left drama school, I chose Leading. In retrospect, this seems to imply that you can only play types like yourself, whereas I've always felt far more comfortable playing characters very different to me. I wonder if Dan Day-Lewis put himself in Character; after all, it is his astonishing ability to utterly transform himself that has resulted in three Oscars.

I never believed that I would ever star in a Western. My incessant childhood practice with a six-gun and a reverence for cowboy programmes meant that, if the time ever came, I would be ready, but the idea of getting the call was a distant dream. So, when I met Séan Brannigan for the title role in *The Pride of Wade Ellison* – his half-hour graduation movie for the National Film and Television

School – I couldn't believe that my dream might come true. It's often said that acting is just 'playing Cowboys and Indians' but Ambridge is, let's face it, very far from Wyoming.

To prepare for the role, my great buddy Kevin Howarth, a master of the broody close-up, brought round four DVDs, *Shane*, *Unforgiven*, *A Fistful of Dollars* and *The Gunfighter*, to give me a proper reminder of the genre. It's an oft-told story – retired gunslinger comes out of pig-rearing retirement for one last (fatal) shoot-out. I practised my Clint voice, real deep and real slow, sashayed around the house with bandy legs for a week, spent an afternoon at a riding stables to get my inner thigh muscles working again, and remembered just how quick I was with a six-gun. We filmed in Black Park, near Pinewood, and at a genuine Western town called Laredo in Kent. Built by enthusiasts, they gather there at weekends for hoe-downs, shoot-outs and sing-songs with the honky-tonk piano. When I asked a fully kitted-up gunslinger if they did the accent too, his pure London reply was, 'Oh no, mate, we don't pretend!'

It was a good script, and the film looked fantastic; me and ma boy (Elliot James Langridge) escaping our burning cabin at night, wading into a lake to bathe the wounds from a horse-whipping, flying out of the livery stable on my prancing grey, challenging the villain to a duel, galloping through the woods and facing four ornery-looking villains for the final bloodbath. I was wired up with six explosive squibs under my shirt for the Tarantino-style climax where I get blown to bits. The squibs were the pride of the film school special-effects department but due to budget constraints we only had two goes at this, and I had to react to the gunshots at the right moment and in the right place – it was no use if my right shoulder exploded while I doubled up from a groin shot. So I was to be seen wandering around the set twitching peculiarly from imagined gunshots until I got the sequence right. I die saving my boy, and the final shot is him riding away from my freshly dug grave, on my horse, wearing my hat. I got buried in *Sharpe's Rifles* in the Crimea too. It's an odd thing, looking at your own grave.

Equally unlikely is me being cast as a bank robber, but in *Locked Up* (winner of Best Foreign Short, Lanzarote Film Festival) that's precisely who I was. Directed by the wonderfully monikered Bugsy Riverbank Steel, we rehearsed and improvised it for many evenings before the two-day shoot, which Bugsy then edited down to a crisp and funny six minutes. A bank-robbing dad and his two sons lock themselves inside their getaway car because number one son dropped the keys when he went to buy himself a haloumi wrap.

I do love playing villains; in another short, *The Club*, I get to give my London hard man, but I have a recurring dream that I'm in a gangster film with Ray Winstone, both of us East End villains, when he suddenly says, 'You're a what, a fucking Earl? Fuck off!' and smacks me in the face. Jung would say this is fear of being found out generally but I don't care, I'd take the beating, just for the enormous satisfaction of being allowed to call Ray a dozy twat!

Although my father's side of the family is 100 per cent toff, my mother's roots were pure Sheffield steel. My mum was sent to a school in the south so she lost her northern vowels, but my two aunts, Pinkie and Bell-Bell, were like female versions of Alan Bennett. Hearing a strong Yorkshire accent always reminds me of family. In *The Turn*, a short directed by Christian Krohn, I was Stanley Kovack, drunken northern has-been stand-up being usurped by a younger, funnier generation, so I just channelled my Yorkshire blood. None of the comedy routines were scripted, so I found myself onstage in a seedy club, having to make up a sequence of lame, tired, sexist jokes that only get boos and heckles from the restless, unsympathetic audience. I loved it!

My co-star was James Phelps, one of the tall, long-haired Weasley twins from the Harry Potter films. A lovely lad, he told me an interesting fact about his fellow child actors on the early Potter films. He said the atmosphere on set was like being at school: in the same way that swots get teased in class for trying too hard, anyone who did too much 'acting' was sent up. Hence, the 'just say the lines' acting technique that became almost a trademark style of the movies.

Doing improvisation with other actors is one thing, but doing it when the other people are real, and you're effectively fooling them, is quite another. I've done role-play a couple of times, spending entire days convincing groups of bright law students that I was in fact a Ukrainian oligarch, trying to wrest billions of dollars from my business rival. It's an entirely different exercise, much more like being a spy or a criminal – hugely exciting. The first time I found myself doing it, though, was purely by chance: 'My name's Don, I'm fifty-four years old, I'm single, and I'm into plastic.'

So began a rather charming student film directed by Wyndham Richardson. Don was a Dorset-accented plastic toy manufacturer with ideas above his station, but at the end of the film he goes out of business and we find him selling his old stock from the layby of a dual carriageway. The camera was using a long lens from the other side of the road, so with a big sign announcing, 'FREE TOYS!' cars kept stopping to see what was on offer, and I strung them along, figuring the director could use this guerrilla footage in the film, which indeed he did.

The quality of these short films varies, but professional productions, like *Locked Up* and *The Club*, have very high production standards and often do very well on the film festival circuit. They're fun too – spending a night in a pub with Nicholas Hoult and Imogen Poots in *Rule Number Three* or being a nasty Glaswegian police interrogator in *Esau Jacobs*. Also, I'm now at an age where I can be useful to young film-makers if they want advice. If not, I'm perfectly happy to follow my sister's advice and just keep my ruddy mouth shut.

Being David Archer: On stage

We once did an *Archers* 'event' at a holiday camp on the south coast. It was fun, we did 'turns' on stage like a talent competition, and performed a couple of scenes from the programme. We all stayed the night so we were able to meet the fans properly and, at dinner that evening, we were encouraged to go around all the tables and chat to people. One woman was quite vociferous in her insistence that I looked nothing like David and that I had completely spoiled her entire listening experience. I told her that I'd heard this before and that I was sure it was just a temporary blip. 'Don't worry,' I said cheerily, 'I'm sure that in a couple of weeks your David will come back to you.' To my horror, she instantly burst into floods of tears. It turned out that her husband's name was David, and that he had died two weeks before. Oh dear.

Events such as the holiday-camp convention, as well as theatre and cruise-ship shows, were organised by 'Archers Addicts', a fan club set up by Hedli Niklaus (Kathy Perks), Terry Molloy (Mike Tucker), Trevor Harrison (Eddie Grundy) and Arnold Peters (Jack Woolley). The club ran from 1990 to 2013 and provided its 10,000 members with books, annuals, diaries, calendars and loads of other merchandise along with a quarterly newsletter, which I used to narrate for the RNIB. When I started, I used to read it first, then record it and edit it properly in Pro Tools, cutting out fluffs and coughs and any outside noise, much like narrating an audiobook. One day though, when a goose honked particularly loudly from the pond outside the cottage, I commented on it, saying it sounded like I was in Ambridge. From then on, I used to sight-read it as though I were simply sitting next to a blind friend, and laugh and make appropriate comments. Much more fun and it was well received.

It's such a shame the company had to close: the membership started to dwindle as the internet provided more and more of what listeners wanted. Celebrity members included George Michael, Norma Major, Judi Dench, Jane Asher and Maggie Smith, and even Jeremy Paxman admitted to listening.

We used to have stalls at agricultural shows, and sometimes recorded scenes there too. The first Addicts' convention was held at Malvern, opened by huge fan and *EastEnder* Wendy Richard. I sang my song, 'Ambridge Time', and the cast threw themselves into the fun of the show – it was a huge success. At the end, one poor woman couldn't find her car. The stewards and police were assembled to help but just as all seemed lost, she suddenly realised she hadn't brought the car, her husband had driven her there. She'd been so carried away by the event she'd gone a bit doolally.

To celebrate the fiftieth anniversary, Archers Addicts organised an enormous day-long event at the National Indoor Arena in Birmingham. There were all kinds of stalls manned by the cast, cookery, skittles, quizzes, the Milk Marketing Board, sound-effects demonstrations, welly-wanging . . . It was like a small village – called Ambridge! Some 3,000 people attended, coming from all over the world. Hedli remembers a bemused sheikh who had been dragged along by his two burka-dressed and *Archers*-mad wives. One person arrived in a hospital bed, complete with drip and attendant nurses. I was amazed by the long queues for autographs and the contented hum of wonder from this vast throng. In the evening, we did a show on stage, MC'd by the late Nick Clarke, such a lovely man, taken by cancer far too young. When Norman and Paddy came on stage, 3,000 people stood and cheered. Just wonderful.

Some people, though, hate seeing us in the flesh. Like the poor widow at the holiday-camp event, for many it ruins the illusion and they even get cross if they see pictures of us in the newspaper. *The Ambridge Pageant* (1991) and *Murder at Ambridge Hall* (1993) were the only full-blown realisations of an *Archers* story on stage – I wasn't involved but when I went to see them, they both fitted perfectly into my imagination because, of course, to me all the actors look like their characters. However, for some of the audience it was a slightly surreal experience – right voice, wrong body. It's such a shame we don't get to do these appearances any more, but apparently the Beeb can't afford it. I know it's a radio show, but the joy on people's faces when they meet their favourite characters, even if they don't look like them, is palpable, and bringing a bit of joy into the world can never be a bad thing, can it?

The Royal Bodyguard
and *Twenty Twelve*

So there I was in 2011, making a decent living out of being a jobbing actor, but still with the permanent sense of insecurity that afflicts most people in the profession. I was much luckier than most having *The Archers* as a constant, but even that was, and still is, subject to the vagaries of the storyline, and if I'm not in it, I'm not being paid. I'd pretty much resigned myself to the idea that the heady days of fame that I'd enjoyed in my youth were over, and that I should be content to muddle along with *The Archers*, voiceovers, computer games voices, travel writing, ADR, dubbing and the occasional lead in short films, or supporting roles in TV and films.

Then I got two auditions in one day. *The Royal Bodyguard* was a six-part comedy series featuring 'Sir David Jason's return to comedy after ten years!' as the publicity had it. It was a leading role, starring in all six episodes. Excited, I learned the lines for the audition and headed up to Hat Trick Productions in Camden to meet the directors Mark Bussell and Justin Sbresni, fresh from the success of *The Worst Week of My Life*. The casting director was Sarah Crowe, who had got me *The Armando Iannucci Shows* and *The Thick of It*, so I was quite hopeful. The audition went okay, but I was in and out like a shot, which usually means I am totally wrong for the part and that I'd ironed my shirt and polished my shoes for nothing.

I went straight from there to the BBC to meet John Morton and casting director Rachel Freck for a really nice part in the second series of *Twenty Twelve*, the comedy about the forthcoming Olympics with Hugh Bonneville. I really wanted the part. This was much more difficult to learn, as the lines are very bitty, full of 'yes, no, yes . . .' and ums and ahs that are all completely scripted and rigidly stuck to by writer/director Morton.

I got them both! A lead in a series with David Jason, name above the title, good money, options on two more series with a 20 per cent increase each time and worldwide DVD sales. I was going to be the next 'Trigger'! Fame beckoned again, and with it the security of becoming a bit of a household name, part of the 'rep' of British actors that work regularly in TV. No more scrabbling about for work, I could put my feet up, secure in the knowledge that all the persistence and work had paid off. Debts could be settled, new car, holiday, the lot. If only I'd known . . .

I started to have my doubts when I received the scripts. I thought that it probably wasn't my kind of thing, but given Jason's popularity, it was bound to be a success. The idea behind it was that it would be a return to a more old-fashioned, safe, non-edgy comedy for the whole family. It relied on a lot of slapstick and silliness. I imagined Norman Wisdom in the role of Guy Hubble, an ageing and hopeless retired Army officer, now in charge of Her Majesty's car park, who, having saved the Queen's life when her carriage horses bolted from the noise of a crisp packet that he had popped, is promoted to the role of royal bodyguard. Wisdom might have saved it, Jason, despite the genius of the falling-through-the-bar gag on *Only Fools...*, sadly couldn't. I played Sir Edward Hastings, a Whitehall mandarin, alongside the wonderful Geoffrey Whitehead as my Hubble-hating colleague, Colonel Dennis Whittington, and Tim Downie as the hapless fall guy, Yates.

I'd heard that David Jason could be tricky to work with but he was utterly delightful on set, generous and complimentary to all.

Our Whitehall office scenes were filmed at Gaddesden Place, coincidentally just down the road from where I was brought up, and in the stables of which I had learned to ride as a child. It was a happy shoot, all of us admiring of seventy-three-year-old David's willingness to throw himself into stunts that actors half his age would have thought twice about, but it felt slow. Good comedy has to take its audience by surprise, and I kept getting the feeling that they would be ahead of us.

This was confirmed at the cast and crew showing of the first two episodes where the laughter was either forced or totally lacking. Sir David did not attend, citing a cold, but it wasn't a good sign. Then there was the scheduling. It might have worked on children's TV, and indeed it went down well with the younger audience, but inexplicably the first episode went out at 9 p.m. on Boxing Day – probably the most pissed, jaded and cynical audience you get all year. I, along with eight million others, settled down with my family to watch it, and within ten minutes the Twitter feed gave depressing forebodings of the disaster to come.

'About as funny as a bad case of the Trotters.'

'This has to be the worst programme on TV this Christmas.'

'The Royal Bodyguard may return next Monday but I doubt any viewers will.'

And indeed a million turned off during the show and the next episode played to half the original figures. The next three attracted a mere two million and the series was axed.

So, no fame, no security, no joining the comedy rep, only the occasional, 'Weren't you in that dreadful thing with David Jason?'

By contrast, *Twenty Twelve* was a huge success, winning awards and flattering praise all round. Proving that success is not judged by viewing figures alone, the first series aired on BBC4 to 400,000 (nonetheless a huge figure for that channel), and when the second series was broadcast on BBC2 it rose to 1.2 million. And there lies the difference between a popular and an artistic success.

Some actors hate them but I generally love read-throughs. It's the chance to meet the cast and crew and to find out the style and tone of the piece, so you're not acting in limbo. Some friends say they get terribly nervous and I've witnessed plenty of well-known names getting deeply uncomfortable, but what with *The Archers* and the amount of narrations and audiobooks I've done, I'm very used to sight-reading, so for me it's like a first performance. With *Twenty Twelve* it was different. I was a huge fan of the first series and had never worked with any of the actors before, so when we all met for the first episode of series two, I came into the room convinced that these were all actually real people, and that I'd be the only one acting and therefore stand out a mile. Thankfully my first line, with Hugh Bonneville, got a big laugh, I relaxed, and it went fine from then on.

When we came to the filming day, slotted in between *Bodyguard* location scenes, it was technically fiendish. We were sat in front of three TV screens, the idea being that in trying to organise a conference call with Sebastian Coe and the Algerian foreign minister, it all goes horribly wrong and Islam is irredeemably insulted. In these situations, you never actually see what's on a screen – it gets added in later, so all of our eyelines had to be on the correct screen at the same time, which combined with the quick-fire banter for which the show was famous, surrounded by a cast who'd been practising it for an entire series, was tricky to say the least. We did multiple takes, sometimes just recording a line on its own, so at the end of the day I had no idea if it had gone well or was a disaster. I therefore arrived at the cast and crew showing a few months later with some trepidation, to be greeted by director John Morton, whose first words to me were, 'Don't worry, you're funny.'

Phew.

Casting

My very first agent was a man called Nick Legh Hepple, who had no experience in the business but was from a PR background. His attitude was that you had to go out of your way to attract the attention of important people, and that would get you work. I took his advice, sometimes to my own detriment. When I heard about a new mini-series being cast, featuring modern-day aristocratic families – I thought I'd be perfect. I went to the boating lake at Alexandra Palace and asked if they had any broken oars. So, the next day I walked boldly into the offices of the production company with a six-foot oar, tied to which was my CV and photo, accompanied by the words, 'I just thought I'd get my oar in first.' I didn't get the part.

They say you usually succeed or fail the moment you walk through the door. My dear friend Jon Dixon had travelled down from Derby one evening and stayed with us in London for a nine o'clock casting the following day. It was a TV commercial for VW and he found himself sitting with about twelve other hopefuls just outside an office with a glass wall, so they could all see what the previous actor was

216

doing. One by one they were called in and Jon saw each of them shake the director's hand, have a little chat, then do the lines, each time two or three times. Then thank yous, smiles, another handshake, and goodbyes. When it was Jon's turn, he walked in, big smile, hand outstretched to the director who had his head down writing something. He looked up, saw Jon, said, 'No,' and put his head back down. After a sympathetic look from the casting assistant, Jon turned on his heel, exited, and went back to Derby. Cruel.

It is always best to do some research before you go up for a part. I was once told by my agent that I had a casting for a comedy series that was 'kind of like the Comic Strip' (the comedy group featuring Ade Edmondson, Rik Mayall, Dawn French, Jennifer Saunders, Alexi Sayle and others). I was up to play a 'student terrorist'. I thought this meant someone at university who was trying to blow the place up. When I got to the casting, they told me it was a school for terrorists, so totally different. Then Peter Richardson, who was directing, said the show was, 'you know, standard Comic Strip sort of stuff'.

Figuring that this must be their direct competition I offered, 'Yeah, I liked their early stuff but I think they've gone a bit off the boil recently.'

Silence and puzzled looks.

'Right . . .' said Peter.

'Um . . . sorry, but my agent never told me who you are. What's actually the name of your show?'

'We're the Comic Strip.'

I just fell about laughing, 'Oh bugger. I'm not getting this part, am I?'

Amazingly, I did, but I couldn't do it because I had an *Archers* episode that day. Damn!

Others that have got away? Boromir in *Lord of the Rings* – I had two recalls, the last one with Peter Jackson – *Downton Abbey* and *Game of Thrones*. It's not so bad when you find the actor who got the part is physically different: Roger Ashton-Griffiths, who got the part as Mace Tyrell in *GoT*, and I are poles apart.

One of my best audition moments was for the part of Major Heyward in *The Last of the Mohicans* with Daniel Day-Lewis. I remember the casting, in an office on Frith Street. The director Michael Mann greeted me with the words, 'Hey, Tim, Dan says hi but he's working out.' So my old mucker had put in a word! I hadn't seen the script so just sight-read some lines. I could feel the director staring intently at me and when I'd finished, he turned to the casting director and said, 'Honey, give Tim a script. Tim, I want you to go to a pub, have a beer and read the movie. Can you be back here in an hour?' Are bears Catholic? Minutes later I was nursing a Guinness in the Dog and Duck, reading the script. 'Oh my God I'm rescuing my betrothed from the Indians . . . oh wow I'm shooting the rapids . . . Christ I go over a waterfall . . . oh oh oh I'm being tortured, bones inserted through my breasts and hoisted over a fire on ropes . . . a mercy shot from Dan puts me out of my pain . . . bliss, a real movie part!'

Steven Waddington got it.

Being David Archer: Writers

Without the writers, there would be no *Archers*. While the overall storyline comes primarily from the editor in discussion with the writers, turning the generality of a months'-long plot line into believable dramatic scenes takes enormous talent and hard work. When faced with tales of great moment and emotion, I hear the actors rise to the occasion and give sometimes sensational performances, but they couldn't do any of that without great writing. However, it's more difficult when absolutely nothing in the slightest is happening and we have to make turnips sexy, and hardest of all is being able to weave Ministry of Agriculture (now DEFRA) advice or propaganda into believable dialogue. Here's how they *don't* do it:

RUTH   David? Where are you off to in the new four-wheel-drive tractor that will plough eight furrows instead of six, thus increasing our profit margins by 2 per cent over the course of the year?

DAVID   Oh I'm just going to spray this new systemic insecticide that provides you with control of pollen beetles in oilseed rape and mustard, aphids in Calabrese broccoli, Brussels sprouts, cabbage, cauliflower, carrots, parsnips, peas, oilseed rape and potatoes and a reduction of damage by orange wheat blossom midge in wheat. I'll be back in time for tea.

It's hard enough trying to make it sound natural even when it's done well.

Our agricultural editor and writer Graham Harvey takes the top prize for negotiating these minefields, and I'm sure the other writers curse him for introducing the plots in the first place.

There have been many scriptwriters over my time, and while impossible to mention them all, those who've been around the longest – Mary Cutler, Joanna Toye, Caroline Harrington, Simon Frith, Tim Stimpson, Paul Brodrick, Adrian Flynn and

Keri Davies have moulded and shaped the character of David more than I ever could. I've oftentimes found myself impossibly moved when reading through a script, and once texted Keri to say, 'You made me cry you bastard!' They really are the unsung heroes – I can make you angry, sad, sympathetic or shout at David in frustration, but without the right words to say, you wouldn't feel a thing.

Sometimes the script gets chopped to pieces. The read-through is timed and has to come in at around twelve and a half minutes. Any shorter and we have to stretch time, but if it's too long, great swathes of dialogue have to be cut. Unfortunately, it's usually the gags that go, as the plot is paramount, and I often feel for the writer when their carefully constructed shtick is deleted at the stroke of a pencil.

Name checks are a bit of a minefield. There's a limit to how many times I can call Ruth 'Ruth' and she can call me 'David' in a single scene, and regular listeners obviously recognise our voices immediately in any case. However, we constantly have to cater for the new listener who needs all the help they can get. Joe Grundy is enormously useful in this respect: his habit of calling us by our full names makes it abundantly clear for the rookie listener exactly who is who.

The Year of the Roth

Despite what happened to Jon Dixon and his wasted trip from Derby to London, theatre, film and TV auditions are usually a lot better than the cattle-market hell of commercial castings – you're generally treated with more respect. They've changed a bit over the years. In the early days, the first question was often, 'So what have you been up to recently?' – which was a tricky one if the truth was watching daytime TV, collecting the kids from school and trying not to kill yourself. Also, you had a fair time to prepare – the scripts would come through the post a few days before and the whole process took longer. Mostly, though, you would just turn up and sight-read and if you did okay you'd get a recall to do it 'off the book'. These days, you can get an email at 6 p.m. for a casting the next day and be expected to produce a memorised and polished performance in one take. However, 'self-tapes' are also more and more common, where you have to film yourself at home and send it in. Often, fifteen minutes after a casting you suddenly realise how you should have done it, so self-taping at least has the benefit of giving you a few more cracks of the whip.

In 2015 Judy and I were on our first Mediterranean holiday in ages. We'd rented a villa with a pool on a Greek island for two weeks and were seven days into unwinding the stress of the last three years when I got an email from my agent asking me to do a self-tape to play the writer Frederick Forsyth in a Jimmy McGovern TV play called *Reg* – the true story of Reg Keys, who had taken on Tony Blair for the seat at Sedgefield in the General Election of 2005. His son had been killed in the Iraq War and Forsyth was helping him on the campaign trail.

The audition comprised the entire part of three monologues. I had two days to do it, so I spent the first one learning the lines while sunbathing next to the pool, the second day we set up to shoot it indoors. I was tanned and swimming-toned, the light inside the villa was gentle and flattering, Judy didn't have to do any off lines, and we did each scene in one take on an iPhone. Two days later I had the part, which was a result considering the wildly expensive holiday was all paid for with a credit card and optimism, and the job exactly paid it off in one go!

I was also delighted because Reg would be played by Tim Roth, and I had just finished filming with his son. Early that year, I'd had a delightful interview with casting director Shakyra Dowling, director Joe Martin and producer Danielle Clark. I was there for the best part of an hour, chatting about the part and life in general. The film was a low-budget British movie called *Us and Them*. Written by Joe, it was a thriller about a home invasion, in which I was auditioning to play a rich banker whose house gets taken over by Jack Roth and his gang, who tie up him and his family and broadcast their torture on YouTube. Nasty stuff, but with a contemporary and poignant message about the haves and have-nots.

I was offered the part but at first I was in two minds. In the plot,

Jack's character half drowns me in my private pool and there's a lot of violence with his sidekick, played by Andy Tiernan. I looked them both up and they seemed to be seriously hard. I was worried in case they were method actors and would be just as nasty off screen as their characters were on. Still, it was a lead in a movie and things had been quiet for a bit so I accepted.

Jack, it turned out, is a total softie and we had the best time. He's a livewire and a seriously good screen actor, bouncing off the walls with energy and generous to a fault to make a scene look good, while Andy is a cuddly, loveable rogue, even when stabbing me viciously in my walk-in wardrobe. Joe is a hugely talented young director who will go far, and the whole cast, from my stoical wife, Carolyn Backhouse, and drop-dead gorgeous daughter, Sophie Colquhoun, to the very funny Danny Kendrick and Paul Westwood (it's impossible not to laugh when a man spends the entire day with 'Wanker' written on his forehead) were a delight to work with. For the first time in my life, I was the oldest, most experienced person on the set, and was often deferred to and consulted for advice. That's a real rarity, and felt good. The film went on to have great success at the SXSW Film Festival in America.

So, I was chuffed to monkeys to find myself in three nice scenes with Jack's dad Tim. The main scene for me in *Reg* was when Frederick Forsyth stands in front of a war memorial, with Reg beside him, giving an impassioned speech to a large crowd about how Tony Blair was a war criminal. When you're in front of a large crowd, and you've got a major Hollywood star next to you, and you've got a long speech written by Jimmy McGovern, and the light's fading . . . that's kind of what you join up for.

When I came to watch it I was alone in a hotel room, and I was terrified. It was so good, Anna Maxwell Martin was amazing,

Roth was quietly mesmeric, the story was tragic and compelling, and I was awaiting my first appearance. *'I'll be crap, I'll let the whole thing down, oh God, oh God . . .'* When it came to it, I was okay, thank goodness. The quality of the production, filming and writing lifted me and I rose to the occasion. This is what it's like, up one minute, petrified the next, and always only ever as good as your last job.

When the next job starred Tim Roth as well, it started to get spooky. *Rillington Place* is a three-part series about the serial murderer John Christie, an update of the 1971 movie starring Richard Attenborough – I played his doctor, Dr Odess. The last time I'd seen Tim he was a spiky-haired Brummie, but six months later, a bald, whispering Yorkshireman of intense creepiness shuffled into a cold, disused office in Glasgow.

'Are you stalking me?' he smiled.

'No, Tim, I'm your new good luck charm. Forget Tarantino, get me in all your productions from now on and I can guarantee your success.'

Being David Archer: Feedback

These days *The Archers* receives a lot of feedback on Twitter and Facebook. There used to be the BBC bulletin boards, known as 'Mustardland' because of the colour of the website. When that started, people used to write reams of often highly articulate critique, worthy of university dissertations, suggesting aspects of the story that I hadn't even thought of. Over the years, these got fewer and fewer and I went off it rather when it all started to get a bit abusive. It started off quite gently – 'David and Ruth Archer, the moral and intellectual vacuum at the heart of *The Archers*' – but after a while some bitter trolls made it unpleasant for everyone and the service was withdrawn, although if you do a search for 'Mustardland' there are independent sites that carry it on. Twitter hashtags and Facebook sites provide more outlets, and it's wonderful that people talk and analyse and argue and feel so strongly about the programme. How dull it would be if they didn't. These days, I have to admit to occasionally basking in the loving endorsements of the David Archer Appreciation Group.

It is said that imitation is the sincerest form of flattery and I was thrilled one day to hear myself being lampooned on *Dead Ringers*, despite the fact that Jon Culshaw didn't seem to sound like me. Have I got any noticeable ticks as David? I honestly don't know.

The Archers spoofs started in 1961 with Tony Hancock's 'The Bowmans' when he forces the producers to use a script in which the whole village falls down a disused mineshaft. These day there are some wonderful spoofs. The *Shambridge* podcast is a bravura turn by Harriet Carmichael, taking on and absolutely nailing all the women of the village. John Finnemore's sketches of 'How *The Archers* sounds to people who don't listen to *The Archers*' is wicked, but very well observed. My favourite, though, because it's so weird, is a series of tableaux done with Duplo figures, called 'The Plarchers' – on Twitter as 'Ambridge Synthetics'. Rob Titchener as Dracula is just perfection!

Before the internet, we used to get letters, and one such has gone down as a classic. There was a fair amount of controversy about the fact that when Pip was born, the whole process was, as it were, recorded live. David was present, and the actual birth was simulated for the scene. Flick doesn't have children but spoke to friends who had been through childbirth, did a lot of research and, because I had attended my son Will's birth, she asked about my experience. 'It was loud,' I said. 'There was a lot of pain.'

When it came to the recording, she really went for it. For my own part I can remember distinctly shedding projectile tears when my first-born appeared, so I used that experience to enhance David's emotion at witnessing his daughter's arrival. A week after this was broadcast two letters were published in the *Radio Times*, one very complimentary and another from a retired major:

> I have attended the births of all five of my children, and I can assure you that my wife didn't sound as if she was being murdered, and that I didn't turn into a snivelling wreck like David, and neither did any of my friends.

It was the phrasing of the letter that made us laugh – how many of the major's friends were at the five births? I imagined them all standing around with their G & Ts, 'Come on Marjory, get on with it, the rugger's about to start!'

Dear old David, he may not be a searing intellectual but he's not thick. He's just more interested in the farm and his family than he is with discussing art, or politics, or philosophy – so he and I are a bit different really. The only things we share are the voice and the love of physical work and making things. I once went to a book launch in Norfolk. The book was a Marxist view of the Roman Empire.

'You're brave,' a posh local ventured to the author.

'Oh, why's that?' he asked, clearly flattered.

'There aren't any Marxists in Burnham Market,' came the entirely accurate reply.

When it came to Q & As, I asked a couple of questions

because the Romans have always fascinated me. Over wine and canapés afterwards, a woman who had been sitting in front of me said, 'It was extraordinary, that voice! I mean it was David, but you sounded *so intelligent*!'

Voice work

I have a recording of me doing a Mother's Pride voiceover for my father when I was about twelve: 'But misery, Mum cannot abide, so in she trots with Mother's Pride.' You then hear my father on talkback saying tersely, 'Again.' I repeat the line. He says 'Again' over and over. I sound terrified.

Little did I know that this was the preparation for how I would be earning the majority of my income for my adult life. Over the last thirty-odd years, I've done thousands of television commercials, radio commercials, corporate voiceovers, stadium announcements, narrations, audiobooks, voice-unders (vocal subtitles), museum audio guides, dubbing, re-voicing, ADR (additional dialogue replacement), loop groups (most movie-screen deaths you hear are me and my friends), language tapes, teaching tapes, training courses, computer games voices, cartoon and animation voices, in-store announcements, documentary narrations, medical instructions, film trailers, celebrity voices – and 'Mind the Gap' on the Piccadilly Line.

There's a recording studio called Side on Great Portland Street where I do a lot of computer games voices. The irony is not lost on me, as the Earl of Portland walks down the street, not owning it, but having spent the last two hours screaming fearful incantations as an undead vampire necromancer.

Winning the Carleton Hobbs award led to my radio career, but also opened me up to this whole other world of voice-related work. My sister Anna, the queen of audiobooks, paved the way and introduced me to a producer called Tony Hertz at Radio Operators, who remains the most original and inventive creator of radio commercials I've ever known. His thirty-second ads were mini dramas, well written, funny, poignant and required acting rather than mere voice technique. For some reason, he rated me and taught me the secrets of the soft sell. When I went off to Plymouth to do *Joseph* in 1979, I managed to get some work for the local radio station, which taught me the techniques of precisely the opposite – the hard sell. Hard sell involves cramming as much information into thirty seconds as you can possibly manage at town-crier volume, in the manner of a crazed salesman who has just discovered that frozen peas at £2.99 a packet are better than sex, and that if you don't RUSH OUT immediately to buy them from your local Co-op you'd be MAD, MAD, MAAAAD!

In the radio studio in Plymouth, there was a home-made, Devonian block of wood beneath the microphone with a series of LED lights stuck on it that counted down from thirty to nought, and I had to get the script across in exactly that time. I have an extremely accurate ability to judge thirty seconds as a result. I also mastered three things.

1. The Clarkson: 'Probably the best frozen peas . . . [one second pause] . . . *in the world*!'

2. The end of advert Terms and Conditions nightmare: 'Peasmayvaryinsizenotallhandpickedpeaswerepickedbyhand somepeasmaynotbesuitableforchildrentermsandconditions apply', and

3. The Voice: that particular and peculiar commercial advert voice that is classless and inoffensive to as many listeners as possible – an everyman voice. I've used it ever since.

The hard sell has gone out of fashion in the UK, but to be a successful voiceover you need to learn all the techniques and be able to do them convincingly and fluently on take one. I've now had a lot of practice, and, despite an inbred reluctance to boast, I have to admit that these days I generally get it right straight away. This can sometimes confuse the room full of people who are there for the one-hour recording session, each of whom feels that they have to contribute. The producer, the writer, the client, the client's mum, the client's twelve-year-old and their dog all have to justify their presence. I'm booked for the hour and I'm happy to take anyone's notes, but we do sometimes go around in a circle: 'Okay, can we get the first line of take six, which I thought was good, then the middle bit from take four, and put the last three words from take nine, because we loved that, at the end?' They play back the result. They look dubious. Then some kind soul says, 'Actually, could we listen to take one again?'

At its best, voice work is a genuine art form. At its worst, it is akin to slavery. Let's start with the hardest.

Corporates

Early days. Brighton in winter. A freezing basement studio. No table, just a wobbly music stand. A three-day job in the cold, sight-reading for eight hours a day – the instruction manual of how to operate a rolled steel mill in Lancashire. Terms whose meanings are like a foreign language, detailed and complex instructions that are, to my mind, gobbledegook, but I know about tools, and I like machines, so I get into a sort of zen-like state where I'm channelling the semi-literate writer of the piece, thinking about things at home, where I'd left the car keys, Charlotte Rampling, all the while sounding hugely authoritative about rolled steel mills. That's the job, that's what your paid to do, sight-read as though you'd thought of it.

Then there are the medical ones. You're meant to be the doctor, so Latin-heavy, didactic tomes of medical philosophy are presented to you on arrival in the form of a weighty, bulldog-clipped A4 script. You're ushered politely into someone's garage and asked to sound like you're the expert. That's when school comes in handy – those hated Latin lessons, those slightly better Italian tutorials with the rather fit housemaster's wife, the years of French and German that seemed at the time to have no point at all, but now mean I can read, on the fly, lines like 'such conditions as Choledocholithiasis, Menometrorrhagia and Bradykinesia . . .' with ease and without hesitation.

Well, that's what it sounds like in the final edit – the original recording is often entirely different: 'Choledodolith . . . Choledotholid . . . Cholethodoly . . . oh bollocks!' It is not just medical terms that can trip you up. With an audiobook, I'll get through three pages without fluffing difficult stuff with long names and multiple character voices, and I'll be feeling just a bit chuffed with myself and bang! I'm suddenly completely unable to say 'the'. Then I'll get into fluff mode. Eventually I get through it and I'm off again. But it's feeling a bit pleased with yourself that's always your undoing.

Documentary narration

This isn't so bad because the pictures do a lot of the work for you. Usually there isn't so much to say, and sometimes the content can be fascinating. I was hugely honoured to find myself narrating a documentary about my father's old friend James Lovelock, the environmentalist; he was equally amazed and happy at the coincidence. My favourite doc narrator is Samuel West: I think he gets it just right. The speaker should not sound as though they're reading it and shouldn't suggest an opinion on the content either; they don't use a special voice and don't perform, but at the same time they command the viewer's interest because of their engagement with the subject.

Audiobooks

Audiobooks can be tough, depending on the material and the studio. Sometimes, you're stuck in a tiny box with no window and an iPad in front of you, so no chance of a quick rest as you turn the page like you used to, blathering on about some mind-numbingly boring subject that will probably never be listened to anyway.

I once did a series of books called *How to Do Business the _____ Way*: the Richard Branson way, the Philip Green way, the Bill Gates way, etc. I was reading about how someone had an idea, wrote it on the back of a matchbox and a week later was a billionaire at the age of twelve. Meanwhile, I was freezing my arse off in a box in Notting Hill earning around 50p a page. Not fun.

On the other hand, you can be in a light airy studio where you can see the producer, reading a wonderful novel, and it's like doing a radio play where you're not only the narrator, but you're playing all the parts too. There's an app on the iPad called iAnnotate, which allows you to highlight all the dialogue with different colours. This makes it slightly easier when there's a Yorkshireman talking to a Geordie, a Scouser and a Scot, and the narrator is from New York. Sometimes it can get really complicated. In *Corroboree* by Graham Masterton, about the early days of Australia, not only are there scores of Aussies and English, but then they go out into the bush where there's about eight Aborigines, male and female, and everyone should be given a different voice. The main character then learns their language, so they're all speaking together, in Aborigine, but it's written in English. It didn't help that I had a bad chest infection at the time, so there's a lot of very butch Aussie women in the audiobook.

I've heard tales of actors who didn't even look at the book before the recording and, having spent three days voicing a story where they'd given their main character a standard southern RP accent, reach the last page only to find, 'said Albert, his Irish brogue softening the cruel impact of his harsh words'.

I've been guilty of this too. One of the first books I recorded was *Dracula* by Bram Stoker. I thought I knew the story so didn't prepare it. I invented characters' accents and voices on the fly. When it got to Mina, I gave her a high-pitched, very girly voice. My heart sank when I discovered halfway through that large extracts are taken from 'Mina's Journal' so suddenly the narrator is a shrill girl's voice, but the dialogue is still full of van Helsing's deep Dutch tones and Dracula's creepy Transylvanian.

Voice-unders

The 'vocal subtitle' is used when you've got a documentary with interviewees speaking a foreign language. Sometimes this is subtitled, but often the dialogue is subdued and an English voice comes in, providing the translation. Producers vary as to how they want this done. Sometimes they want you to match the colour and emotion of the speaker, and 'act' the lines, but more often the brief is to just provide the words, with no expression at all. There's a skill to this, as sometimes reading it totally flat can be a performance in itself and detract from the mood of the interview.

TEFL and ELT

Teaching English as a Foreign Language and English Language Teaching are recorded as learning aids for foreign students. Usually they consist of simple words and phrases, depending on the level that is being taught, from beginner to expert. At higher levels, you're doing Dickens and Shakespeare. Probably the most demanding job in this discipline is reading the rubrics: 'Chapter three, page nineteen, exercise five. One.'

The king and queen of Rubrics are Ken Shanley and Nicolette McKenzie, who both seem to adore doing it, and are peerless.

I was once booked to go to a studio in Milton Keynes to do some pickups of a session I'd recorded the previous month. The weather was appalling – huge snowdrifts and abandoned cars, treacherous icy roads, and driving, horizontal sleet. It took me nearly three hours. I staggered into the studio to be told, 'Ah, Tim, thanks so much for making it through in this weather. Very simple really, we just need you to record the alphabet.'

'The alphabet?'

'Yes, just A, B, C etc. Can't think how we failed to do it last time.'

'Right.'

I sat in the booth and when the green light went on I read the alphabet.

It took five minutes. I then got back in the car and drove home through the arctic waste, another three hours. An actor's life for me . . .

Mind the Gap

'Tim, job for you tomorrow at two, studio in Horsham. Station announcements,' says the lovely Tania from Hobson's International voiceover agency.

I got there early.

'So, station announcements. Which station is it?'

'It's the Piccadilly Line.'

'What, Mind the Gap?'

'Yup, and the rest.'

So for something like fifteen years I and fellow Hobsonian Julie Berry were the voices of the Piccadilly Line between King's Cross and Earl's Court. I achieved English icon status with this: 'Please mind the gap. This is Holborn. The next station is Covent Garden. Please stand clear of the closing doors.'

My boys grew up to the sound of their father watching out for them on the tube, which they both found strangely comforting. I use the Piccadilly Line almost every day, and when brash foreigners used to take the mickey out of my warnings, 'Ho ho ho, Mind ze Gepp!' I'd fantasise about seeing them fall down the gap, and I would lean down and whisper, 'I warned you!'

One day I was listening to *I'm Sorry I Haven't a Clue* on the car radio – they were on my favourite round, 'Mornington Crescent', when Graeme Garden introduced this piece of incidental information, 'On the Piccadilly Line, commuters hearing a recording of the phrase, Mind the Gap, are listening to the voice of Tim Bentinck, who plays David Archer in *The Archers*.' Now that is what I call fame!

People often ask me if I got paid every time it was played. Oh, I wish. Sadly, it was a £200 buy-out. You win some . . .

TV voiceovers

Some people have made a great deal of money from voiceovers and I've done all right, but mostly from the less glamorous types of job. My first one wasn't a voice but a whistle.

'Tim, can you whistle?'

'Yes?'

'Okay, Soho Studios tomorrow at nine.'

I walked in.

'Oh hi, Tim, can you whistle?'

'Yes, I think that's why I'm here.'

'Great, it's just we employed an actor to play a milkman, but it turns out he's the only member of your profession who has a complete inability to whistle, so we need to re-voice him whistling cheerfully as he delivers the morning pinta.'

'Okay.'

'Right, so we'll just show you the film; if you want to whistle along we'll take some level.'

'Fine.'

I watched a milkman get out of his milk float, go around the back, pick up two bottles and put them on a doorstep. I whistled along cheerfully.

'That's perfect, Tim, we actually put a tape on that and it sounds great. You're done, mate.'

I've been in the studio for five minutes max. I've earned £2000. It doesn't usually work like that.

I once did a TV voiceover for L'Oréal. So, I did take one. And it was fine.

There were seven women in the control room all looking baffled, desperately searching for something to criticise. We did another take because we could, they looked happier, then a third one which was

236

pretty slick and everyone was smiling. Then the client, the represent-
ative of L'Oréal in the UK, early twenties, earnest, serious, justifying
her presence, says, 'Sorry, but you're not saying L'Oréal correctly.'

'Okay, fine how do you want it?'

'L'Oréal.'

'L'Oréal.'

'No, L'Oréal.'

'L'Oréal.'

'No, like this. L'Oréal.'

'Okay, so do you want it more French-sounding? More in the
area of L'Auréalle with a sort of vocal Gallic shrug? Or would you
rather it was inclining more towards the cheerful Anglicised timbre
of a 'Lorry-al' sort of sound?'

'It's L'Oréal.'

'Right. Okay, Steve, let's go again.'

I think we did twenty-six takes. The nature of the deal was that I
would get paid a studio fee to record it, but if my voice was accepted
I would get a buy-out, which was a whole lot more, so I was
concerned to say L'Oréal in every conceivable way known to man.
As we left, I felt a lack of enthusiasm and thought I'd blown it. I
went on holiday. On my return, I got a call to come back and do it
again. Only one person there this time, the agency producer.

'Is it the way I said L'Oréal?'

'No Tim, not at all, they *loved* the way you said L'Oréal, they
adore the whole film. It's such a powerful commercial. Natalie
Imbruglia's wonderful, you're wonderful. No, it's the way you said
mascara.'

'How did I say it?'

'Mass-cara.'

'How do you want me to say it?'

'Ms-cara.'

'Mscara?'

'That's it.'

'Okay Steve, let's go. "The first two-step mscara from L'Oréal . . ."'

Cut to a month later and Judy and I are watching TV and the L'Oréal ad comes on. I haven't told her about recording it and I say, 'Oh this is me . . .'

As it comes to an end, there's a pause, and I say, 'There you are – because I'm worth it!'

And Judy says, 'Yes, very good darling. But . . .'

'What?'

'Why did you pronounce it *mscara?*'

Dubbing and re-voicing

This is one of my favourite types of voice work. There are two types of re-voicing, each demanding different skills. Dubbing usually refers to replacing foreign dialogue with English, and re-voicing when it's English to English, for instance, when the director has decided that he hates the actor's voice so replaces it entirely. This happened to Oliver Tobias in the 1983 film *The Wicked Lady* when director Michael Winner, without telling him, got my old *By the Sword Divided* chum Mark Burns to completely re-voice him in a starring role. Oliver didn't find out until the premiere.

The effectiveness of a foreign to English dub is almost entirely down to the translation. You have the raw translation in front of you, but that will rarely sit with the mouth movements of the actor, so you watch the footage without sound, and try to imagine what English words will convincingly replace the original. The reason I love it so much is that you're doing two things at once, being completely technical about getting the lip synch right while giving a performance that's as good (or in some cases better) than the original. My most high-profile dubbing work was voicing Chow Yung Fat from Mandarin to English in *Crouching Tiger, Hidden Dragon*. Mandarin is quite easy as the speakers don't move their mouths too much, unlike Japanese, which is completely impossible.

I cut my teeth on hundreds of episodes of dreadful German TV series such as *Derrick* and *Black Forest Clinic*. These were done using the 'band' technique, where you would just sight-read scrolling words at the bottom of the screen as they passed a vertical line, and they would be in synch. I could get through mountains of work in a day, and it was great training for what was to come.

I've now re-voiced three French actors speaking English – it seems Americans are bad at understanding a strong French accent, and I've had to tone it down for them, while still remaining 'vay Frenche' – Gérard Depardieu in *Battle of the Brave*, Xavier Duluc in *A Tale of Two Cities*, and most recently, and I'm proud of this, working with Paul Conway for a week in the Soundsquare Studios in Prague revoicing Marc Lavoine in ten episodes of the Eurocop drama, *Crossing Lines*. I've re-voiced Depardieu in a number of productions, and apparently he asks for me as our voices do have a similar timbre. Oddly, we have the same shaped face, apart from the nose, which in his case is becoming more cauliflower-like as the years go by. I once had a dream where I was on a film set, Gérard was in front of the camera, miming, and I was squatting on the floor, just out of shot, providing his voice. And that is kind of what it's like.

ADR

'Additional dialogue replacement' is a catch-all term that encompasses any vocal sounds that were not actually recorded during the filming. There's another art called Foley, which is recreating all the sounds, like car doors, chopped-off heads, footsteps, creaking doors etc. On a big movie, you can be sure that practically nothing recorded at the time gets into the final mix: everything is done in post-production.

Loop groups are also a part of that. I've had regular employment in this most invisible, and usually unheard, area of voice work for over twenty years. My first encounter with this world was working on Mel Gibson's *Braveheart* where I was amazed to find that the screams and battle cries of the massed armies of the English and the Scots were created in full by multi-tracking twelve big-lunged actors in a Soho studio.

There are two requirements for this job: a willingness to sacrifice your throat for the cause because dying horribly, screaming military commands and being a tribe of Orcs all day long needs strong vocal chords; and an ability to improvise period dialogue, modern dialogue, do all English-speaking accents and preferably have another two languages as well. It can be great fun. I've often heard directors say that the improvised scenes we invent on the spot for the characters in the background are far more interesting than the principal dialogue. Our regular company is made up of leading West End actors, film and TV stalwarts and improv specialists. Despite the fact that practically none of it will ever be heard above a mumble, it keeps our improvisation skills up to scratch, makes us laugh a lot, and sometimes produces little gems – everything from fiendish East End burglary plans that are utterly plausible while Tom Hardy is being both the Krays to mechanics' detailed comparisons of different types of early twentieth-century motor cars while his lordship is arseing around in the Downton foreground.

Unfortunately, for many years the Internet Movie Database (IMDb) had me as 'Best Known For . . . Conjoined Gnome Left' in the animated film *Gnomeo and Juliet,* not David Archer or any of the lead parts I've had in TV and film. This is because one day we were providing all-purpose background Gnome chatter and the sound editor said, 'Oh and we need two voices to replace the temp dub that the director did for these Conjoined Gnomes.' I volunteered, as did the resultant Conjoined Gnome Right, Neil McCaul, and we got a credit in the film. The IMDb's algorithms put at the top of your credits the highest grossing film you've ever been in, not the biggest part you've ever had, so if I'd died my major acting legacy, for the rest of internet time, would have appeared to have been Conjoined Gnome Left. Fortunately, IMDb have now allowed me to alter this, saving me from further ignominy, but it's one of the things that drove me to write this book – to put the record straight.

Computer games

I used to play a lot of computer games. Judy didn't. She hasn't the slightest interest in shooting things, whereas my *Desert Island Discs* luxury would probably be a Mongolian war bow. This led to a period in our lives where we would hardly see each other in the evenings, which I regret. So when *Myst* came out, I was delighted that we would play the game together. *Myst* was a completely different kind of game. Set on a beautifully drawn, photorealistic island, it involved a series of fiendish logic puzzles that unlocked doors, rooms and chambers to allow you to progress to the next level. What spoiled it totally was the dreadful acting. The game designers thought that it would be fun to provide their own jokey little dramas between levels, the appalling amateurishness of which meant that all involvement in this brilliantly created other world was entirely lost. Thankfully this has all changed now.

As the industry grew, and games creators started to make serious money, it finally dawned on them that their creations were being let down by the low standard of dialogue. Put it this way, if you're confronted by a ten-foot Vampire Necromancer wielding a blood-steeped battle axe, the effect is totally ruined if it sounds like an insurance salesman from Basildon. So they introduced writers, actors and directors, who brought with them all the hard-learned rigours of our profession. These days, the major games writers produce dramas that can be as good as a movie.

Every actor's bucket-list job is probably Bond. When Timothy Dalton got the gig, I knew I would never get the call, not least because they were never going to cast another Timothy with a two-syllable surname. However, I have got that credit on my CV as I am the voice of James Bond in *The World Is Not Enough*. Of course, in the movie it's Pierce Brosnan, but he didn't want the computer game gig, so they cast around for a voice match and I got it. Brosnan's got a great voice, and it's hard to match as it's sort of Irish, sort of English and sort of American – very hard to pin down, so before each line of the game they would play me his voice in my headphones so I could tune in to it. So yes, professionally, I have uttered the line, 'The name's Bond, James Bond.' Die happy.

In 1988, I played a Finnish race announcer in the TV movie *The Four Minute Mile*. The character had to deliver the very first example of a mile time starting with 'Three minutes . . .' and I had to learn some Finnish. Once you've learned the Finnish for 'Three minutes, fifty-seven point nine seconds' you never forget it. Recently I was doing some dwarfish computer voices at Mark Estdale's Outlook Media with the producer on a video link down the line in Helsinki, and I told him this story.

'Oh, yes please, let's hear it,' he enthused.

'Kolme minuuttia, ja viisikymmentäseitsemän pilku yhdeksän sekuntia,' I announced with pride.

'Aha! Yes, yes, yes! And with a Swedish accent!'

While listening to *The Archers*, you can always play the game of telling how many Orcs I've been recently by the raspiness or otherwise of David's voice.

Animation

This is a different skill. It's more like radio drama but the fun is that your character is brought to visual life with the skills of the animator. I did an American children's series about Robin Hood in which I was the Sheriff of Nottingham and Richard the Lionheart. The Sheriff was my well-used snarly, imperious, evil posh voice, à la Severus Snape, but when it came to Richard, for whom I was being deep, warm and kindly, the note I received from the director, who was listening in 'down the line' at four in the morning somewhere in California, was, 'Can the King have less accent?'

'Sorry, what accent?'

'Less British accent?'

'But he's the King of England!'

'Yeah, but he sounds kinda evil.'

This is the problem with my fellow thesps getting good work in Hollywood playing bad guys. In American movies, practically all the villains are now English. With the exception of Harry Potter, if you're a toff, you're the bad guy, which probably harks back to the American Revolution. She said 'British', but she meant English, and not Scouse or Bristol or Geordie, but posh, sneery, superior – basically Alan Rickman at his best. It seems the rule about class war is that it's fine to take the piss out of people who used to oppress you, and since the English oppressed just about everyone, including the Welsh, Scots and Irish, and the toffs oppressed the workers, the posh English are fair game for anyone, any time. So that's why the King of England sounds like he's from Pasadena.

I've trodden the movie premiere red carpet only once. I auditioned for the part of Roger Radcliffe, the owner of Patch and a hundred other Dalmatians for Disney's *101 Dalmatians II: Patch's London Adventure* and was quite astonished to get the part. Astonished because the bulk of the role was singing a close-harmony duet, and in that department I'm a journeyman at best.

Technically it was fiendish. We recorded it at the famed Air Studios in Hampstead, often used for orchestral movie scores, and we did it live with my 'wife', the American actress Jodi Benson, a 'Disney Legend' who was at the end of an ISDN line in a studio in Los Angeles. The problem with this was latency, or delay. No matter how fast the signal comes down the wire, there is always a slight delay, so we were singing either ahead or behind each other. The studio engineer had to get it, by trial and error, so we were both singing at exactly the same time. I was also at the absolute upper limit of my vocal range and the song was musically tricky, and it was for *Disney*, so everyone else involved was the very best in the business. Intimidating.

The film won an award for Best Musical Score, so I guess take 103 must have been okay. When it came out I was invited to the premiere at Grauman's Chinese Theatre, downtown LA. My dear friend Tony Armatrading had moved to California some years before so this was an opportunity to visit him, too. The slightly deflating thing about being 'the voice of . . .' in a Disney film is that on the red carpet no bugger knows who the hell you are, so all the rent-a-celeb mums had brought their kids and were being snapped by the paps, and Tony and I just sauntered in unnoticed.

We settled down in our tortuously uncomfortable seats to hear myself in my only Disney movie ever. So excited. The curtains drew, the titles rolled, on comes Roger, he opens his mouth . . . and it isn't me. I've been replaced! This guy's got a high-pitched voice that isn't anything . . . oh . . . oh, wait a minute . . . oh, it *is* me! Christ! Nearly had a thrombie. It had been months since I'd done it and I'd forgotten that I'd pitched it like a fourteen-year-old.

The party afterwards was interesting. The theme was 'London' inasmuch as there was a guy on stilts outside dressed as a guardsman and two 'Bobbies' in Keystone Cops outfits giving it plenty of Dick van Dyke. Inside it was just an American party, which is much the same as any other party only louder – those open plains. I was keen to meet Jodi after singing a duet with her and recording scenes of marital love and happiness when we'd been a thousand miles apart. I felt there was a bond. And she was like, 'Yeah, like it was such a pleasure working with you,' with that long emphasis on the 'you' that Americans do when they don't mean it.

The Equity voiceover strike

In 1997, we were told by Equity not to work for anyone who wasn't adhering to the long-established Equity agreements on voice work. The person who was seen to be responsible for this was Enn Reitel. He had been probably the most successful voiceover artist for many years and the story goes that after an article about him appeared in the press, in which he said he sometimes couldn't get in the front door because of all the cheques piled up behind it, some admen got the hump and started asking why they were paying actors all this money.

The arguments are pretty simple. On the one hand, if a TV commercial has persuaded someone to buy your product, then part of the reason for that is the performance, in that one showing, of the voice behind it, who should therefore get paid for that one performance. So, if the ad is shown a hundred times, the voice artist should be paid x times 100. On the other hand, the advertising industry was saying that paying someone thousands of pounds for saying 'Blooper Soap is Best' is ridiculous, and they could get the tea boy to do it, it doesn't require any skill and the product is sold by the filming and the writing.

So Equity went on strike, and the admen got the tea boy to do it. And very effective he was.

Up until then, I had been regularly employed, not so much on TV ads but on radio certainly, selling products with a kind of class-less but nevertheless educated southern English accent, the idea being that a voice of enthused authority was what people wanted to hear. The success of the new, post-strike amateurs proved the opposite, particularly among the young, for whom posh and enthusiastic were the opposite of cool. A perfect example was a telly ad for Vodaphone. The end line was, 'Use it, don't use it, it's your call.' Great line, and delivered with the kind of laid-back attitude of a rude boy sitting at the back of the classroom with his feet on the desk. It was saying, 'Look mate, there's this thing, right? Just saying. Up to you if agree with me. If not, cool.' That voice wouldn't be right for selling Bentleys or Ferrero Rocher, but it's perfect for mobile phones.

My income plummeted and, although things have got better since, no one's having problems with their front doors any more. Enn bought a stud farm and retired. You can still hear the difference in today's voiceovers, for which the preferred performance is not to sound as though you mean it, which wouldn't be cool, but as though you've been told to read it, which is acceptable.

Even with reduced rates, it was a lucky day when Anthony Hyde turned down the Radio Rep job and I got it instead, and with a bit of luck, as long as the old dulcets hold out, I may continue to be employed making odd noises in front of a microphone.

Radio drama

Since I've been in *The Archers*, the huge output from my days on the Radio Rep has dwindled and now BBC radio drama has almost disappeared. I do the odd play but the powers that be frown on *Archers* regulars turning up in other work: they think David will be heard no matter what I do. That's fair, I suppose. I can hardly complain I'm not on the radio enough, and these days I get to flex my radio-acting chops in a huge variety of roles for Big Finish, who have the licence to make *Doctor Who, Torchwood, Survivors, The Prisoner, Sherlock Holmes, The Avengers* and much more. I love working for them, I die almost every production I'm in, often more than once, I get to do all the accents and characters in my repertoire, the lunch is superb and it means that I have now worked with every living Doctor bar Matt Smith – and if I'd got a part I was up for in *The Crown* I'd have the full set.

Being David Archer: Technique

The older generation on *The Archers* had the experience of recording onto acetate disc, which meant it couldn't be edited – if the actor fluffed they either soldiered on embarrassed or, disaster, they had to start again from the beginning. The first hour and a half was spent in rehearsal, with the last thirty minutes or so devoted to the recording itself. It was effectively a live performance, which, together with the lo-fi quality of the broadcast, is part of the difference between the acting style of those early years and the more naturalistic style of today.

Also, in the last sixty-odd years, our language has changed so much. In usage and accent, early *Archers* recordings sound like a forgotten world. However, certain things remain the same. Telling a story within the time constraints means the structure has hardly changed, and the subjects are much the same – farming, intrigue, gossip, love, feuds, natural disasters, etc. These are the eternal archetypes and the scenes are about the same length as they have always been. The difference is the freedom we have in recording, which allows us the opportunity of invention – occasionally what we say isn't necessarily what is written on the page. As long as the cue for the other actor is the same, it can be liberating sometimes to be a bit free with the lines. Also, adding grace notes like pauses, deliberate stumbles, ums, errs, 'sort ofs', 'you knows', 'but . . .' or 'so . . .' can loosen up the script.

We can only do that because of digital recording – nowadays if you make a hash of it, the results are so easy to edit. I do a lot of technical work with music and voice recording, and I know how quick editing is compared to the razor blades and sticky tape of years gone by. Make a mistake? Pause a second, go back to the beginning of the sentence, say it again. Today, a fluff is just a deleted region of a digital waveform. The taped mistakes of the past are now only heard as the crunching of straw underfoot.

At Pebble Mill, in the days of tape, there was an 'edit room' where actors would wait, coats on, suitcases in hand, taxi waiting, to hear if the edit was clear and they could race for their train. If it wasn't, they'd have to go back into the studio to re-record, never a popular demand.

If you listen to a playback of a natural conversation in which the speakers don't know they're being recorded, natural speech patterns have a rhythm and a song that is almost impossible to replicate. I say 'almost' because sometimes an actor's job is to get as close to that as possible, and occasionally you can achieve it. Being in a drama for a very long time means you can just immerse yourself in the reality, and say it the way you think it. The lines in the script aren't just words to say: they're clues as to how you're thinking, what people are saying to you, why you might want to reply. The words on the page are simply the things that come out of your mouth as a result. You just have to react.

The cast are all very good at sight-reading. This helps with audiobooks and narration of any kind, especially when you turn up to a studio for a three-hour booking and you haven't been given the script in advance. The trick is to read ahead to see where the sentence is going, your heart sinking if it's a medical one, and that sentence is heading inexorably towards

Patients were treated with lymphodepleting conditioning chemotherapy (intravenous cyclophosphamide [60 mg/kg] daily for 2 days followed by fludarabine [25 mg/m^2] daily for 5 days, followed by a single intravenous infusion of autologous TILs and high-dose interleukin-2 [720 000 IU/kg] every 8 h). (*Lancet*)

Of course, it's nothing like as bad as that in *The Archers*, but Bovine Spongiform Encephalopathy still springs effortlessly off my tongue!

Quiz shows

I learned two lessons from quiz shows. One, you can't win 'em all and, two, quit while you're ahead.

Call My Bluff (1996)

I'd been brought up on *Call My Bluff*, which started in 1965. I have great memories of Robert Robinson chairing the panel game, with team captains Frank Muir and Arthur Marshall, but that era came to a close in 1988. I really enjoyed the format, in which two teams of three were given a word that no one had ever heard of, and asked to give definitions. Two definitions would be false and the opposing team had to guess the correct version.

The show was resurrected in 1996 with Bob Holness as chairman and Sandi Toksvig and Alan Coren at team captains, and I was asked to do one episode in this new incarnation, on Sandi's team.

I wasn't very good. I'd always loved Frank Muir's technique, which would start, 'You're on a desert island . . .' or 'You're a daffodil . . .' and I thought I would copy him. I also thought I should throw in as many accents as possible to prove what a versatile and varied performer I was. All I remember is Alan Coren saying, 'God, is this an audition?' In the break, he tried to convince me that there were such things as 'Bentinck's Chocolates'. I said no it's Bendick's, as usual, but he was adamant. Exhaustive Google searching has come up with one tantalising reference, but nothing more. Have you ever heard of them? After all I based my one-man show around the misconception!

Hidden Treasures (1998)

This was such fun – working with the Toby jug of loveliness that is Henry Sandon. Chaired by Lars Tharp, *Hidden Treasures* was a radio antiques quiz that each week came from a different stately home. We were in Harewood House, but the problem really was the format. Antiques are visual, and describing them doesn't have the same impact. We were asked to bring along an interesting *objet*, and that went down well as I brought along a fascinating naval journal written by an ancestor, Captain William Bentinck, which contains this tantalising entry, which I read out: 'Breakfasted with Sir Jos. Banks, where I met Capt. Bligh, late of the ['Discovery' crossed out] Bounty, taken by Pirates going round the world.'

This led to historians contacting me and the eventual loan of the two volumes to the University of Nottingham for transcription. I love the idea that Bligh told his fellow officers that he'd been 'taken by pirates' rather than cast adrift by a mutinous crew.

University Challenge (2004)

'How would you like to do *University Challenge: The Professionals*?' asked the impossibly glamorous and brilliant Kate Oates, producer of *Emmerdale* and then *Coronation Street*, but at that time working as producer at *The Archers*.

'Oh definitely! Are we "The Archers"?'

'No, you're "Actors". You're representing the entire profession.'

'Strewth, that's quite a responsibility.'

'Yes, and you're the captain.'

So, a few weeks later I was sitting at our kitchen table at home with Charles Collingwood (Brian), Louiza Patikas (Helen) and Felicity Finch (Ruth) with four battery-operated doorbells in front of us, being quizzed by the late, very much lamented, Nick Clarke, who was armed with the *University Challenge* quiz book, and being filmed by Will and Jasper to add to the mood. My worry was that we would be embarrassingly bad and have to live with, 'Oh yes, you're the thick one on *University Challenge*,' and have thespians across the country telling us that they knew all the answers. So I learned the periodic table, the kings and queens of England, British prime ministers, US presidents, the romantic poets and all the major artists and composers, and doled out subjects for revision to the others. A professional and competitive approach.

A luxury minibus was sent to drive us all together up to Manchester, and we continued our preparation on the journey. During this trip, Charles suddenly got rather serious.

'Now look, chaps, I've done a few of these things, and I'll just say that in my experience it's not a good idea to have anything to drink before you go on, it takes the edge off the speed of thought.'

We all agreed that this was sound advice.

When we got there we found we were up against a team of 'Soroptimists', a term we had never heard of but it turned out they were from a global women's charitable organisation. They were pretty nervous and they were also huge *Archers* fans, so they were doubly intimidated when Charles sauntered charmingly up, glass of red in his hand and said, 'Hello ladies, how delightful to meet you. Of course, this is all a bit of fun, but if I can offer a bit of advice?

I've done a few of these things and in my experience it never hurts to have one or two glasses of the old vino before the show – takes the edge off the nerves, you know.'

Charles was almost a professional cricketer, and what he doesn't know about gamesmanship isn't worth diddly squat.

Well, we stormed it. I was on fire. Not one thing that I had prepared came up, but I was so in the zone that, supported by Collingwood on sport, what I didn't know anyway I guessed and got lucky. We agreed that we were all bad at classical music, so if any such question came up we'd say Beethoven. 'And the first starter for ten . . .': immediate result.

Oh, how I wish I'd left it at that.

A Good Read (2006)

This was not a quiz show, but it was another opportunity to sound like a dunce. It didn't help that my fellow guest on the Radio 4 programme was Andrew Graham-Dixon, a man who knows how well qualified he is. His introduction took up a fair amount of the programme: his degrees, awards and achievements were a good read in themselves. Then Sue McGregor got to me – 'The voice of David Archer and Mind the Gap.' That was it. No mention of degrees or awards or education, and my choice of book didn't help. I'd gone for levity and chosen *Bryson's Dictionary of Troublesome Words* because I'm a bit of a grammar Nazi, an apostrophe abuse spotter and a spelling fiend. The problem was it sounded like I needed an American to help me speak my own language. Then I had to wax lyrical on Graham-Dixon's choice, the monumentally clever poem *War Music* by Christopher Logue, based on Homer's *The Iliad*. I love poetry and can write sonnets in the style of Shakespeare, French Dada-ist poems that are really English pop songs, and translate

French erotic novels into English, but in-joke translations of Homer are for the classics scholars, not me.

Sue's choice was not much better: *The Turn of the Screw* by Henry James. There had recently been a film based loosely on the premise called *The Others*, which is wonderful and spooky and scary – all the things that the book is not. I left nineteenth-century fiction behind a long time ago, for a very good reason – life is too short, and outside Hardy, Conan Doyle and Dickens I haven't got the patience, so I wasn't much help there either. I suppose I was vaguely amusing, but the invitations to literary symposia didn't flood in after the broadcast.

Through the Keyhole (2008)

Humiliation.

So, there I am on the computer about five in the evening when the doorbell rings. Will shouts up that there's a cab for me. Wrong street, I say. 'It's for Tim,' he says. Still wrong street, different Tim. 'It's for Tim Bentinck,' he says.

I come downstairs. It's a large Mercedes waiting to take me to Riverside Studios for the *Through the Keyhole* interview. It's just that nobody bothered to tell me. The car satnavs me to the studios and drops me round the back so I have to walk round.

'Hi, I'm here for the recording.'

They put me in with the audience.

'No, I'm in the show?'

'Who are you?'

'Tim Bentinck, I'm one of the stars?'

'Oh, you're late.'

Um, yeees!

I'm shown into a tacky green room with some curling sandwiches and fizzy drinks. The only high point of the evening is that two of the other celebs are England rugby internationals, so now I've got a free pass to watch Wasps any time I want. I go into make-up and, since I've just got back from Australia and am fairly tanned, ask the make-up artist not to put too much slap on. She is clearly miffed.

A woman comes in. 'Darling, darling, you're so gorgeous, here let me massage you, isn't this fun?'

I feel I ought to know her so I give plenty of 'Darling, darling, yes indeedy' in return.

Then she says. 'Years ago, I went out with Eric Clapton and for the first four hours I had no idea who he was. Do you know who I am?'

'No darling, no idea, sorry.'

'I'm Paula Hamilton, the model who was in the VW ad where I put the keys in the dustbin. Now I'm a recovering alcoholic. Who are you?'

'I'm Tim Bentinck. I play David in *The Archers*.'

'Oh God, I love your voice I love that programme' etc., etc., gush, gush, until she finds herself next to Sir David Frost's PR man, after which I don't exist.

So now I'm on. I'm hidden in the wings while a film of my house is shown, and the 'celebrity' panel has to guess who I am. I'm in a chair looking into the TV camera and watching my own face on screen. It is deathly pale, the make-up woman's revenge. The studio audience clap if the panel is getting warm and stay silent if they're not. For some reason, the film shows a lot of military stuff in the house, swords, etc. so they think I'm a soldier. They have to be told I'm an actor.

'Is he a TV actor?'

Silence.

'Is he a film actor?'

Silence.

'Is he a theatre actor?'

Silence.

Having done thirty years of telly, film and theatre and forgetting that I'm on camera, I start to say, 'Oh for fuck's sake.' I see myself in shot halfway through and turn it into 'Oh for fahahaha . . .' smiley, smiley.

'Well, what other kinds of acting are there?' says Gloria Hunniford, who I've met at least twice and claims to be an *Archers* fan.

'Radio.'

'Oh, radio!' they sneer.

Eventually, they get around to the longest-running series in the world, a national icon and the most successful show on Radio 4, broadcasting to five million people daily.

'Is it Nigel Archer?' (There is no such character.)

Eventually they have to be told.

In the edit pause, David Frost comes backstage and says he used to live next to my father in Carlisle Square. 'No, David, that's the DUKE of Portland, my father was the Earl, as am I.' This is not going well.

So I come on. I want to say to the panel, 'Don't worry, I've never heard of you lot either,' but my natural politeness prohibits me. I do say, 'So, thirty years of telly out the window then.'

'Oh, have you been on television? What have you been in?'

This is the dread curse of the nearly famous actor. If you start to reel off the names, they always go, 'didn't see that' or 'never heard of it' or 'oh, who were you in that?' – you're on a loser to nothing. Actually, the usual phrase is, 'What might I have seen you in?' To which my answer now is, 'I don't know, what have you watched?'

So then Frost asks me about the banjo and guitars and recording equipment in my room, ending up with, 'Have you ever had a hit?' I have to admit that I haven't.

'So, Tim, you're an inventor.'

I tell them about how I spent a fortune on patents when I was younger.

'So, Tim, you're the voice of Mind the Gap on the Piccadilly Line?'

I tell them the story of getting only £200 for twenty years of being the station announcer on the whole Piccadilly Line.

'Can you do it for us?'

Oh God. Okay. 'Please Mind the Gap. This is Holborn. The next station is Russell Square. Please stand clear of the closing doors.' Big round of applause.

'Well, Tim, it's been great having you on the show.'

So, I'm the guy that no one's ever heard of, who is a failed songwriter, a failed inventor and whose only claim to fame is that he says 'Mind the Gap' on the tube. Thanks a bunch.

The mixed blessings of being a radio star.

Celebrity Eggheads (2012)

I'd always wanted to meet Judith Keppel. When she was the first person to win the jackpot on *Who Wants to be a Millionaire?* I fell for this gorgeous, posh, coolest of women. We also had a history in common. The first Earl of Portland had been ousted from the affections of King William III by Judith's direct ancestor, Arnold, and poor Hans Willem retired hurt to the country where he died only a few years later.

So, there we were, Charles Collingwood again (captain this time), Andrew Wincott (Adam), Charlotte Martin (Susan), Rachel Atkins (Vicky) and me, lined up against Judith Keppel and the other members of 'arguably the most formidable quiz team in the country'.

The host, Dermot Murnaghan, announced that the first subject was 'Science'.

'Ambridge Academicals, who wants to start off?'

'I'll do Science,' I piped. I didn't care what the subject was, I wanted to go face to face with Judith and didn't want anyone getting in before me.

'Okay, Tim, and who would you like to take on?'

I have the recording, and what I said was this: 'Well, I'm going to choose Judith simply because our families have history. It goes back to 1689. Keppel took on Bentinck then – a certain Arnold Joost van Keppel got rid of my ancestor Hans Willem Bentinck from the favours of William III, so I think it's revenge time, Judith!'

She was delighted. As we walked together round to the booth that's separated from the main area, she said it was the best challenge she had ever faced, and we've since become good friends. And I beat her, so Bentinck/Keppel honours are now even.

We didn't win the competition, though, the blame for which I lay squarely on Collingwood's shoulders, but never mind, we had fun in Glasgow.

On the plane home, I found myself sitting next to Sandra Dickinson, who'd been doing a different episode. We were getting along fine; her squeaky American voice was very cute. There was a pause and then she said, 'Have you ever thought about having your moles removed?'

Well, of course, I've thought of nothing else since, Sandra.

Celebrity Mastermind (2012)

Only a month later, it was time for the big one. I would get to sit in The Chair! When they'd asked me for my chosen specialist subject, I'd said 'Winnie the Pooh' for the sole reason that I wanted to be the only

person who had ever sat in The Chair and said 'Heffalump'. They said
the subject was too small, so it had to be 'A. A. Milne and Winnie the
Pooh', but at least it wasn't 'The Extended History of World War
One' or 'Everything that Tolstoy Ever Wrote' – after all, there are
only two Pooh books. So I learned them. I went through them both,
imagining what possible question could be asked after each para-
graph, writing it down and giving the answer. Then I learned what I'd
written, like a script. For Milne, I figured they would only ask two or
three questions, and they were likely to be about his upbringing,
where he lived, his schools and teachers, so I learned that too.

In the week before the recording I started to get the serious
wobbles. By a horrible coincidence, there were two *Mastermind*-
related things on telly, which didn't help at all. Harry Enfield and
Paul Whitehouse did a sketch where Harry passed on every question,
and Paul couldn't even remember his chosen subject, and an actual
episode where a woman did this for real: a total brain fade, rabbit in
the headlights, panicked freeze.

There's nothing you can do to prepare yourself for the General
Knowledge round, but I really swotted the Pooh questions and figured I'd do all right. I was up against actor Guy Henry, Bucks Fizz's
Cheryl Baker and astronomer Mark Thompson. Cheryl and Mark
were very relaxed and we agreed that all we wanted was to not make
total prats of ourselves, but Guy was clearly in it to win it, pacing
up and down outside in the Manchester rain, smoking furiously.

It's an odd thing, but with these TV game shows, no matter how
apprehensive I may be feeling beforehand, by the time we walk out
onto the set I'm usually completely calm and really looking forward
to it. I suppose it's because TV and film sets are my favourite places,
and I'm very familiar and comfortable there.

We had to wait for Cheryl to have a hairpiece fitted and she was first on. She did okay on James Taylor and got 10. Then it was me. The Walk To The Chair. I remembered my name, and my subject. The questions came fast. Milne's early life – I knew his house, where he went to school and his English teacher. Now Pooh. Correct, correct, correct. 'Heffalump' – I smiled! And then came the one to separate the men from the boys. There's a poem in the first book in the chapter on finding Eeyore's tail that goes,

> Who found the tail?
> 'I,' said Pooh,
> 'At a quarter to two
> (Only it was quarter to eleven really)
> I found the tail.'

I'd noticed that this could be a trick question, and John Humphreys nearly got me.

'At what time did Pooh find Eeyore's tail?'

'A quarter to t . . . eleven!'

'Correct.'

Phew. All correct and no passes!

Mark was next, on the history of coffee, and did okay. Finally, it was Guy's turn, 'The Life of Peter O'Toole'. He did better but got a few wrong and I was in the lead.

General Knowledge. Going well, sailing along, then an impossible question about an obscure Turkish town. No idea. Pass. And this is when the brain starts to let you down: your concentration dims because you're thinking about the previous question.

'Who is the current presenter of *A Question of Sport*?'

Oh. Tennis player, blonde, you know . . . thingy . . . damn, pass. I knew it was Sue Barker.

'Hero of Troy and sailed on voyages of adventure?'

I heard 'Troy' and said 'Paris'. Odysseus. I KNEW that!

'Who famously interviewed Richard Nixon on TV after Watergate?'

I heard 'TV interviewer' and got an image of Princess Diana and Martin Bashir.

'Martin Bashir?' David Frost. OF COURSE I KNEW THAT!

I was pretty sure I was now losing to Guy.

'What oil is used to stop cricket bats from drying and cracking?'

Aaaah. I could smell it. Things from your past that at the time seem completely pointless, like German, chapel, and in this case compulsory house cricket when I'd much rather have been swimming, last in to bat, lying in the grass playing with worms, and rubbing the bat with . . .

'Linseed oil.'

Correct.

I won by one point. Standing next to Humphreys, holding the trophy as the *Mastermind* music played out, was as close as I'll ever get to winning Olympic gold.

Guy was livid.

Pointless Celebrities (2013)

Kellie Bright played Kate Aldridge in *The Archers* from 1995, and I was delighted to find myself on *Pointless Celebrities* with her, as she hadn't been cast in the programme for a while and was now an award-winning star of *EastEnders* – she has since turned superstar as the runner-up in *Strictly Come Dancing*.

It was a 'Record Breakers' episode, so we were up against Linford Christie (100m British record holder), Sally Gunnell (400 m hurdles British record holder), the tallest man and woman in Britain (seven foot seven and six foot ten), Janet Ellis and Ayo Akinwolere from

Blue Peter (longest-running TV series), and me and Kellie (world's longest-running drama series).

What a clever game show it is, a great leveller, not relying so much on education as a wide-ranging life experience, helped occasionally by getting lucky with a subject you know about.

Linford and Sally went out first – we had beaten the fastest man and woman in the country. Then we beat the tallest, then *Blue Peter*, and now Kellie and I were going for the money. We had to name obscure counties in New York State. Now I'd worked there, and led my Trailways bus tours all around it, and I couldn't even think of a well-known one. For some reason, the name Hoboken came into my head, mainly because Jasper was writing a song once and asked me what rhymed with 'broken'. I knew it was a district of New York City, but we couldn't think of anything and it sounded good, so we said it anyway.

Clang! Big red cross.

We didn't win the money for our charities, but we got the *Pointless* Trophy, which stands proud next to the *Mastermind* pyramid – a lifetime of trivial achievements in clear plastic.

So, when they asked me again, exactly a year later, of course I came back for more – my first indication of the advisability of quitting while you're ahead.

Pointless Celebrities (2014)

The great thing about going out in the first round in *Pointless* is that you're paid the same and you get to go home for supper. Dame Jenni Murray and I were teamed together as part of a whole Radio episode, and were joined by Ken Bruce, David 'Kid' Jensen, Liz Kershaw and two modern DJs of whom I hadn't heard. Just because you're a bit well known doesn't stop you being slightly smacked-of-gob when meeting the superstars of your youth. Kid Jensen! Ken

Bruce I knew from before and is every inch the gentleman he sounds on Radio 2, although balder.

Our first task was to name a country whose first vowel is an 'A'. I toyed with Kyrgyzstan, but wasn't totally sure of the two Y's and plumped for Zambia. Jenni unfortunately said Wales, which is a Principality, so out we went. Poor Jenni was distraught, and my limo driver had barely had time for a fag.

University Challenge (2015)
So, quit while you're ahead.

One day I got an email from *University Challenge* asking if I'd like to be on a Christmas Special team of former students from the University of East Anglia. I accepted like a shot.

I'd been waiting for this. I'd done the Professionals game but that's not the same as being on the uni team; this was the real deal, and my whole life of watching the programme, shouting the answers and learning from each one had been my preparation for this. I'd nailed it the last time so this would clearly be my intellectual zenith.

We were up against a formidable team from Manchester, with comic Lucy Porter and Jesse Armstrong, who wrote the first episode of *The Thick of It* that I was in. My captain was Labour MP Caroline Flint.

I had no idea of the first three starter questions, and nor did any of our team. Manchester, and Lucy Porter in particular, were very quick. I finally knew an answer, pressed the buzzer . . . too late. I thought, *Gamble, just go for it early, and get the answer in the time it takes Roger Tilling to say your name.* Bzzzzz. 'UEA, Bentinck.' Answer. 'No, you lose five points.' So, we're now on *minus five*! They're on fifty-something.

'What Woody Allen film has a name derived from an instruction manual?'

Everything You Wanted to Know About Sex but Were Afraid to Ask – I press the buzzer!

'Manchester, Armstrong.'

'Er . . . Everything You Ever . . .'

Bugger!

I got us back to a massive plus five points by knowing the board game 'Go' and also redeemed some credibility as a university graduate by casually tossing out 'Machiavelli' for another ten. We ended on 35 points. They got more. Sort of 150 more. In the broadcast, they didn't cut me quipping, in a stiff upper lip sort of way, hoping for a laugh, 'It was close,' and Paxman's waspish retort, 'No it *wasn't*!'

Being David Archer: Perks of the job

There are perks to being in *The Archers* – you do get invited to some rather special things. We once did a live performance onstage for a show called *The Great Event – Forty Years of Broadcasting for Her Majesty*. The green room was packed with stars – and us! Stirling Moss, Frank Bruno, some of the 1966 World Cup football team, Seb Coe and Steve Cram, Cliff Richard, Wogan, you name it. It's weird being a radio star – nobody knew who we were – until we went on stage and then all the people we'd previously been asking for autographs were suddenly our best mates.

After the show, we were lined up to shake hands with Her Majesty and her family. Now the thing is that the Queen's grandmother is a Bentinck, so I was prepared for her to say something along the lines of 'Are we related?' the answer to which would have been, 'Yes, ma'am, we're seventh cousins', but she said nothing. Then came Philip, irascible as ever. I was introduced, 'Timothy Bentinck, sir.'

'Hmm, that's a familiar name?'

My cue! 'Yes, sir, that's possibly because . . .' Then I couldn't think how to refer to the Queen when you're talking to Prince Philip. I mean he obviously knew she was the Queen, and I couldn't really call her Elizabeth, seventh cousin or no, so instead I said, ' . . . your wife's grandmother was a Bentinck.'

'YOUR WIFE'? What was I thinking?

Anyway, he didn't bat an eyelid at that but just said grumpily, 'Oh, Bentinck. I thought you said Bentine.'

He meant Michael Bentine, who among many other things was on *The Goon Show* – the Duke of Edinburgh, Goon fan.

Then came Diana, and I suddenly realised what the whole obsession with her was all about. The way she looked at me, I saw that she was immediately madly in love. I was the only one. Her marriage with Charles was a sham and she and I were destined to elope in secret to a desert island and damn the consequences. I was weak at the knees – and then she spoke. The conversation went like this:

'Gosh, a radio star, how exciting.'

'Yes, it means you don't get recognised in the street.'

'Oh God, I could do with some of that.'

'Well, your royal highness, perhaps you'd like to move to Ambridge and be our radio princess, and never be seen again.'

She smiled, leant towards me slightly, and whispered, 'Sounds divine.'

I was besotted.

Charles was next.

'I love the way you use a bicycle pump and cork for the champagne-popping sound effect. I was allowed to do that for the Goons once you know.'

I couldn't believe it, Goon references from both father and son, but I also suddenly felt so sorry for him, the 'I was allowed to . . .' summing up an entire life of never being 'allowed' to do anything he really wanted to at all. I got cheeky, seeing as how he was now clearly the cuckold in this three-way relationship.

'Well, your royal highness, perhaps you'd like to come up to Ambridge and do our special effects for us?'

He gave me a rather old-fashioned look then came up with this cracker.

'Sounds intriguing, but I think I'll stick with this. I get to travel more, do you see?'

Brilliant.

Other benefits include, I suspect, getting off a driving ban because of being in *The Archers*. I'm a good driver – you don't pass your HGV test unless you are – and what with driving tourists round America and VW Beetles round Europe, I've had a lot of experience, but sometimes you get caught out by those pesky cameras. These days cruise control and a more adult perspective has cut down the problem but in my more impetuous thirties, I once got up to twelve points and was facing a ban. In these cases, you can plead 'Exceptional Hardship' and in the dock of the civil court at Market Harborough, having explained that I was in a 'long-running drama series on Radio 4', I felt the decision might be going my way when one of the magistrates leant across and whispered to her colleague, 'I think it's David!'

I wasn't banned, but driving for the next three years knowing that just one flash of a camera would mean the certain loss of my licence radically changed my driving behaviour.

As 'David' I've opened fetes, done after-dinner speaking, reviewed the papers on *Broadcasting House* and done a load of 'celebrity' TV game shows. It's also helped hugely when publicising my children's book, *Colin the Campervan*. This fame only goes so far though, and I'm never going to be asked to eat dead lizards in the jungle or go stir-crazy in *Big Brother*, to both of which I'd say 'Thank God' were it not for the huge piles of cash involved.

To be honest, I'm very happy with not being recognised in the street, although I do secretly relish occasional delicious moments like once when at a dinner party, having spent most of the evening chatting about anything but acting with a charming but rather tiddly countess who, over coffee, joined in someone's conversation about *The Archers* and announced loudly to the whole table, 'Oh my God, can you imagine actually meeting someone from *The Archers*? I mean, really, if I did I think I'd probably DIE!'

Travel journalism

After our *University Challenge* triumph – the Actors one in 2004, not the UEA debacle, I received an email from Frank Barrett, editor of the travel section of the *Mail on Sunday*. He was inviting me to join him for the annual Irish Tourist Board Pub Quiz, held between representatives of the press. The *Mail* had won the previous year, and were determined to do so again. I figured I'd just got lucky with *University Challenge* but Frank was insistent, and an *Archers* fan, so I felt I couldn't let him down.

We got to the final round. Sports. We were neck and neck with *The Times*, so every point counted. The final question was, 'What is the animal on the top of the Calcutta Cup?' This is the annual rugby match between England and Scotland for the oldest rugby trophy ever, and the animal is an elephant.

'Lion,' said Frank firmly.

'No, it's an elephant.'

'No, it's a lion, I can visualise it.'

'How can it be? It's Calcutta. India. If it was going to be a large cat it would be a tiger, but anyway it's not, cos it's an elephant.'

He looked at me viciously.

'Are you sure?'

'I'm absolutely sure.'

'An elephant?'

'An elephant.'

'Look, this is pretty crucial, you know, because we're neck and neck with . . .'

'Frank, it's an elephant.'

Grudgingly he wrote it down. It was an elephant. We won by one point.

'Can you write?' Frank asked.

'Yes.'

'Where in the world would you like to write about?'

'Wow. Well, I've always wanted to go back to the land of my birth. Tasmania.'

'Okay.'

When Frank says, 'Okay,' he means it.

A few months later, Judy and I flew business class to Tassie. Courtesy of the Tasmanian Tourist Board, we stayed in all the very best hotels, had amphibious plane trips that landed on narrow rivers, had zip-wire adventures, walked Maria Island, had two weeks' free car hire, and were shown the very spot where I was born – under a red Mazda in the Campbell Town hospital car park. Oh, and the food and wine were out of this world, and I was commissioned to write further travel articles. Not a bad result for an elephant!

Writing about that trip was easy, but the deal was to write about Sydney too, where we had a two-day itinerary, arranged by the NSW Tourist Board – a crammed seventy-two hours. Everything was painstakingly planned down to the last tiny detail. As it turned out, all went well but these tight itineraries can be a recipe for disaster: if everything goes well, all you ever feel is relief, but if the car breaks down, the hotel's half-built or a child suddenly goes cold turkey for wifi, you experience that dreadful frustration of having catered for every eventuality except what usually happens – Murphy's Law. I'm thinking of starting a company called 'Bentinck's Serendipity Tours': no expectations, so no disappointments.

We had an itinerary-free trip to Ireland when the boys were young, driving round the Ring of Kerry and just finding somewhere to stay each night. One night we saw a battered sign pointing towards the 'Portland Hotel'. Obviously, we had to stay there. They'd had a massive party the night before, so at dinner, when I asked for the wine list, the waiter pointed at a side table with two bottles sitting on it.

'What would you be wanting, the Blue Nun, or the French?'

When Will locked himself out of his room, the cheery and untroubled solution was to completely remove the French windows, retrieve the key, put the window back, then walk round to the door and unlock it.

Judy and I did a similar thing in Croatia once; Ryanair were offering flights to Trieste for 4p, so we just up and went, hired a car and simply drove south. When it got dark we looked for a hotel. Luckily the Serbo-Croat for hotel is *hotel* so asking directions was fine. One evening we clearly crashed a meeting of the local paramilitaries doing gun drill, which was exciting, but the wine choice was similar to Ireland: under the heading of 'Red Wine' was the single word, 'Merlot'.

This sort of adventure makes for fun copy in the paper, as does becoming a PADI qualified scuba diver in the Cayman Islands on your sixtieth birthday, but being sent off on a journalists' jolly to New Zealand in 2010 was an eye-opener. Travel journalists get treated like royalty, way ahead of an earl or an actor. The *Mail on Sunday* has the highest circulation of any paper in Britain, so a complimentary article about your hotel or restaurant is priceless advertising, and learning the tricks of the trade from my new seasoned professional friends was an education. Airline upgrades? Damn right, from Business to First on Etihad, which allows you to have a stand-up shower, starkers at 30,000 feet, an extraordinary experience, although getting back into T-shirt and jeans instead of flowing white robes is the equivalent of wearing a shell suit to a polo match.

I was in New Zealand with the bunch of real journos to tour the country's rugby stadia before the following year's Rugby World Cup. On the first day, we were given a choice: tour the vineyards on the islands north of Auckland, or fling yourself off the highest building in the southern hemisphere. I have a phobia of heights, which is odd as one of my childhood pleasures was climbing trees. In fact, the instant and categorical reply from all of us was: 'Vineyards.'

Two of the things that journalists and actors seem to have in common is getting full value out of a freebie and a taste for fine wine. Having spent the whole morning not spitting out any of the delicious samples, our defences were down when our young Kiwi guides suggested that not experiencing the Sky Tower's controlled wire SkyJump descent from 192 metres at 85 km/h was Pómmie wimping-out on a grand scale. 'Mate, we had a ninety-year-old granny do it last week!' So, pathetically we all succumbed.

My Dutch courage lasted until I was on the platform where, dressed in a superhero costume with full harness, I ventured out onto the windy diving board, mortality staring up at me from below. I heard a click as a carabiner was attached to my harness and, with a cheery pat on my back, I heard, 'All right, mate, you're good to go.' I was clinging on to the safety rail with the grip of a crocodile's jaw. All I had as assurance that I wasn't going to simply plummet to my death was the word of a Kiwi teenager. Mentally saying goodbye to all my family and friends I leapt into the void, fell for twenty feet . . . and stopped dead – for a photo opportunity! I was hanging in front of the café at the top of the tower, where safe people, sensible people, people who were drinking beer or coffee, could snap away at the rictus grins of terror on the faces of the mugs who thought this was a good idea. Then I fell again, 85 km/h straight down. And instead of splattering myself on the Antipodean pavement, I was brought gently to a halt, and landed delicately on my feet.

I have the film of it. I said one word, and it began with 'F'.

Inventions

When I announced to my father that I wanted to be an actor, he said, 'A freelance, eh? That's very brave.' I thought, brave? From a man who's been through a war, wounded twice and a POW? I just didn't get it. Now I do. He was talking about security – a proper job, a steady income and a decent pension at the end of it. These days the difference between freelance and employed is not so great, but it's meant that I've spent my whole adult life trying to come up with a business on the side, a lottery win – or an invention.

The best inventions are the simplest, as they are the most likely to find success – one-piece plastic moulds, like the book-holder-downer that fits on your thumb, the tennis-ball-thrower for walking the dog, or the cable tidy for phone chargers. If you can get the invention patented, it's even better as you're the only person allowed to make it. Hence 'The Hippo'.

As they grow, children get heavier. The 'terrible twos' can turn your delicate, angelic little baby into a lumpen refusenik who demands to be carried everywhere, especially when you're also toting five bags of shopping. When Will reached that age, I discovered that one of the things that men tend not to have is wide, child-bearing hips. I'm fairly strong but the dead weight of a child on your side is pretty heavy; I felt like I needed a sort of shelf – so I built one.

I made the first Hippo prototype out of wood, cardboard and coat-hanger wire, with a wide hessian strap to go over my shoulder. It worked, so then I made one out of wood, which was more comfortable but way too heavy. This was 1986 – long before the internet, and also pre-*Dragon's Den*, so finding out if there was anything like it on the market was much harder to do, but a couple of trips to Mothercare and John Lewis's baby department assured me there was a gap in the market, so I went to a patent agent.

The skill of drawing up a patent is to create an 'inventive step', that is, you have to cast your net as wide as possible so that no one can make a slightly different version of your idea, but at the same time not intruding on anything that has gone before. It's a real skill, and you pay for it. You also pay for the patents themselves. At the time, I was earning quite well, with *The Archers*, telly shows and commercials, and the money I could have put into savings accounts or pensions went into the patents.

Eventually, with the help of my brother-in-law John Emerson, I teamed up with one of the greatest industrial designers in the world, Sir Kenneth Grange, who had designed the InterCity 125, the first UK parking meters, Kenwood food mixers, Parker pens, London taxis and a host of other design classics. He took the concept and created a plastic mould, a beautiful lightweight design that worked perfectly.

By the time we'd finally got a product ready to pitch to manufacturers, the patents were about to need renewing, at a cost of £10,000, and I was no longer so flush. I was offered a one-off payment of that amount by a company and there was a chance that

I could have earned a percentage of every item sold in perpetuity, but I lost my nerve. This is why I'm not a businessman.

Kenneth included the Hippo many years later in an exhibition of designs that never got off the ground called *Those That Got Away*. With the patents lapsed, another company came in with a similar, and I have to say better, product, the Hippiechick, that you can still get today. Damn. It was fun while it lasted, though, and now I have a wall full of Hippos.

I had caught the inventing bug, though, and I carried on coming up with ideas. The next one was an orrery – well, sort of. An orrery is a mechanical representation of the solar system, with planets going around the sun on their unique orbits. Mine was a desktop object to show what part of the world was in sunlight.

My desire to invent has long been entwined with my passion for electrics and technology. From a very early age I used to wire things up, often with dangerous results. At boarding school, I took the power from the central light fitting and ran multiple lights around the room, twisting the wires together using Sellotape as insulation. When it fused the whole house, I was in serious trouble.

When computers came along, it was clear I was going to have to get involved. I wrote my first program within minutes of opening the box of my first computer, and I wrote my first website in 1996 – I couldn't understand why people were paying thousands or millions of pounds to people to write their 'Start-up Sites'. It was just HTML and I could write a site in a day, but as usual, I failed to monetise my talent and just made pin money from doing websites for friends. I bought a Psion 3a for its electronic diary and address book, but it came with a programming manual for its inbuilt language called OPL, which is a doddle. I typed in a sample program which converted miles to kilometres and started to expand it. Six months later I'd written an immensely complex program, called Conversion Calculator Pro, that converted absolutely everything to absolutely everything else. On Compuserve there was a thing called a Bulletin Board, and in the Psion section, people were posting their programs. I put up my Conversion Calculator, with a nag screen to encourage people to register for £10. Within a year it had become one of the most downloaded programs ever.

I also wrote an *Archers* adventure game in a weird language called Professional Adventure Writer, and missed another opportunity when I wrote a comprehensive relational database program called Agent that could be used to run a voiceover agency, but I only sold it to two companies. I wrote it for my then voiceover agent, Sheila Britten at Castaway and she continued to use it until she retired in 2012 – not bad for an Amstrad programme! I sold the PC version to another agency, Speakeasy, but maintaining the systems took up a lot of time, and as I was pretty busy acting at the time, I never got serious about selling it to anyone else.

I also came up with an early virtual reality concept that would be a strap-in fighter simulator that hurled you all around and upside down as you played. I worked out how this could be done, but it wouldn't fit in a bedroom. I have had other virtual reality ideas that lay dormant, and are now on the market courtesy of someone else.

I still think my 'Your Satnav' website concept is a good idea – it used to be possible to replace the generic voice of a satnav with one of your own, so you would use our app to record your daughter saying, 'Turn left, Daddy', etc. and we would then send you the code for TomTom, or Garmin, and you would have a personalised satnav. I don't know if it's still possible these days but, if so, go for it. As far as I know, no one's done that one yet.

I did create a little bit of a stir with Faceliftbook – a social networking site for the over-fifties that, following a chance joke at a dinner party just after I'd turned fifty, I created with a service called Ning. I put a link to it on Twitter, it got picked up by Christine Hamilton who had zillions of followers, and it suddenly took off. People really bought into the idea that this computer thing that our generation had created was now being completely taken over by our children, and we wanted a different place to play. However, the site was nothing like as sophisticated as Facebook and, of course, I didn't monetise the idea, so when Ning wanted to charge me an annual fee, I ditched it.

One of my ideas that I think could have a future is Minute Songs, an app for smartphones and a website where you can record or upload a song that is under a minute long. The idea is that this would appeal to the Twitter generation and be the musical equivalent of 140 characters: 'The Haiku of Music'. I'd often find, when I was writing a song, that once I'd done the first verse and chorus, that was enough. As ever, I got a job, put the idea on the back burner for a while and I ran out of steam. Interested? Let's do it!

Being David Archer: Rob and Helen

At the time of writing, the Rob and Helen story about domestic abuse has just reached its climax. Every now and then a real headline-grabber is needed to attract the next generation of listeners. There tends to be a perception that listening to *The Archers* is for old people, and indeed the demographic favours the over-thirties, so to stop it dying with a generation an injection of high drama is needed to up the profile.

When Sean O'Connor came in as the new editor in 2013, he followed through with his intention to make it more like Thomas Hardy, with a return to the traditional values of the programme and centring it on Brookfield, with Jill back at the heart of the story. However, Hardy didn't really do the kind of gentle, non-confrontational, happy tales of prize marrows and milking that are the familiar and beloved staple for most listeners: his books were in a way the *EastEnders* of their time, involving love, death, rivalry, deceit and shocking events. Sean is a great storyteller, so tales of the 'Great Flood', the will-they-won't they-move-north epic and the pressure on David and Ruth's marriage after Heather's death were like Marmite to the audience, loved by some, hated by others.

As Sean said in a *Feedback* interview, 'One thing that will always be true of *The Archers* – there is no consensus.' There really is no pleasing everyone, but the Rob and Helen plotline almost confounded that theory: it was the most intriguing story in the programme for years, brilliantly written and acted while bringing to the fore the little-discussed subject of emotional domestic abuse. While other stories dominated, in the background the listener was drip-fed the slow erosion of Helen's confidence and individuality, with Rob's charming but horrifically controlling dominance slowly undermining her entire personality. Then their story took centre stage, culminating in the stabbing, then her arrest, imprisonment and trial.

Of course, I am being hugely generous here because it meant that David and Ruth were almost unheard for months, and I was slowly going broke! But from the programme's point of view it was really remarkable, getting front-page headlines, dominating BBC Radio's output for months, and attracting so many donations for Refuge, the charity for domestic violence.

Relevant storylines in *The Archers* are nothing new and, after all, the raison d'être of the programme was to help farmers get the country fed after the war, dishing out propaganda and advice about modern farming techniques, which it continues to do. This, though, was different, and for me the most poignant reactions were from women who said that they had had no idea they were in such a relationship until the slow burn of the real-time story echoed the slowly dawning realisation that they were just like Helen – that's powerful storytelling.

Music

I suppose it must have all started because we had a piano in the house, and as a child I used to bash it. 'STOP BASHING,' my mother used to yell. Then I learned 'Chopsticks', so they arranged for me to have piano lessons. I still associate them with fear. When I'm standing in the wings waiting to go on stage, that terror conjures up sitting next to some fearsome gorgon of a music mistress waiting to pounce on my every mistake. All I remember of those lessons was scales, scales and more scales – and criticism. How that didn't put me off music for life I have no idea.

A teacher did manage to put me off being creative in another area. I still have a drawing of a robin that I did at Berkhamsted Junior School when I was about ten. It's a perfectly adequate drawing of a bird – with a beak, a red breast, wings and legs – instantly recognisable as a robin. Below this in red ink are the words: 'This is a very <u>BAD</u> drawing – 1/10.' I never drew again.

When I left Berkhamsted and went to Harrow, I stopped piano and took up the guitar. I tried guitar lessons for one term but found I was being taught classical Spanish guitar, which involved scales again, when all I wanted to learn were heavy-metal riffs and James Taylor. From then on, I learned from books and by ear.

It's said that there is a correlation between music and being good at accents and languages. I play mostly by ear, in the same way that I can hear an accent in my head and reproduce it. It's a gift, in the sense that being 'gifted' is something you're born with. It's far more laudable to become proficient by grinding hard work.

The first exercise I worked at for my own pleasure was a twelve-bar blues called 'Trouble in Mind' – the absurdity of a thirteen-year-old public schoolboy singing what was effectively a slave song is not lost on me. Now, in my sixties, still living with the daily insecurity of being a jobbing actor, blues songs resonate with just a little more validity; while remaining resolutely optimistic, I have had my black-dog days, and the blues satisfies a fundamental need in me. Being lost in music is amazing. When your hands are doing things over which you have no conscious control, other than simply feeling the music in your head, it is lovely.

At school, I attempted to make an electric guitar out of oak, but it was far too heavy. My lovely pa, who was terribly pro youth, gave me an electric guitar for my birthday, which was probably even heavier than the oak one I had abandoned. It was something out of the fifties, massive, horrible, with the thickest set of strings possible. I was barely able to hold down a chord, let alone bend the screaming solo riffs of my dreams out of it. It wasn't until I bought a Fender Strat with ultra-light strings that I finally realised how bloody easy it is to be a rock god. If you can look good at Air Guitar, that's all that's required – feedback, distort and howl-around do the rest.

Thankfully the hell of scales, plus my love of computers, ultimately reaped their reward when I found out about Musical Instrument Digital Interface (MIDI) and digital recording. This meant I could play piano without being able to play the piano. Not only the piano, but the entire orchestra. It's like being a musical god: just using a small musical keyboard, I could record multiple tracks of any instrument – drums, violins, brass, woodwind – all playing along together and sounding very like the real thing, just by knowing my scales from fear of a harridan's bollocking.

I became obsessed, playing around with more and more equipment and programs. Judy didn't see me in the evenings as I spent every available minute writing and recording songs. Why? Because I was going to make a fortune out of my smash hit Novelty Song, wasn't I? My model for success was Joe Dolce's 'Shaddap You Face' or Men at Work's 'Down Under'. If it could be a Christmas hit, so much the better. I wanted to be like Hugh Grant's dad in *About a Boy*, who lived off the royalties of his Christmas song for life, as did all his offspring.

I once found myself in the office of a music producer who sat and dutifully listened to my latest effort, 'Russian Rap', full of internal rhymes and clever comedy, three-part harmony and multi-tracked with the full band, all played by me. There was a pause.

'Tim,' he sighed, 'your education is standing in your way.'

The songs were part of the constant theme of my life: the need to make some money outside of acting which will keep some dosh coming in when I'm too old to act any more. So far, my songs, inventions, computer programming, website creation, ideas for apps, playwriting, book-writing, translations, lorry-driving and the rest haven't cracked it.

If they made a film of my life, the guy playing me would get paid more than I did living it. Hey ho, mustn't grumble. Music, as well as acting, has opened doors to friendships and more, and let's face it, guitars are sexy as hell.

However, you don't expect David Archer to be able to sing and play guitar.

I discovered this when I did my one-man show, when in between anecdotes I would sling my guitar round my neck and belt out ballads with my incredibly complex pre-recorded backing tracks. It slowly dawned on me that the only thing people had really come for was to hear about *The Archers*, and every time this bloke called Tim Bentinck, who they'd never heard of, slung his axe and started to warble, they'd switch off.

These days, I have decided to spare the nation and I just play for fun.

Being David Archer: The Great Flood

Regular listeners tend to be disappointed that I often don't know as much about what's going on as they do. That's really because I'm not a regular listener. I listen if it's on in the car or if I'm doing work around the house, but only occasionally do I put a note in the diary to listen to something special. One such occasion was the 'Great Flood'.

Judy and I sat down in front of the fire to listen to the omnibus edition on iPlayer through the stereo on good speakers. There had been some criticism that listening to the individual episodes was confusing, but the omnibus was really an hour and a quarter radio play, and it had everything. Even Judy was in tears at the end. Creating epic soundscape audio drama is usually the preserve of the likes of Dirk Maggs but this was a technical masterpiece, and the production team of director Sean O'Connor, engineer Andy Partington and writer Tim Stimpson deserve enormous credit. When Charlie Thomas

(Felix Scott) went underwater and was pulled out by Adam (Andrew Wincott), there was a genuine feeling that we were nearly drowning with him.

I remember the scene when Eddie was down the culvert – Trevor Harrison had a nasty backache and used the pain to add realism to the scene. He was on his knees with his head between two concrete breeze blocks, close to the microphone, hurting badly, while Liza, the spot-effects person, poured water over his head – now that's commitment. I was on a separate mike shouting encouragement. Listening to it we heard a very wet and pained Eddie down below and David clearly above him, which is an extraordinary effect to achieve in radio; far and near, left and right is easy but up and down is much harder.

Also, I wasn't used to hearing it in stereo, as for some unfathomable reason the DAB broadcast of the programme, which I get in the car, is in mono, which makes a nonsense of the amount of time and effort we put into the soundscape we try to create. Stereo, eyes closed, big speakers with the sound turned up – better than a movie any day!

It's often the case that Ambridge has its own microclimate, and while the village suffered terrible inundation, the rest of the country was puzzlingly flood-free. It was an interesting call by Sean to run this story, and had to do with something the programme tries hard to avoid – bandwagonning. The previous year the UK had suffered from severe flooding with loss of life and the ruination of homes and businesses. If Sean had run the story then, it would have seemed trite and insensitive when real tragedies were happening around the country. By telling the story the following year, they were able to do what *The Archers* does best: combine drama with information and suggest causes and lessons learned from the real thing, without being perceived to be exploiting genuine tragedy.

In order to make everything and everybody sound wet, there was a lot of water in the studio. Signs were put up saying 'Caution. You are now entering a Splash Zone!' I have pictures of us all dressed in hats, Barbours and wellies, standing in huge buckets of water – for once our workplace looked more like a damp farmyard than a recording studio.

When the studio at the Mailbox was built, they included a huge picture window to the corridor outside, the idea being that the public would be able to see us at work. They could have saved a lot of money by asking the actors first, as the curtain has remained resolutely closed since day one – there is no dignity involved when standing in front of a microphone, wearing a silly hat and standing in a bucket.

The title

So there you are, as Churchill said, 'buggering on' like everyone else, and then suddenly you're a lord. It's quite a peculiar experience.

If a title does not come directly from your father, you have to prove it. When the last Duke of Portland died in 1990, my pa was theoretically then the Earl of Portland, Viscount Woodstock and Baron Cirencester, but in order to convince the College of Heralds, he had to prove that all the other branches of the family, going back ten generations, had died out, and that some South American De Los Bentinck wasn't going to suddenly appear claiming his seat in the Upper House. Pa knew that there was no material benefit coming, but he was fed up with English toffs saying, 'Oh, he calls himself a count,' when in fact we were one of only two families entitled to do so. Most of all, he wanted a political platform to warn the world of the impending environmental catastrophe that was inevitable unless humankind, instead of putting its short-term best interests first, chose those of the planet.

Proving that people really had died when they were meant to have is more difficult than you might think. My father once found himself in a graveyard in Malta, where the headstones of the British had been torn out by angry Maltese and stored in a shed. He was looking for a certain Cavendish Cavendish-Bentinck, who was said to have drowned at sea, his washed-up body buried somewhere on the island. Pa never found him. He gave me various research tasks, and I remember sitting in the Reading Room of the British Library, feeling very Holmesian, flicking through a book, looking for a name that, if found, would mean I was a lord.

Eventually, after a long time and much expense, Pa took his seat in the House of Lords. He would come up from Devon on the train and stay at the Lansdowne Club. The job is unpaid and he was always broke, but he never claimed expenses. I get furious when I hear of lords' fraudulent claims as the whole point about being a lord used to be that it was beneath you to claim for things that you could perfectly well afford, so no one did. Or as Lady Anne Cavendish-Bentinck said when I asked her what it meant to be a lord, 'It means not being a shit.'

The whole family was there to support my father when he made his maiden, and only, speech in 1993, urging the noble lords to 'keep their green hats always on', and we were enormously proud of him – I gave him a lucky sixpence. He made a tremendous speech about the environment in Trafalgar Square in 1971 and his views were always ahead of and therefore out of kilter with everyone else. In his obituary, he was described as an 'intellectual eccentric', but everything he believed in and railed about has come true. As he predicted, his once alternative views on pollution, carbon emissions and climate change have become mainstream worldwide political policy. In that speech, he said: 'We know that if civilisation and population are allowed to continue unmodified on their present expansionist courses, they will cause an ecological catastrophe which will destroy that civilisation and most of our descendants. And yet we do nothing. Why is that?'

His novel *Isoworg* – the International Society for World Government – starred the Bond-like hero, Thorne. The book was written in the mid-sixties and within the first two chapters he foresees: the internet, *'Thorne was connected to a network of computers that housed the sum of the world's knowledge'*; the iPhone, *'he communicated with it via a radio device the size of a cigarette case'*; and Wikileaks, *'the job of Isoworg spies was to discover the secrets of all the world's governments and publish them in the newspapers'*. He certainly didn't think he was eccentric, he just knew that he was right and everybody else was wrong. It turned out that he *was* right.

The great sadness was that he only had four years to live, pancreatic cancer getting him seventeen years after he'd quit cigarettes with the words, 'Giving up smoking is like giving up life.' I was devoted to him, not only because, from the age of thirteen, he was the only parent I had, but also because he was the most extraordinary person I have ever met. I've spent my life hoping he would be proud of me.

When he became the Earl of Portland, I was given the courtesy title of Viscount Woodstock, which for someone of my generation, brought up on the Woodstock festival, was about the coolest title you could possibly have, but for a jobbing actor in a left-wing meritocracy, it was also fraught with danger. When Pa died and I became the 12th Earl of Portland, it was even worse. I imagined the press getting hold of it: 'Lord David Archer takes his seat' . . . 'Not another Archer in the Lords!' So, I kept my head down and never spoke in the House.

The preconceptions are completely understandable; if, on day one of a new stage job, someone had told me that one of the cast was a duke, or an earl, or a viscount, I wouldn't think that they were a proper actor at all. I'd imagine them tooling down from their estate in the chauffeur-driven Bentley and having a go at 'this acting lark' in a painfully amateur and condescending way, probably because they'd bribed the producer. That was my terror. You're only as good as your last job, and if anyone thought that of me, that last job would be exactly that, the last. So, I tried to keep as quiet about the title as I possibly could. Thank God for 'Mind the Gap' – you don't do that sort of job unless you need the work.

Let me dispel a few common myths. 'When you're a lord you can . . .'

1. '. . . get a table at a fancy restaurant.' False. Firstly, whenever I have rung a restaurant, no one has said, 'Are you a lord? If not, I can't help you.' I have to confess that right at the beginning it went to my head slightly. I had a credit card with 'The Earl of Portland' on it until someone said, 'Is that a pub?' And the first and last time I tried the restaurant trick, I was brought soundly down to earth. I tried to book a table at the Ivy and was told that the waiting list was three weeks. I rang back ten minutes later with a much posher voice and said, 'Oh, hello, it's Lord Woodstock here, I'd like to book a table for two for tomorrow night.' 'I'm very sorry, *my lord*, but at the moment the waiting list for the Ivy is six months.' Wrist duly slapped. Whoever still thinks that 'Everybody loves a Lord' is probably a hermit living on Sark. I was seriously regretting having booked a package holiday with the title, when the rep started calling out the names of the tour group at the airport. We would be with these people for the next ten days – and they'd hate us from the off. Luckily 'Viscount Woodstock' came out as 'Visco-nut and Wodstick', which is what Judy has called me ever since.

2. '. . . get a first-class upgrade on a plane.' You're far more likely to be asked to pay for an upgrade than anyone else because you're a flaming lord, and can *bloody well afford it!* Also flight bookings can't cope with titles. On my boarding card, my name is often given as 'MR THEEARLOFPORT'.

Why people spend huge sums of money on bogus titles or 'Lordships of the Manor' I can't imagine. Mind you, Americans go weak at the knees for a lord. I once had a bizarre time in Miami Beach when I was doing a lecture tour on 'English Eccentrics' for the English Speaking Union – people came out in their millionaire facelifted droves to see me. For them, it was like being in Downton for the evening. They were expecting someone in gaiters, preferably beheaded, so I was a confusingly modern anachronism. When I met them at the yacht club before the talk, they'd brought along a resident English 'lord' to check that I was the real deal. He said 'toilet' very early into the cross-examination and scuttled away when I gave him a knowing look – I thought it unfair to ruin his gig.

I don't think I've ever made a single penny out of being an earl, but there are some advantages. For a start, you get your own frigate.

Each Type 23 Duke Class frigate of the Royal Navy has an affiliation with the family of the ship's name, hence when the first HMS *Portland* for sixty years was commissioned in 2001, Judy and I were invited to begin our association with the ship. I was asked to design a flag based on the family coat of arms and colours, and I also told them of the family motto, 'Craignez Honte' (Fear Dishonour), under which she sails to this day. The strangeness of being both an earl and an actor is that in the morning, before heading down to the commissioning ceremony at Portsmouth, I had been doing a radio commercial for Finish dishwasher tablets. I arrived at the recording in a smart suit.

Someone asked, 'Off to a wedding?'

'No, actually I'm going to the commissioning of a Royal Navy frigate.'

'Blimey. Why?'

'Because it's mine.'

Being piped aboard is a privilege. I grew up on the Hornblower books and am a devotee of Patrick O'Brian's tales of Aubrey and Maturin, so being a part of the birth of a Royal Navy frigate was beyond my wildest dreams. We inspected the ship's company. Lined up on the helicopter deck, they were all at attention as the Admiral of the Fleet, Vice-Admiral, others with scrambled egg hats on, the ship's captain and me, the Earl, walked up and down, chatting to the sailors of the first company of HMS *Portland*. This was all new to me. The Admiral stopped and turned to one of the men. So did the Vice-Admiral, so did all the others, so I had to as well. It's at this point that you realise why Prince Charles always fiddles with his cuffs. I asked a sailor what his job on board was.

'Communications technician, sir!'

Desperate to say something vaguely intelligent, I imagined what might happen if all your sophisticated electronics had been disabled and you were back to basics.

'Do you still learn Morse code?' I thought this was pretty clever. He looked at me as though I was the most stupid, inbred, brainless twerp he'd ever encountered.

'No, sir,' he replied witheringly, 'we use semaphore.'

Judy and I, and the boys, have been welcomed aboard many times since for social events and for 'Thursday War', when simulated engagements are carried out. For the 'war', our arrival on board was very different. We were greeted at the quayside by two Pacific 24 rigid inflatable fast-attack boats and given all-in-one survival suits to don over our clothes. We then headed out to sea to rendezvous with the ship – at full speed. We came alongside doing a good twenty knots and they lowered a rope ladder down the side. I think it was a bit of a test to see what this posh actor chappie was made of. We were convinced we were going to end up in the briny, but despite looking a bit like Teletubbies, we made it!

We've spent the night on board at sea, and we could not be more impressed and humbled. The young, now 40 per cent female crew are hugely brave, bright, efficient and friendly, and I feel like a child playing Cowboys and Indians by comparison.

Being David Archer: Pip, Josh and Ben

As the father of two sons, the closest thing to daughters I've ever known in real life are my nieces: Anna's daughter Sophie, at the moment studying at LAMDA on the way to a promising acting career, and Sorrel's twins Melanie and Amelia, both the best working mums in the world. Gorgeous girls all three, but I've never known that very special father–daughter relationship. David's bond with Pip is the closest I'll get until I have a daughter-in-law, and it has been an education. Nothing I have learned as the father of boys is in any way relevant to bringing up a daughter. They don't do as they're told and their world is a closed book. I've always joked that I'm so glad I never had a daughter because I wouldn't have been able to cope with the boyfriends, and in the ghastly Jude, and now Toby Fairbrother, all my fears have been confirmed, but I also think it would have made me a more rounded parent, so for this gift of a fictitious and complex daughter, I am eternally grateful.

There have been three Pips. The first one was a loudspeaker, as were all our fictional children. Before they were allowed to come and work in the studio, the children would be pre-recorded at home by recording assistant Sonja Cooper. She would sit with them and patiently get them to say the line in the way she wanted, and after multiple attempts finally come up with a selection of takes that would fit. The chosen take would then be played in to us on loudspeakers in the studio. This requires a special technique – instead of reacting, we had to, as it were, *pre*-act because you knew how the child was going to say the line, and it was the same each time. When they were tiny, it was just a gurgle coming out of the speaker and we would cuddle a pillow. I still have the manky old one I also used in my one-man show. Once, after a scene of mutual cooing over baby Pip with Paddy (Jill), I drop-kicked it across the studio. Paddy nearly had a fit.

After the pre-recorded Pips came Rosie Davies, then Helen Monks and now the wonderfully monikered Daisy Badger. Helen is a brilliant comic actor, as shown so well in a fat suit and Wolverhampton accent as Germaine in Caitlin Moran's *Raised by Wolves*. As usual, some listeners loved her, others thought her voice too high and her accent too West Midlands. When Daisy took over in 2014, the contrast couldn't have been greater, as Daisy's voice is very different – more mature and more RP. She's taller too which means I can stand up straight. My son changed as well when Josh also grew about a foot overnight from Cian Cheesbrough into lanky Angus Imrie. I have to admit that I had been a giant in my own family, as Felicity, Helen and Cian are all normal height, while I'm something of a cloud breather. Now it's Flick who feels she's in a family of giants – I think we should buy her some high-heeled wellies for Christmas.

At the moment, Ben is the unheard one. A loudspeaker for years, he then appeared for a while in the form of a bubbly lad called Thomas Lester but has yet to be cast in his adult form. Such is the nature of this ongoing saga, he may well be running the farm in another six months.

And now, sometimes almost word for word, David is having the same arguments with Pip and Josh as Phil used to have with David, and Dan with Phil – the same generational conflict, the arrogance of youth, new farming practices versus the tried and tested traditional techniques, and, charmingly, sometimes calls from younger voices to return to some of the old ways, putting the environment before profit, exactly as my own father had done for real in the 1970s.

One of Jill's lines in the clip we did in front of the Queen was, 'There's always been Archers at Brookfield.' What if Pip marries a Fairbrother – will it become *The Fairbrothers*? Over Jill's dead body, I think. John Peel wanted it to be renamed *The Grundys*. Or maybe Josh or Ben will want the farm and there'll be an inheritance struggle with Pip, just like we had with Kenton, Shula, David and Elizabeth. Whatever the future holds, one thing is for sure, for every listener who approves of the story, there'll be another who thinks it's rubbish, but I hope listeners keep shouting at the radio for many years to come.

An earl abroad

In the year 2000 we had a family adventure. To date, it was the most extreme example of the complete 'otherness' of possessing a title. August and September 2000 were two quite extraordinary months that culminated in an experience in Jamaica that almost no one outside the royal family will ever have. All as a result of inheriting a title from a distant cousin. It brought home quite how odd it is being a jobbing actor and a hereditary peer at the same time.

It had started in France. We'd hired an old mill house that slept nine – pool, pond, streams, etc. and had some close friends to stay. An *Archers* episode clashed with the flight so Judy and the boys flew out, while my friend Noël and I drove down the following day – twelve hours solid through the night. In ten days, we made a spoof Jackie Chan movie with the boys as Jasper Chan and his trusty sidekick Wilbur Force. Judy played harem queen Darling Jeeling. The other cast included Noël's wife and son, Sarah and Jack, old chum Jon and my sister Sorrel came in the second week and my other sister Anna, her partner Arnold and daughter Sophie came for a day. All were used in the film. We returned via Paris and Parc Astérix. I have been on the Goudurix. I know terror.

When we got back I had a week's *Archers* in Birmingham. I then flew to New York where I was collected in a limo and driven to the Holiday Inn, Yonkers. The next morning a talkative cabbie took me to Pearson Education in White Plains, where I was seated in a tiny office with a blue screen taped on the wall behind me and lights were shone at me for eight hours while I sight-read on autocue a grammar guide for an interactive educational CD-ROM. To this day, I have no idea why I couldn't have done that in a tiny office in the UK. At the end of the day I went back to the Holiday Inn with another talkative cabbie and ended up eating a hamburger in the bar with an even more talkative travelling jewellery salesman called Joe. We were then joined by a talkative tart who suggested a threesome. I honestly couldn't take the talking and went to bed alone.

While in New York, I visited old haunts from working there in the 1970s and found myself in the Manhattan Mall where I bought some soft loafers and a pair of Sta-Prest™ cream trousers – I had Jamaica in mind . . .

Two years earlier, I had received a letter from a man called Earl Levy (Earl is his first name, not his title), a Jamaican property developer, asking me to come to Jamaica as the Earl of Portland to endorse some building project that he was doing. The parish was called Portland, and it was named after Henry Bentinck, 1st Duke of Portland, a distant cousin, who had been the Governor of Jamaica for six years in the 1790s. I was suspicious, and when the *Daily Mail* rang up to ask me about it, I was flippant, which earned me a ghastly article sounding like I was broke and desperate for money. I heard nothing more and presumed that Earl Levy had read said article and thought *not a proper earl.*

A year later I got another letter, apologising profusely for the delay, with beautifully laid-out plans for the regeneration of the bay of Port Antonio in Portland, and an itinerary of things we were to do on our week-long trip, all expenses paid, to Jamaica.

So my Sta-Prest™ trousers, loafers and I caught the red-eye to London. I went to Amsterdam the next day for three days to celebrate a friend's fiftieth birthday, came back to London on Monday to re-voice St Peter in a TV movie called *Saul of Tarsus*, went with Kerry Shale that night to see Otis Lee Crenshaw at the Jazz Café in Camden, played a Catholic priest on *The Armando Iannucci Shows* on Tuesday, and flew to Jamaica with Judy, Jasper and Will on Wednesday.

That last section of the sentence sounds straightforward, but it wasn't. We had four free first-class return tickets to Kingston, courtesy of Air Jamaica. However, as luck would have it, that week the Air Jamaica 747 was being serviced, so we were on a chartered Belgian 767 (two engines not four) with a Swiss crew and staff, and one Air Jamaica stewardess who sat the entire way in the front seat of first class and got the food before we did. The plane eventually took off seven hours late. Four of those hours were spent on the tarmac.

Problems encountered before the Belgian 'City Bird' took off:

1. Nose wheel needs changing. 3 hours.

2. PA system not working. 2 hours.

3. After boarding and taxi-ing to runway, warning light flashes briefly signifying possible starter motor fault. Regulations require return to departure gate.

4. Tow truck to get us back to departure gate attached to front wheel breaks down and bends connecting rod – can't detach from wheel so stuck. 2 hours.

5. Panicky passenger starts shouting: 'WHAT IS WRONG WITH THIS PLANE? THIS PLANE IS NOT SAFE. WE ARE ALL GOING TO DIE. MY WHOLE FAMILY IS ON THIS PLANE. I AM NOT GOING TO SACRIFICE MY FAMILY. WHY ARE YOU TRYING TO KILL MY FAMILY?'

6. Jasper has had enough and bursts into tears, needs comforting. I recognise David Baddiel. He and I help calm things down. Baddiel is baffled by my mumbling about being a Catholic priest one minute, then being . . .

We finally took off and were served alcohol for the first time. The Swiss crew would have been crap on a sixty-minute trip to Brussels but a nine-hour transatlantic flight was beyond them. Even in first class the seats were like rock and I don't remember the food. Belgian. Probably chips and mayonnaise. I didn't sleep as I was intent on swatting up on Jamaican history.

On the tarmac in Kingston, I was walking from the plane when an airline official asked me, 'Are you from London?' so after thirteen hours of Swiss service I answered rather tersely, 'Of course,' and walked on. She started talking to Judy, who called me back. It turned out she'd said, 'Are you Lord Portland?' Profuse apologies. Not a good start.

We were fast-tracked through passport control and customs, and with a cheery wave to Baddiel, who was in a long queue, we were met at the baggage carousel by Earl Levy and his wife Beverley. It was a further hour till all our bags, and Judy's hats, arrived.

Earl was short and wide, silver hair and glasses, a slightly sensuous mouth and Jamaican accent. He was of Spanish/Scottish descent and his family had been in Jamaica for 300 years. Beverley was charm itself. We felt welcome.

Finally, we walked out into the Jamaican night, the air filled with the smell of small fires, humidity and heat, and were met by a white stretch limo that only just fited in the airport car park. This was more to do with the size of the car park than the size of the limo, but it was very long and the boys perked up. We drove with Earl and Beverley through the evening to our hotel for the night, before the journey over the mountains the next day to Port Antonio in the parish of Portland. We arranged to meet the following morning to go and visit the Governor of Jamaica. We, jetlagged and knackered, hit the hay immediately. I, however, having slept badly for a few nights and jetlagged from New York and now jetlagged back the other way, didn't sleep a single wink.

I had a long swim and lots of coffee in the morning and hoped that that would cure it, but it didn't really, I was feeling very spacy. I put on the Sta-Prest™ bought on Broadway, the handmade blue blazer that earned me such derision in *Night Must Fall*, suede shoes from *Casualty*, a $100 shirt from Palm Beach and an old Harrovian tie. Judy looked like an English rose with a brilliant hat. The boys were boiling so they were in white shirts and trousers. I realised this was not going to be the informal chat over coffee that I had imagined when the limo, having negotiated the long winding drive, pulled up in front of Government House, where a reception committee and the whole Jamaican press and camera crews were waiting to greet us. The driver got out, went around to the boot, got out a red carpet and unrolled it up the steps to where the governor was waiting. It was rather like doing something from the Armando show, but this time it was for real.

We were ushered into a large reception room with three huge sofas and large French windows, all open. Despite the breeze and the early hour, I started to sweat. Just as I found on *By the Sword*

Divided, once my shirt had saturated it was better because the wetness was cooling, but my face was completely soaked. After initial pleasantries, I was introduced to Bev Cook who presented me with her book, *The Maroon Story*, a history of the Jamaican Maroons who escaped slave communities to live in the hills and resist the British. We stood in the centre of the room while she delivered a prepared speech that blamed the white man and the aristocracy in particular for all that was wrong with Jamaica. She told me in so many words that my wealth(!) came from the sweat, toil, torture and death of her slave forebears, and her book would give me a better idea of who I was, who she was, and what the hell I was doing there in the first place.

I had to answer, in front of two video cameras from Jamaican TV, reporters, Earl Levy, the Governor, Bev, my family, etc. Luckily I had looked up the Maroons on the internet, so I was relatively clued up. I did a lot of 'had no idea of the connection with my family', a great deal of 'How fascinating, I shall read it with enormous interest', a fair amount of 'my deep gratitude to Earl Levy and Air Jamaica for inviting me', and a smattering of 'I was Joan Armatrading's brother's best man so I'm not like the kind of earl who knows nothing of black culture . . .' This probably would have sounded patronising if they'd ever heard of Joan or Tony Armatrading, but they hadn't.

We were then shown around and given the history of the place, which was fascinating. At one point, the Governor said I sounded a bit like a Jamaican – the improv was slipping and I reverted to Prince Charles mode sharpish. I thought that was the end of the official functions. How wrong I was.

A limo arrived to drive us over the mountains. As we wound our twenty-foot absurdity through shanty towns and isolated shacks, the reaction veered between serious aggression and stoned welcome.

We arrived at Trident Castle, which we thought was a hotel but turned out to be Earl Levy's personal folly: an enormous, white-painted, twenties-built, eclectic beauty. Four guest rooms, each one different, and each with a theme. Our bedroom was the size of a large London flat with en-suite, squash-court-size bathroom. We couldn't stay long though. The Titchfield School Choir was waiting to sing for us, so we hurriedly got the boys into suits and got back into the limo.

As we rounded the corner to the school, we were greeted by a sign saying 'Titchfield School'. Underneath it was the Bentinck Cross, our heraldic cross. This was getting weird. We were greeted by the school's head and teachers, and again all the Jamaican press and two TV cameras. We were taken on a tour by two beautiful young girls who related the history of the school, which was in an old British fort, and we were shown the cannon and the dormitory buildings that now house the classrooms. It was a sobering sight to see such well-dressed, well-behaved teenagers with so few resources. It made me ashamed to think of the state of schools back home. Their school ties had Bentinck crosses on them too. I presented them with a framed print of the Marquis of Titchfield that I'd brought from home, and that had somehow survived the Belgian City Bird.

We stood in the sweltering sun for fifteen minutes while the choir sang, 'When the Going Gets Tough, the Tough Get Going' and I'd have happily stood there for an hour. It was beautiful. Four-part harmony and counterpoint. I want to record them. They'd be number one.

By this time, I was starting to feel extremely weird. I hadn't slept for seventy-two hours and my brain wasn't functioning properly. However, instead of heading gratefully for the castle, we were taken to the main civic building in the town centre to re-enact the signing of a peace treaty in 1846 between the Duke of Portland and the Maroons, who had been waging guerrilla warfare on the British for a century. I am the Duke's third cousin nine times removed, so not much of a link there, but despite my explanation to Earl Levy at the very beginning, I was seen as his direct descendant.

The Colonel of the Maroons, the MP for Portland East, the MP for Portland West, a few other guys in shades and gold watches and I re-enacted the signing and posed for the cameras. Then I was brought forward for the TV cameras and asked, 'So, Lord Portland, what are you doin' here?' This was accompanied by the *tooth suck*. Okay. What the hell *am* I doing here? I dried up at this point. The brain wasn't working, I was operating on my last vestige of mental capacity, and was being asked the *one thing I couldn't answer*.

He asked *me*, I thought, looking wildly at Earl, who brilliantly saved the day by giving me a three-point prompt: redevelopment of area, ancestral link, Bentinck cross on school ties. I compared them favourably to my own boys' ties, got a laugh, started to warm to it. Five minutes later, I was flying and it all sounded good, but I've seen the footage and careful editing could make me look either like a heart-warmingly human, concerned, knowledgeable, dignified aristocrat – or an inbred idiot.

That night I slept, and slept, and slept.

Halfway through the most glorious breakfast on the sunny terrace above the rocky seashore the next morning, Earl announced the arrival of the national TV crew who wanted to do an interview with me. Slightly better prepared, I had finally got to grips with what I really *was* doing there, and said that I'd do all I could to raise awareness of the regeneration projects in tourism in the area, specifically the dredging of the harbour to allow big cruise ships, and the building of hotels and tourist facilities. I also kind of intimated that the image of the Earl of Portland being supportive of the County of Portland would lend said county more credence with investors. This was all stuff I'd gleaned from Earl the previous night, shortly before passing clean out over brandies.

We swam that morning in the Blue Lagoon, except it wasn't blue. It was thick brown due to the recent rains. We couldn't see our hands in front of us it was so muddy, but that helped make the idyll a bit more real.

In the evening, there was a massive party in our honour. All of Jamaican society was there and I found myself flirting wildly with Errol Flynn's widow, Patrice, at seventy-three still formidably sexy and redolent of that old Hollywood excess. In this slightly Deco castle, we could have been in a black-and-white movie together and Bogart could easily have approached us with a whimsical line. Instead, a different Errol appeared: Errol Ennis, the MP for Portland West. He was an imposing figure, six foot four with a Stetson hat.

'So Lord Portland, your wife tells me you an actor.'

'That's right, I am.'

'Mm-hm. What sort an actor?'

'Well, everything really, I do theatre, TV, films, voiceovers, improv, radio, you name it.'

'Uh-huh.'

There was something about Errol that told me he didn't buy into this Earl of Portland thing. The only Earl he knew in Portland was his friend and my host Mr Earl Levy, and I could sense that Errol was here to suss me out.

'I've been in a radio series called *The Archers* for the last sixteen years . . .' I volunteered in a vain attempt to big myself up.

'You in *The Archers*?' His eyes opened.

'Yes.'

'Who you play in *The Archers*?'

'David.'

'You David Archer?'

'Yes.'

'Ha!' He turned around, bent down, slapped himself three times on the thigh, then turned back to me.

'You know when I was in Wembley, '82 to '93, I never missed an episode!'

We got on like a house on fire after that. Great guy. I was glad that he liked me for what I did, rather than what I supposedly was, and I think he was glad that I didn't fit the cliché of what he'd expected.

On the next day, we found ourselves, along with an affable, humorous, Scottish attaché, being driven in a British Embassy Range Rover, with Union flags flapping on each side, to be shown the regeneration that had already begun in St Antonio. A large friendly crowd was gathered beneath the canopy of a petrol station because of the tumultuous rain, and I made a speech from a balcony on the other side of the road. By this time, I'd got it down pat and suddenly understood the whole thing of what it must be like to be a politician. Judy looked gorgeous in another wonderful hat, the boys had been stunned into an understanding that this was a bit serious and were on top form. We looked the business.

I was soon touring a house that had been newly reconstructed to the way it was in the eighteenth century, and was crowded with dignitaries. Emboldened by my new confidence in my role, when I was handed a guitar by someone who had seen from my website that I can play, I accepted the challenge.

'What you going to play?'

'Well, I think I should sing some reggae.'

'Bob Marley?'

'No, this is one of mine. It's called "Easy Money".'

And in that week's 'Hangin' Out' section of the *Sunday Gleaner*, there's a photo of me with axe slung low, in full voice, and with Portia Simpson Miller, the future first female Prime Minister of Jamaica, looking on in bemusement. The article begins, 'The Earl of Portland, an accomplished guitarist, sings reggae . . .'

Now that's a clipping to cherish.

As for the disadvantages of a title, people do have preconceptions, which I completely understand, but when you don't know that *they* know about the title, it can be tough.

For instance, the great adventure on the Australian Tourist Board ad had a downside. I like to think of myself as a 'Good Company Member' – someone who works hard, is generous and trustworthy, generally the kind of person who's fun to be on tour with. That's the image you want as an actor because the opposite is what is known in the trade as an arse.

On the Australian job there was something wrong from day one. There's an Aussie adage that goes, 'If we're not taking the piss out of you, it means we don't like you.' And they weren't taking the piss. We toured Australia for four weeks, being filmed in all the most exotic locations the country has to offer. People were perfectly polite, but I never felt included, wasn't asked out with the crew in the evening, never felt part of the team. I tried and tried but couldn't break through. On the last night, there was a wrap party and we all got pretty legless.

Late in the evening one of the sparks said to me, 'So, I hear you're a fucking lord?'

'How did you know that?'

'Everyone knows it. You're gonna have to make your mind up, mate, you can either be an actor or a fucking lord, you can't be both.'

Turned out the producer was a friend of my sister-in-law, who had inadvertently spilled the beans. If I'd have known I could have diffused the situation by explaining where the title had come from and who I really was.

So you might well ask, 'What did you do with your privileged position of power?'

Well, when I took my seat in the House of Lords in 1997, I knew that the large majority of hereditary peers would be thrown out within the next few years. My dilemma was, do I become a politician and abandon acting, just to lose that position almost immediately? Or do I pretend it never happened and just take people to lunch in the Peers' Dining Room occasionally?

As a cross-bencher I was approached by the Liberal Democrats to join their party, and schmoozed by a number of peers who wanted my vote on various issues. I felt an onerous responsibility. I was torn between a sense of duty to continue what my father had started, and my own survival. I've always believed that if you're going to do something, you should do it properly, but I've never wanted to be a politician. The truth is that while I care passionately about a number of things, I believe that actors shouldn't use the accident of fame to presume they have a mandate to spout about political matters they've only read in the newspapers. We shouldn't pretend we know any more about a subject, or are any more important, than someone banging on in the Horse and Crown. The only people from my profession who have the right to be taken seriously about politics are Glenda Jackson, who gave up the business for twenty-three years while she was an elected MP, and more recently my friend Tracy Brabin, who stepped in to become an MP after the tragedy of the murder of Jo Cox.

My views on hereditary power are divided. On the one hand, the idea that you should be able to decide government policy because of an accident of birth is utterly absurd. On the other hand, when they got rid of the old peers, they threw something out with the bathwater that I'm not sure has been replaced by the new system's babies: duty. In Thomas More's *Utopia*, the author floats the idea that anyone who seeks political power should automatically be disqualified from holding it. This simply doesn't hold up nowadays. I would hope that the vast majority of people who go into politics are there out of a genuine altruistic desire to make a difference, and deserve nothing but respect, but to quote Lord Acton, in 1887, 'Power tends to corrupt, and absolute power corrupts absolutely. Great men are almost always bad men.' I think I'd rather be told what to do by someone who didn't want to tell me, but thought it was right, than someone who made up policy in order to keep their seat.

The old hereditaries didn't come down to London and work long hours over tortuously dull documents of legislation for no reward because they wanted to, but because their fathers had told them that they *had* to; it was their duty. Present incumbents might tell me that this spirit survives, and if so then I stand corrected, but what we have now is still not a democratic alternative.

Power is sexy. I had no idea that was true until I entered the Upper House like a new boy on his first day at school only to be immediately treated like a house prefect, called 'M'Lord', respected, taken seriously and listened to. When it was taken away, I felt a palpable sense of loss. I was only there three years and I never gave a speech. Imagine what it must be like for a lifelong politician who is put out to grass. It must be like being sent to rehab after decades of intravenous drug use.

I've been invited to two royal garden parties at Buckingham Palace; one was as 'The Actor Who's in *The Archers*', the other as

'The Earl of Portland'. I'm prouder of my work than I am of my title. If the inheritance of an earldom from a distant cousin had carried with it the responsibilities of running an estate, or the duties of a position of power in the government, I hope I would have risen to the challenge and fulfilled the requirements that came with the job; but, as Stephen Fry once said when I did take him to lunch in the Peers' Dining Room, 'Your problem, Tim, is that you have a title, but you aren't entitled to anything.' And that's it in a nutshell.

The only time the title ever gets used is for charitable work and, even then, people are more impressed by me waffling about Ambridge than they are by the presence of a turfed-out peer.

Being David Archer: And finally . . .

There's a group of listeners called 'Archers Anarchists' whose conceit is that the programme is a documentary: there are no actors and everything that happens is real. In their book, there is a page devoted to each character. It takes the mickey out of each one of us, and their treatment of David is no exception. The last line of the entry, though, has always pleased me, ' . . . still, at least he has a good shout on him'.

It isn't real, and we are all actors, but 'Being David Archer' is in some ways like having an alter ego. It gives me an idea of what it's like to be a farmer, and I'm humbled by that, as they lead a much tougher life than I do. By 'farmer', of course I mean the people who get up at five and get their hands dirty. They are at the mercy of nature and the weather, supply and demand, imports, radiation from Chernobyl, food fads, crop failure, disease – there aren't many who choose farming as a career if they weren't brought up with it, and so many stay in it with no profit, holidays or treats, just simply for the love of the land and the animals. They have my utmost respect.

To live and breathe this parallel, fictitious life in real time, to play the part of young upstart, then young parent, now older man, beginning to feel the next generation taking more and more control, is more like another life than an acting job, and I feel hugely privileged to have been allowed to do it for so long. Who knows what kind of man David will become in the future? If I'm lucky enough to continue to portray him on the wireless, one thing is for sure, he'll always be six years younger than I am, and for as long as I can manage it, he'll always have 'a good shout on him'.

The present

I have loved Being David Archer, but I have also enjoyed my simultaneous life Being Tim Bentinck, with its chequered history of ups, downs and everything in between: TV star, stage actor, voice artist, out of work, tiny parts, big parts, silly voices, singing, writing, inventing, computer programming, journalism, building houses, earl, son, husband and father.

Through it all I've managed to earn enough to keep the wolf from the door, and sometimes even feel a bit flush. I am at least proof to any budding actor that there is a living to be made from this mad profession without necessarily being famous. It's depressing hearing young people say that all they want to do in life is 'be famous'. I remember very well in our first year at Bristol, all of us felt that fame seekers were the ones who went to RADA, but we just wanted to perform great plays, entertain people, and play Cowboys and Indians, and if fame and fortune came our way it would be a bonus, a by-product, but not the thing itself.

My work continues to be eclectic. In 2015, Judy and I both published our first books. *Designing and Making Hats and Headpieces* took Judy two years to write and is a comprehensive how-to book revealing the secrets of the traditional couture milliner, with step-by-step tuition and hundreds of photographs. It's already become something of a classic. You can see her beautiful creations at www.judybentinck.com. My book, *Colin the Campervan*, involved far less work. It's a story that I wrote for the boys when they were young, and which had sat on my computer for twenty years.

We had our own 'Colin' for many years, which I used to sleep in, parked in a field opposite Pebble Mill in Birmingham, to save on hotel bills when recording *The Archers* in the 1980s and 1990s. I modified it, putting in front seats taken from a scrapped Rover, cutting out the partition wall and, as the heating was almost non-existent, installing a gas central heating system, which was fine for the back but meant you still needed to wear moon boots in the winter and scrape the frost off the inside of the windscreen. The boys and I loved it. Judy absolutely didn't.

The book was a sort of wish-fulfilment for us all, turning an old rust-bucket into a state-of-the-art supervan with a personality. It's a sweet story and has been well received, so a sequel is on the way.

In 2015, I translated a French novel into English. The author, Laurence Casile, published as Laure Elisac, is an English teacher who lives in Lyon and improves her English by listening to audio-books. She wrote me a letter after enjoying one of the books I'd narrated, and after some fun correspondence asked me if I would like to translate her novel. It's called *Oh Lord!* and is the story of English aristocrats and their friends gathering at a country house in Kent for New Year celebrations and sex! Translating sex from French is a challenge, as they approach it in quite a different way: it's more of an art form. The gay sex was an eye-opener, but the most difficult thing was the food. They were all culinary maestros, in a way that the English upper classes simply are not. No spotted dick or custard, no gargantuan slabs of venison, no kedgeree, but lots of garlic, *fines herbes* and, for some reason, blinis galore. It took me the best part of a year to do, but I loved it, and it was like being paid to learn French all over again.

In recent years, I've flown to Budapest to be garrotted by a seven-foot Hungarian called Vlad in the TV series of *Dracula*, played a heart surgeon with a heart problem in *Doctors* (he was also having an affair with a nurse young enough to be my granddaughter, which was weird), 'moonlighted' as a lawyer in *EastEnders*, mastered the art of autocue as the newsreader in *Fast Girls*, worked with David Tennant in *The Politician's Husband* and Brian Cox in *The Game*, been a police superintendent in *Gangsta Granny* and a Bristolian metal detectorist in *Gilt*, was made up to look like Ludovic Kennedy in *Lucan*, had a nervous breakdown in *Redistributors*, and spent three days in Gloucestershire, starring in a delightful film, *The Dead Dog*, as an eccentric gay duke and a week in Cape Town Brigadiering in *The Last Post*.

Then, after 'The Year of the Roth' and my first movie lead role in *Us and Them*, I have now achieved legendary status in the eyes of Jasper's Japanese friends by being almost the first person you see in J. K. Rowling's *Fantastic Beasts and Where to Find Them*. In this business, some people who get to the top disappear up their own fundaments, while others remain modest and charming. When Eddie Redmayne came up to me in the make-up chair and said how much he loved my work in *The Archers*, he definitely got put in the latter category. This credit, together with being the voice of Victor Saltzpyre the Witch Hunter in the computer game *Vermintide*, Kor Phaeron in *Warhammmer*, and, my first TV *Doctor Who* credit, the voice of The Monk, now ensures my place in Comic Con conventions forever!

The present

I narrated an audiobook for Marco Pierre White in which he talks about how writing was cathartic and, in visiting his past, he was better able to make sense of who he was today. I have found this too, so much so that I've been to a therapist for the first time. The thing that has become apparent was the traumatic effect that the years 1965 and 1966 had on me. First, being rejected by all my friends in my last year at Berkhamsted Junior School, when they learned that I was going to Harrow, then the overpowering strangeness of boarding school, and just after Christmas in my first year, my mother taking her own life. One minute I had a mother, and the next she was gone, and life was supposed to continue as normal. I've really been coping with that ever since. It may well have informed my choice of career.

To make up for a lack of funeral, we recently had a sort of memorial for my mother Pauline, celebrating her life. One of the main reasons for this was because her grandchildren knew so little about her. As my sisters and I told stories, read out her poems and played the audio clip we have of her, all of them (Sorrel's son Warwick and twins Amelia and Melanie, Anna's Gully, George and Sophie, and our own Will and Jasper) saw things in her that they recognised in themselves — looks, mannerisms, but most of all a palpable shared sense of humour.

When Pa was wounded and taken prisoner during the war, he was reported missing in action. She wrote this when she thought he wasn't coming back:

SONG OF A LONELY CARAVAN DWELLER

> Why speak? For who will heed my voice?
> The sea, the marshes, can they hear?
> Why read? To dull a mind tormented,

313

There's still an ever listening ear.
Why sing? My songs are sad with seeking,
Longing for what can never be.
Why laugh? Such bitter empty laughter
That ne'er an echo answers me.
Why walk? Each path a fresh reminder,
Each tree, each cliff, a memory wakes.
Why eat? To live: They say life's precious.
Keep the heart beating while it breaks.
Why pray? Or seek to find an answer
Knowing my faith be all too small.
Why cry? My grief is never silenced,
There is no coming to my call.
Why write? The ink stares back, bleak, lifeless.
Words have no power to ease the pain.
Why sleep? When all my dreams are nightmares
In which I cry to you in vain

As I write, fifty years on from losing her, life goes on. On the good side, in the last year I've done three movies, four tellies, a load of voice work and some great family stuff in *The Archers*. On the bad side, we seem to be becoming a land without empathy and a world without truth. Beyond charitable work and donations, I feel guilty and frustrated that I am unable to do anything about it.

Meeting Judy was the best stroke of luck that ever happened to me. I loved her then and I love her more with every day that passes, and Will'm and Jasper are an endless source of joy and pride. I am surrounded by a loving and close extended family and good friends. So, whatever happens in the real world or in the little village of Ambridge, I count my blessings daily.

Acknowledgements

Writing this book has been hard because I've met and worked with hundreds of people through my life, and anyone who's bought it and searched in vain for themselves is going to think I'm a forgetful, ungrateful bastard. So, just so I can show my face in the green room when it comes out, dear *Archers* cast, I love you all, but here are those that must be mentioned in dispatches, or tearfully recited at the awards ceremony I will never attend:

My *Archers* family have been closest to me, and Richard Attlee (Kenton), Alison Dowling (Elizabeth), Judy Bennett (Shula) and Paddy Greene (Jill) feel much more than just colleagues; my new family Felicity Finch (Ruth), Daisy Badger (Pip) and Angus Imrie (Josh) grow and develop as characters alongside me, and my thirty-five years in Ambridge so far would not have been the same without the fun and friendship of Charles Collingwood (Brian), Angela Piper (Jennifer), Andrew Wincott (Adam), John Telfer (Alan), Michael Lumsden (Alastair), all the Grundys – Trevor Harrison (Eddie), Ted Kelsey (Joe), Heather Bell (Clarrie), Ros Adams (Clarrie), Barry Farrimond (Ed), Emerald O'Hanrahan (Emma), Philip Molloy

(William) and Becky Wright (Nic) – the Tuckers, now reduced to one, Ian Pepperell (Roy), the wonderful Snells, Carole Boyd (Lynda) and Graham Blockey (Robert), Sunny Ormonde (Lilian), Souad Faress (Usha), Stephen Kennedy (Ian), Eric Allan (Bert), John Rowe (Jim), Michael Cochrane (Oliver), William Gaminara (Richard), the now legendary Louiza Patikas (Helen) and Tim Watson (Rob), and new Archers family member, Buffy Davis (sex goddess Jolene). I have had the joy of listening to the sexual innuendo of chilli with Charlotte Martin and Brian Hewlett (Susan and Neil), the wonderful freshness of the younger members, Joanna van Kampen (Fallon), Ryan Kelly (Jazzer), Lucy Morris (Phoebe), Hollie Chapman (Alice) and the Yorkshire whirlwind James Cartwright (Harrison), and those Fairbrother boys Nick Barber (Rex) and Rhys Bevan (Toby) are top lads.

Recent replacements like Troughtons David (Tony) and Wiggsy (Tom), as well as Perdita Avery (Kate) and Will Howard (Dan) have become part of the team, as have those playing new characters, Eleanor Bron (Carol), Simon Williams (Justin) and Anneika Rose (Anisha). It's lovely having Annabelle Dowler back as Kirsty, but we still miss William Sanderson-Thwaite's Chris Carter and Tom Graham's Tom Archer, and hope that the Tuckers – Lorraine Coady (Hayley), Rachel Atkins (Vicky), Amy Shindler (Brenda) and Terry Molloy (Mike) – and Hedli Niklaus (Kathy Perks) will soon return. The new Freddie and Lily Pargetter, (Toby Laurence and Katie Redford) are fresh new voices and although David had few scenes with them, Carolyn Jones (Ursula), Rina Mahoney (Jess), Isobel Middleton (Anna) and Michael Byrne (Bruce) were such an integral part of the brilliant Rob/Helen story.

And just so the long-time actors who crop up every so often don't hate me for not mentioning them, where would we be without

Acknowledgements

Hazel Woolley (Annette Badland), James Bellamy (Roger May), Lewis Carmichael (Robert Lister), Snells Leonie (Jasmine Hyde) and Coriander (Alexandra Lilley), Amy Franks (Jennifer Daley), Charlie Thomas (Felix Scott), Annabelle Schrivener (Julia Hills), Alf Grundy (David Hargreaves), Horrobins Clive (Alex Jones), Bert (Martyn Read) and Tracy (Susie Riddell), Wayne Tucson (Clive Wood), Lucas Madikane (Connie M'gadzah), Mabel Thompson (Mona Hammond), Martyn Gibson (Jon Glover), Satya Khanna (Jamila Massey), the wonderfully annoying Graham Ryder (Malcolm McKee) and, of course, the star of the whole show, Sabrina Thwaite?

Without the tireless and patient work of the *Archers* staff, there would be no programme. To thank everyone I've worked with since 1982 would be a book in itself, but, though now retired, Jane Pritchard was our friend almost from the start. The present staff are editor Huw Kennair-Jones, business manager Ailsa Acklam-Drury, producers Kim Greengrass and Jenny Thompson, agricultural advisor Graham Harvey, assistant producer Hannah Ratcliffe, production coordinators Sally Lloyd and Andrew Smith, production management assistant Sandheep Johal and casual production coordinator Mel Ward. Directors Julie Beckett, Rosemary Watts, Peter Leslie Wild, Marina Caldarone and Gwenda Hughes are our present guiding hands and we hope Jenny Stephens and Sue Wilson will come by again, and, driving the ship, Andy Partington, Vanessa Nuttal, Liza Wallis and Kathryn Shuttleworth. The late and much lamented Mark Decker was studio manager at Pebble Mill and designed the new studio at the Mailbox, which was then run with the same dedication and efficiency by his successor, Michael Harrison. Thanks to you all, past and present.

There's one character I'd really love to return, as I want to know what happened to him: the drug addict Luke, cared for by vicar

Alan Franks. Played brilliantly by Tom George, the bravest and sunniest of men, it would be lovely if Luke turned out to be as great a guy as the lad who plays him.

I'm so grateful for the guidance and support of all those who have gone before and are now no longer in the programme and the recent death of dear Sara Coward (Caroline) is particularly hard to bear. June Spencer (Peggy) is an inspiration to us all and I will never forget the kindness of unsung longest-serving continuous character Lesley Saweard (Christine), who together with Paddy and the eternally young Pat (Pat Gallimore), took me under their wings when I first arrived. Felicity Jones left and went to Hollywood (there's no coming back after *Star Wars*), Lucy Davis left and went to US TV, Sam Barriscale left and came a cropper with the tractor, poor old Heather (Margaret Jackman, previously Joyce Gibbs) passed away in a motorway services, Kim Durham (Matt Crawford) left but has recently returned, Tamsin Greig got famous but sensibly left the door open, and I'm still waiting for the call from the Broccolis. They'd have to work around the milking though.

When my father died having only completed a tiny part of his life's story, I was determined to record something of my life for the future interest of my boys and any grandchildren. So when I got an email from literary agent Robert Dudley asking if I was interested in writing an autobiography, I'd already written quite a lot and had something to show him. If it weren't for him, these musings would never have reached book form, so for that, Robert, my eternal thanks.

He in turn found the interest of Andreas Campomar at Little, Brown who, with fellow editors Howard Watson and Claire Chesser, have magically turned my conversational, hyperbole-fuelled ramblings into a book. It's a bit like magic and I am humbled by their attention

Acknowledgements

to detail and ability to construct a story out of a series of observations. My deepest thanks to you all.

To all friends and family for help with historical details, especially Lucy Bird for arcane dance terminology!

To my parents Henry and Pauline I owe a huge debt of gratitude. Beyond obviously giving me my life, they were both wildly creative and so much of me is down to them. To my adored and multi-talented sisters Sorrel and Anna who had to put up with the antics of a permanently performing pest, and to all my dear friends who have probably heard all the stories in the book, many times over.

To Will'm and Jasper who have had to put up with a lifetime of parental insecurity, never knowing how close we were to insolvency, and consequently having to endure a father prone to wild mood swings, please accept my forgiveness and know my love.

But the greatest thanks of all to my beloved Judy for her support, patience, understanding, forgiveness and love, and without whom I would be nothing.

For more information about Tim, including photos and video clips of his work, please visit www.beingdavidarcher.net.